Creative Embroidery Techniques

using

Colour Through Gold

The Elephant Thief: *sample for piece of work designed and stitched by Daphne, which is held in the Madeira Collection.*

Creative Embroidery Techniques
using
Colour Through Gold

Daphne J. Ashby and Jackie Woolsey

Guild of Master Craftsman Publications Ltd

First published 1998 by
Guild of Master Craftsman Publications Ltd,
166 High Street, Lewes,
East Sussex, BN7 1XU

Reprinted 1998, 2000

ISBN 1 86108 083 2

Photographs by Zul Mukhida

Charts originated by Simon Rodway

Line drawings by John Yates

Designed by Mind's Eye Design, Lewes.

Typeface: Sabon

Colour reproduction by Job Colour srl – Gorle (BG) – Italy

Printed in Hong Kong

We should like to dedicate this book to our respective husbands, Hedley and Jeremy, without whose help, patience and support, this book would not have been possible.

Daphne J. Ashby &
Jackie Woolsey

ACKNOWLEDGEMENTS

Our grateful thanks are extended to the following companies for their generous provision of materials, used in the pieces illustrated in this book:

Coats Crafts UK Ltd: threads
Madeira Threads UK Ltd: threads
Gütermann: threads
Impress Cards: cards
Framecraft Miniatures Ltd: clock, tray and mirror set
Kernow Crafts Woodturning: wooden pot
Selectus Ltd: ribbon
Zweigart: congress cloth

We would also like to thank Daphne's niece, Linda Gurmin, for her work in stitching the Parisian, Hungarian and Hungarian variation stitch samples shown in Figs 2.47, 2.49 and 2.51.

MEASUREMENTS

Throughout, measurements are given in both imperial and metric systems. For each project, please use only one system as the two are only equivalents and can never be exactly equal. Where products can only be bought using one system, equivalents have not been given. As the original pen holder, letter rack and jewellery box (pages 72, 75 and 95) were made to metric dimensions and the imperial equivalents cannot be exact, it is recommended that the metric measurements are used for these items.

Contents

INTRODUCTION

Everything has to have a starting point and, for this technique, mine was a City and Guilds embroidery weekend in 1987, entitled 'Colour'. The premise was that we should use the primary colours – red, blue and yellow – together, or one of the sets of complementary colours. Complementary colours are those which appear on opposite sides of the colour wheel: red and green, blue and orange, or mauve and yellow.

These were bright colours that I had not really used in abundance before, never having been very adventurous with colour. Driving back home that weekend, I tried to think how I could progress from one colour to the next, as we had been instructed to do during our exercises.

Years before, when craft shops were not so easily found, I always welcomed a visit to the Cotswold area, as I knew an excellent shop in Chipping Campden. On one of these visits, I purchased a length of coin net (now more often known as congress cloth), not knowing what I was going to do with it. Now I got it out once more. It was fine enough to use my machine embroidery rayon threads, and the idea came that I could use several threads in the needle at once and progress through the colour range by changing one thread at a time for a different colour.

After a quick experiment, I found that three threads, doubled to give a thickness of six, were ample to cover the congress cloth. My first sample – with red, blue and yellow, worked in rice stitch and overlaid with gold metallic thread – proved successful and I was quite excited by the results, using what were, to me, untried colours.

In my following pieces I used other stitches and very soon found that, just as an artist mixes his paints to get new colours, I was mixing my threads.

My second set of samples – using the complementary colours mauve and yellow – proved rather startling, so were abandoned. Going into the garden later the same day, I noticed the spring flowers coming alive. By the pond was a large clump of golden alyssum and, through the top of it, I could see just a few mauve aubretia flowers. This showed me what was wrong with my complementary colour samples: I had used the two colours in equal amounts. I now realized that when using complementary colours, more of one should be used than the other. The sight of a few red tulips against a very green background backed this up.

I worked about eight different samples, using the primary colours with different canvaswork stitches. Looking at the completed sheet from a distance, I could see the mauves and oranges appearing. To add richness to the samples, I overlaid the colours with gold metallic threads. I found that just a double thickness of the Madeira gold No. 12 thread was sufficient.

On my next visit to college, I produced my sheets of samples. My tutor took one look and called it my 'colour through gold', and that is what I have called it ever since.

I have gone on to use this technique with many of my students. (One in particular found it very therapeutic during a long illness.) At first, I used the stitches just as they were shown in the many good canvaswork stitch books I had on my bookshelf. However, I gradually realized that these could be altered in so many ways; by enlarging, reducing, making them multicoloured, using blocks of stitches, overlaying with gold, using gold underneath, adding extra stitches, etc. The list goes on and I am sure there are many variations that I have not thought of.

A recent student asked how I kept finding new patterns and designs and I assured her that one idea leads to another. I have tried to show how you can use colour through gold with other techniques, for example machine embroidery, hand stitchery and ribbonwork, and also to show that it is an ideal technique to embellish things for the home, for fashion items, cards and boxes.

Daphne J. Ashby

PART ONE

TOOLS AND TECHNIQUES

CHAPTER 1

Materials and Equipment

Fig 1.1 Congress cloth (coin net) is available in a variety of pale colours and black.

FABRIC

The background fabric used throughout the book is congress cloth (sometimes known as coin net). It is 100% cotton and a really good fabric to use. The threads have been treated with a fixative, so they do not slip or stretch and the stitches made on them do not distort. It can be obtained in a variety of pale colours and in black. Unlike evenweave and block weave fabrics, congress cloth is not available in different counts per inch.

The stitches and ideas presented in this book could, of course, be used with other, coarser (lower count) canvases if you find the congress cloth too fine. You would need to experiment with the number of threads required in the needle to cover the canvas adequately and, of course, remember that the finished items will be larger.

As with all forms of embroidery, a quality fabric is easy to use and gives good results. There are some cheap canvases on the market which have quite a fine texture (high number of threads) but they lack the quality of congress cloth and are not pleasant to use.

THREADS

The threads used for the samples and embroidered items in this book are rayons and, again, these vary in the way they handle and in the results they achieve. I have used the relatively cheap Indian rayon threads, as well as the more expensive Madeira, Coats and Gütermann threads.

Some of the more expensive threads, such as Madeira Sticku no. 30 and Madeira rayon no. 40, are produced on normal size reels as well as on larger cops, and Coats Marlitt thread comes in skeins.

Throughout the book, threads can be substituted one for another. The rich, vibrant colours are a joy to use and, if you cannot find the colour you require in one brand, it is possible to use a thread from a different manufacturer.

Unlike stranded embroidery cottons, different manufacturers do not produce equivalent shades, nor do they all use a system of numbers for shade identification. It is, therefore, not possible to provide tables of equivalent shade numbers, or even to provide numbers for all of the threads used, though where possible we have done so.

With most threads, using three strands doubled (i.e. six thicknesses) will give adequate coverage, and throughout, metallic gold thread is used as a single strand doubled. The thicknesses required for the threads used are given in each project.

Remember, whichever thread you use, diagonal stitches cover the fabric much better than those worked horizontally or vertically. If you are in any doubt about how well the background is covered, add an extra thread.

Indian Rayon These threads are relatively inexpensive, available in a large range of colours, and easy to use. Three threads doubled over to give six thicknesses are ample to cover congress cloth.

Fig 1.2 *Indian rayon threads: available in a large range of colours, but with no identifying number.*

Fig 1.3 Madeira threads are available in a number of thicknesses: no. 30 and no. 40 are shown here.

Madeira Rayon no. 40 This is much more expensive, but very nice to work with, and available in a large range of colours. Again, three threads doubled to give six thicknesses will cover congress cloth.

Madeira Sticku no. 30 This, as the number suggests, is a slightly thicker thread than the no. 40 and is also quite expensive, but good to use. When working multi-layered stitches, you may feel that two threads doubled over would be ample to cover the fabric.

Gütermann Dekor This is a 100% viscose thread which, like the Madeira threads, is quite expensive, but a pleasure to use. It is available in 100 different shades. Use three threads doubled to cover congress cloth.

Fig 1.4 A selection of Gütermann Dekor threads.

Anchor machine embroidery thread This is a 100% polyester thread. It is good to use, but has a limited colour range. Use three threads doubled to cover congress cloth.

Coats Anchor Marlitt This is a much thicker thread and only needs to be used double. There are 88 colours in the range.

METALLIC THREADS

For metallic threads too, there are many different makes and thicknesses. I prefer to use a thread that only has to be doubled, such as Madeira no. 12 or Madeira no. 15. These numbers denote the thickness of the thread; often a second number denotes the colour variation. Some of the very fine gold threads require more strands in the needle to give the required thickness and while they do give good results, they are more difficult to handle.

BEADS AND RIBBONS

Modern beads are well-produced and evenly-sized and can, therefore, be used everywhere. They are available in a glorious range of colours.

There is also an enormous range of ribbons available, though the only ones used in this book are metallic gold polyester lamé ribbons, in 3mm and 35mm widths.

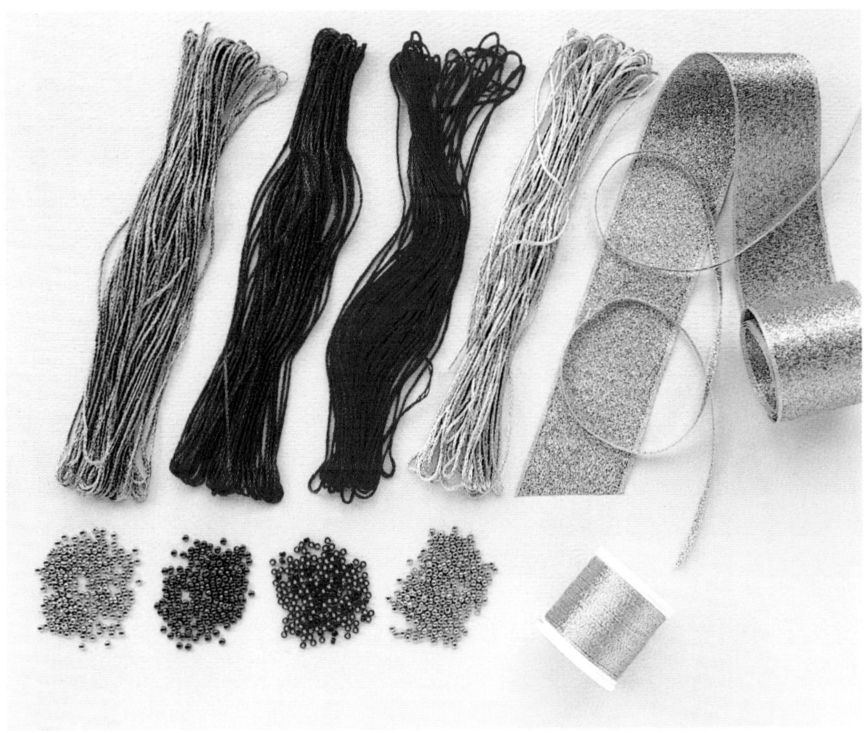

Fig 1.5 *Use beads and ribbons to add texture to your work.*

EMBROIDERY FRAMES

It is essential that congress cloth is attached to a frame in order to work the stitches and for every project I have recommended the size of frame required. The frames are all rectangular and should be simple, flat, wooden frames, which can be re-used and into which it is easy to fix (and remove) drawing pins or staples.

STAPLES, DRAWING PINS AND MASKING TAPE

Congress cloth can be attached to an embroidery frame with staples or drawing pins. If pins are used, it is advisable to cover the heads with masking tape to prevent the very fine rayon threads from catching on them.

EMBROIDERY STAND AND SANDBAGS

It is always easier to work with two hands when using multiple threads, so try to support your frame. Ideally, use a metal or wooden floor stand and secure your frame in that. (*See* Suppliers, page 164.)

If you do not have a stand, you can make yourself a sandbag by filling a fabric bag – 12 x 7in (305 x 178mm) – with $2^{1}/_{2}$ lb (approx. 1kg) of silver sand (available from garden centres). Place your embroidery frame on the table so that the area to be worked protrudes over the edge, then place the sandbag on the top edge of the frame to weight it securely so that you can have both hands free. It is best to make an inner bag to contain the sand for security and to use a patterned fabric for the outer cover, simply to make it more attractive.

Fig 1.6 *Securing the frame with a sand bag leaves both hands free for embroidery.*

NEEDLES

You will need a no. 24 tapestry needle for the colour through gold technique, as its larger eye comfortably holds the multiple threads required for most of the projects.

A beading needle is helpful when adding beads to a piece of work and a small, fine, curved needle will be useful in making up the pen holder, letter rack and jewellery box (*see* pages 72, 75, and 95).

SCISSORS

Always have a pair of really sharp embroidery scissors to hand, as well as larger scissors for cutting fabric.

FINE PAINT BRUSH AND FINISHER

These are very much optional items but are extremely useful when cutting congress cloth very close to stitches; applying needlework finisher to the edges of the cut canvas prevents fraying.

INTERFACING AND PADDING

Extra heavy interfacing or pelmet vilene is used as a padding when inserting finished work into mounts or cards.

I have used iron-on vilene where a fabric needs the additional strength of a backing, for example, when cutting into the corners of a mount to create a frame.

CHAPTER 2

GLOSSARY OF STITCHES

RHODES STITCH

Rhodes stitch is a fairly bulky stitch, built up with a series of diagonal stitches. The lower end of each stitch moves one square to the right (as indicated on the chart), while the top part of the stitch moves one square to the left. As each stitch crosses over the preceding stitch, the centre of the stitch becomes raised.

Following Fig 2.1, start by bringing the needle up at position 1 then taking it down at position 2. Continue around the square, bringing the needle up at the odd-numbered squares and taking it down at the even ones, following the numerical order. Note that the final stitch repeats the first, but brings the needle up at position 2 (33) and down at position 1 (34).

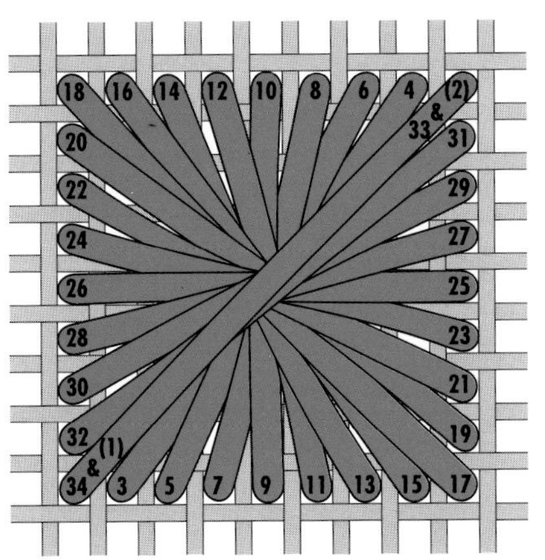

Fig 2.1 Working a Rhodes stitch.

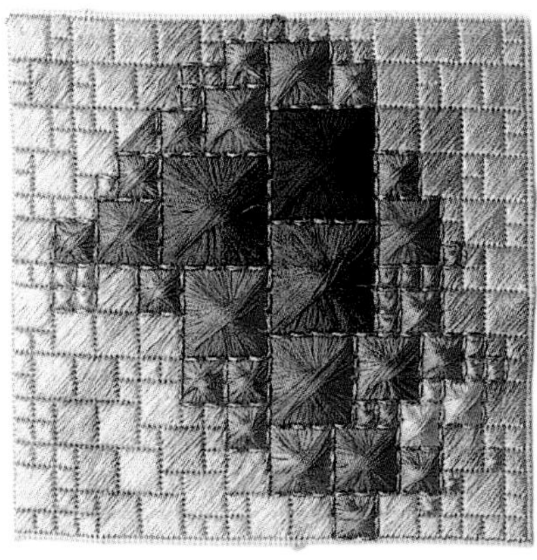

Fig 2.2 This sampler shows a traditional Rhodes stitch worked in varying sizes and sometimes with two colours threaded in the needle.

VARIATIONS AND SAMPLES

The following samples all use straight stitches, either as a border or a background, to add interest to the overall design. They were all worked using Gütermann Dekor threads in maroon (5400), deep pink (5435), yellow (1850), cream (1195) and hyacinth blue (5900), and Madeira thread for the metallic gold (no. 12, colour 33).

Rhodes stitch is usually worked over a square area of canvas, the size of which can vary. A mass of Rhodes stitches worked in sizes varying from a square of four threads to sixteen or even twenty-four threads can give an interesting effect. Try mixing the threads in the needle, say two of one colour and one of a contrasting colour. (*See* Fig 2.2.)

As well as changing the size and colours of the stitch, different effects can be achieved by changing its basic shape. The sample in Fig 2.3 is based on an octagon and the sample in Fig 2.4 on a triangle. This triangular Rhodes stitch was invented to imitate the design on the fabric used to line the jewellery box (*see* page 95). (*See also* Figs 2.5 and 2.6.) A tile pattern was the inspiration for the rectangular Rhodes stitch shown in Fig 3.1 (*see* page 46).

Fig 2.3 *Rhodes stitch worked to form an octagonal shape.*

Fig 2.4 *A triangular variation of Rhodes stitch.*

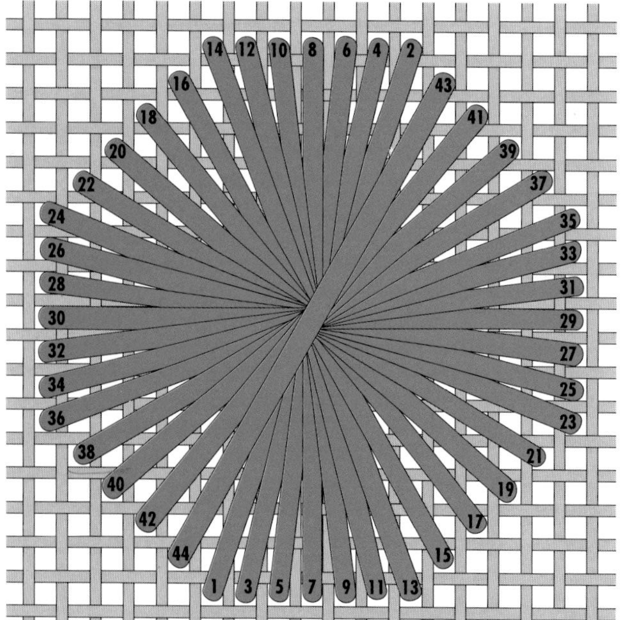

Fig 2.5 *The placement of stitches is varied to form an octagonal shape.*

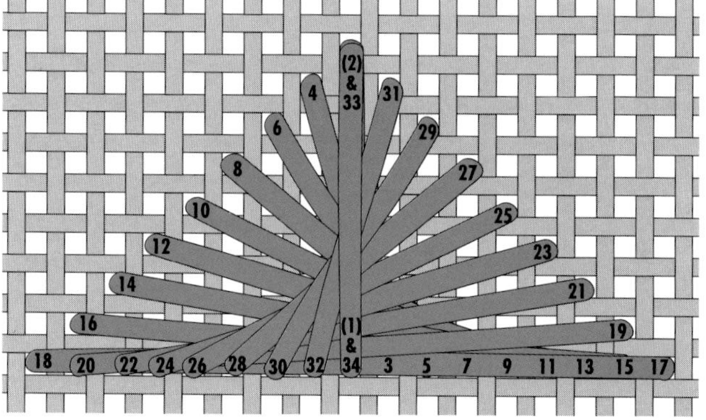

Fig 2.6 *The placement of stitches followed to work a triangular Rhodes stitch.*

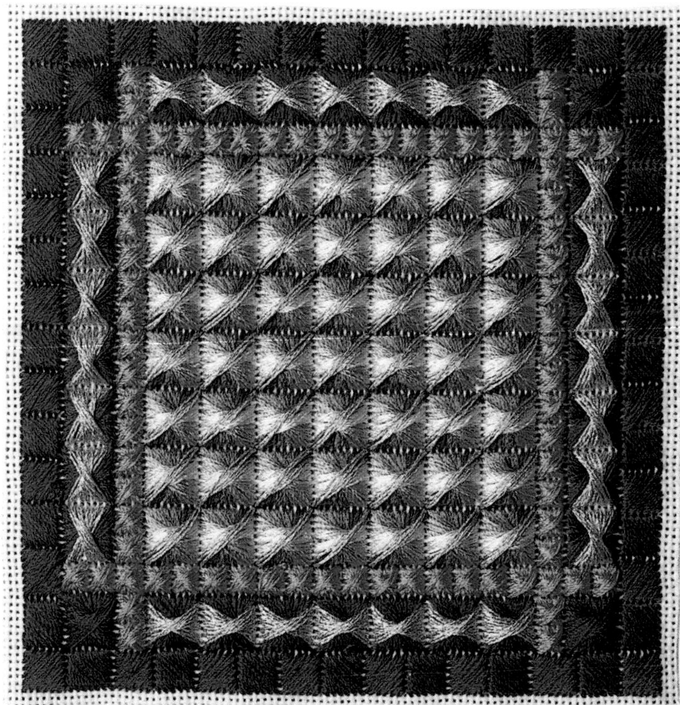

Fig 2.7 Changing colour as you work a stitch alters its appearance. The border in this sample is worked in two colours and the centre in six.

A change of colour also alters the appearance of the stitch. The border on the sample in Fig 2.7 is worked in two colours – vertical stitches in maroon and horizontal stitches in metallic gold – and the centre is variegated. The first three vertical stitches of each Rhodes stitch square (needle positions 1–6) are worked in maroon, the second three (positions 7–12) in deep pink and the last three (positions 13–18) in hyacinth blue. The first three horizontal stitches (19–24) are worked in yellow and the second three (25–30) in cream. The square is then finished with two metallic gold stitches, the last stitch overlapping the first stitch of the square. (*See* Figs 2.8 and 2.9.) The smaller row of traditional blue Rhodes stitches form an inner framework. Turn the sample through 90° and see the overall effect when the stitch is turned on its side.

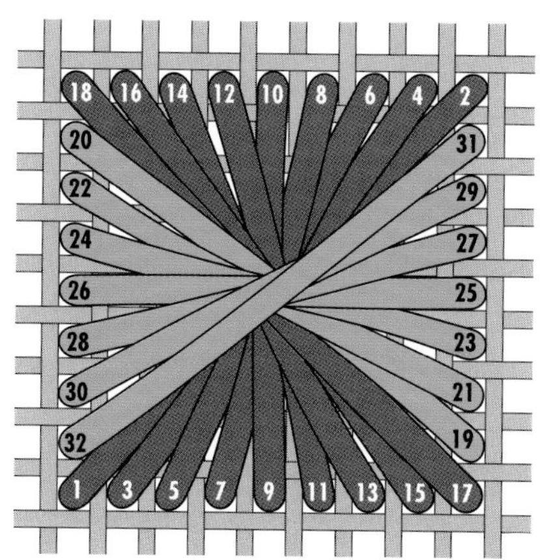

***Fig 2.8** Placement of stitches to work the two-colour Rhodes stitch shown in Fig 2.7.*

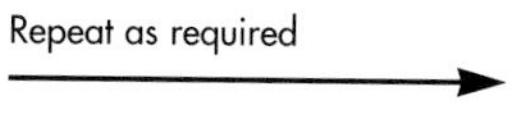

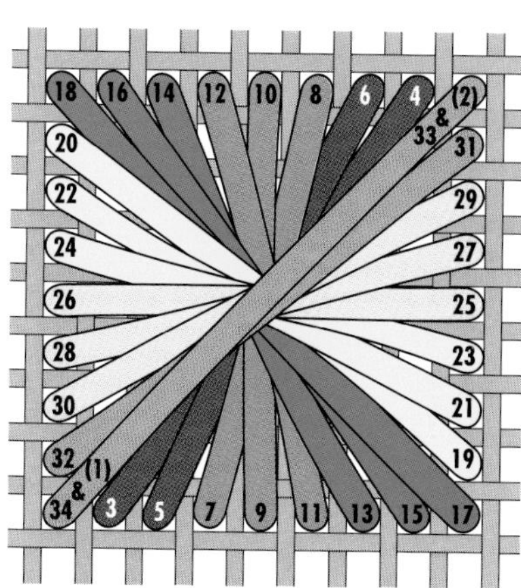

***Fig 2.9** Placement of stitches to work the six-colour Rhodes stitch shown in Fig 2.7.*

Look now at Fig 2.10. Here only the vertical stitches are worked and, when one set has been worked, you move four threads down and to the right for the second half stitch (*see* Fig 2.11). Thus, the first colour makes a diagonal across the design.

Fig 2.10 *Half Rhodes stitches worked to form a diagonal line.*

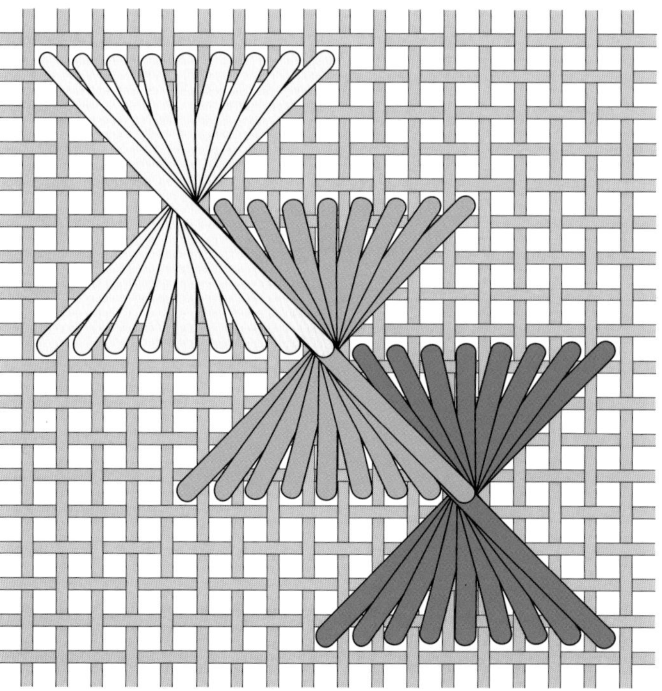

Fig 2.11 *Placement of stitches followed to produce the central design shown in Fig 2.10.*

Look at Fig 2.3 again. The centre octagon is worked in maroon and the north, south, east and west ones worked in blue. Those in-between are worked in two colours. The blue-and-cream octagons form an upright cross and the pink-and-cream ones form a diagonal cross. To create these effects, follow Fig 2.12. Try using groups of each of these colourways to create another pattern.

Pink over cream. Work sections E–F and G–H in cream, following the correct stitch sequence. Follow this by working sections A–B and C–D in pink.

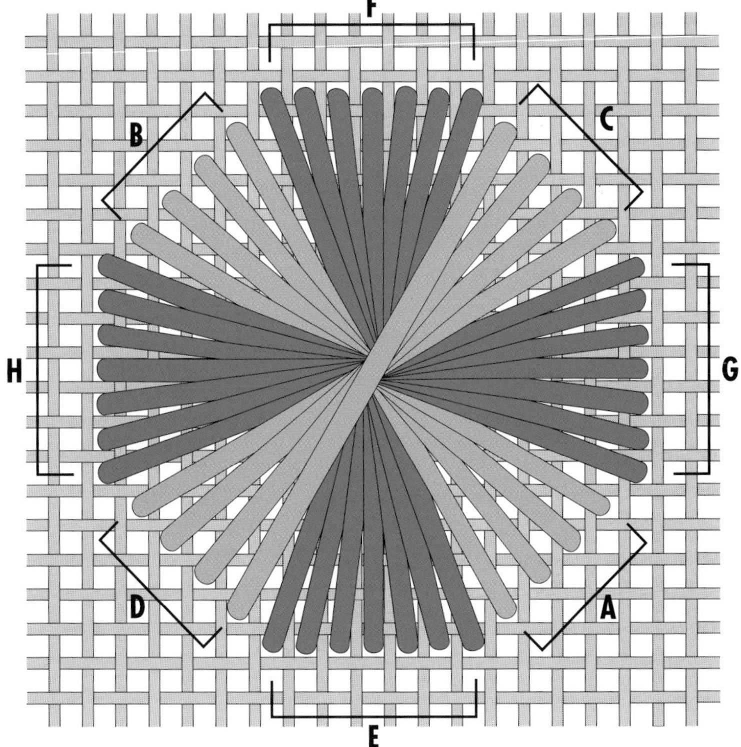

Blue over cream. Work sections A–B and C–D in cream, following the correct stitch sequence. Follow this by working sections E–F and G–H in blue.

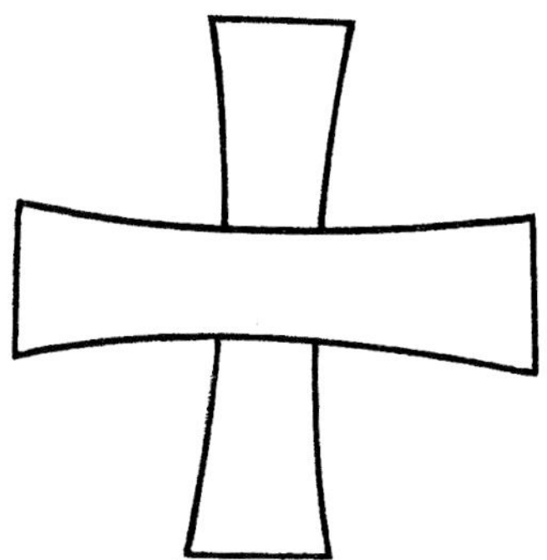

Fig 2.12 Placement of stitches to give the upright and diagonal crosses shown in Fig 2.3.

The evening bag on page 130 uses Rhodes stitch worked in blacks, greys and creams, with metallic gold thread. The small black squares, worked over four threads, form a type of Greek key pattern which surrounds the design. The central background is worked in variegated colour and, like the sample in Fig 2.7, uses a metallic thread to complete each square, which adds to the richness of the design. The remaining metallic stitching is worked in a horizontal straight stitch.

CUSHION STITCH

Cushion stitch, sometimes known as Scottish stitch, is a square stitch made up of diagonal stitches. The squares can be worked all facing in one direction or in alternate directions. Threads worked in alternate directions reflect the light differently and appear to alter in colour.

Cushion stitch can be overlaid with the same colour or with a contrasting one, but the overlay stitches must always be worked in the opposite direction from those in the background squares. When this is to be done, groups of four background squares are worked with each of the centre stitches pointing into the centre of the resulting square. Then either the inside or the outside corners can be overlaid, which leaves a coloured diamond in the centre.

Variations and samples

In all of the samples shown, Indian rayon threads in deep mauve, pale mauve, cerise, cream and pale orange, and Madeira metallic gold thread (no. 12, colour 33) were used.

Looking at the sample in Fig 2.13, the four corners of the border show the inside corners (in pale mauve) overlaid with gold and the side borders show the outside corners (in deep mauve) overlaid. (*See* also Figs 2.14 and 2.15.) The centre panel shows another idea, with the inside and outside corners overlaid alternately. Worked in this way, the stitch becomes known as cross-cornered cushion stitch.

Fig 2.13 *Sampler showing cushion stitches with both inside and outside corners overlaid.*

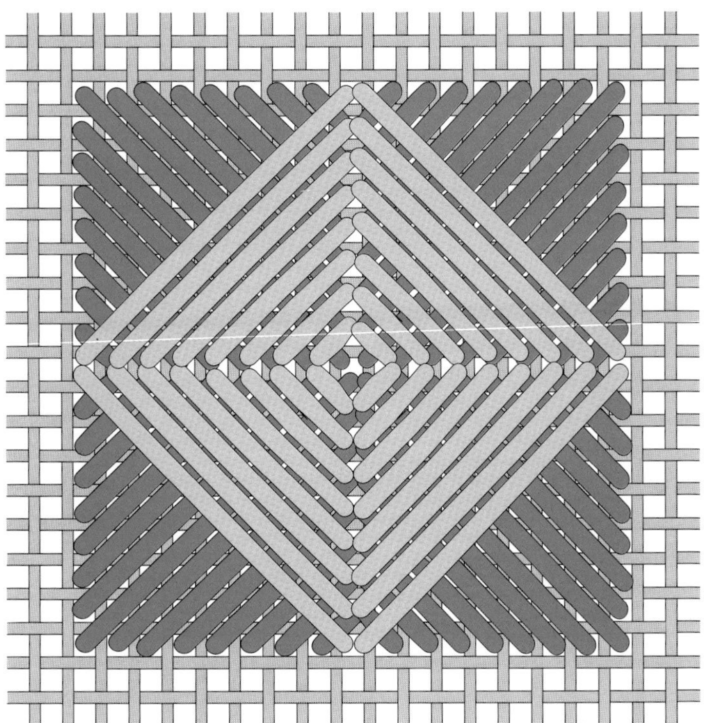

Fig 2.14 *Cushion stitch with traditional inside corner overlay.*

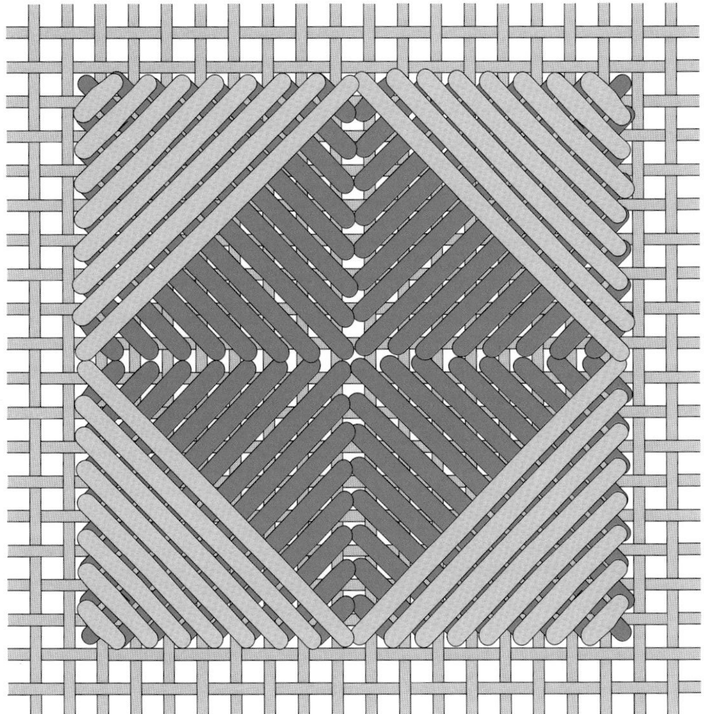

Fig 2.15 *Cushion stitch with traditional outside corner overlay.*

***Fig 2.16** Sample showing two- and three-colour cushion stitch with gold overlay.*

The sample in Fig 2.16 has colours added for working the background cushion squares. The four corners of the border have a two-colour background, where the centre stitch plus two stitches either side of it are worked before the colour is changed and the square completed (deep mauve for the centres and pale mauve for the corners). The centre panel uses a three-colour square for the background. When using various colours, it is best to reduce the amount of overlay stitching to avoid covering all the detail created by changing the colours of the threads. In the border corners, a diagonal stitch plus one either side are overlaid, and in the centre panel, the diagonal stitch plus two either side are worked, leaving an attractive centre cross and a striped corner. The side borders show a triangular pattern, using only two background squares in each group, alternating cerise and deep mauve. (*See* Figs 2.17, 2.18 and 2.19.)

Fig 2.17 *Placement of stitches for the two-colour cushion stitch with gold overlay shown in Fig 2.16.*

Fig 2.18 *Placement of stitches for the three-colour cushion stitch with gold overlay shown in Fig 2.16.*

Fig 2.19 Placement of stitches for the border pattern shown in Fig 2.16.

In Fig 2.20, the sample shows a centre square with a four-coloured background (deep mauve in the centre, followed by cream, cerise and pale orange) and only part of the corner and part of the centre overlaid. (*See* Figs 2.21 and 2.22.) The centre of each side area shows cushion stitch used in one colour (cream) without an overlay – note the apparent change of colour with the direction of the light.

Fig 2.20 Laying the threads in different directions causes the light to reflect differently which gives an apparent change in colour.

Fig 2.21 *Placement of stitches to work the centre square shown in Fig 2.20.*

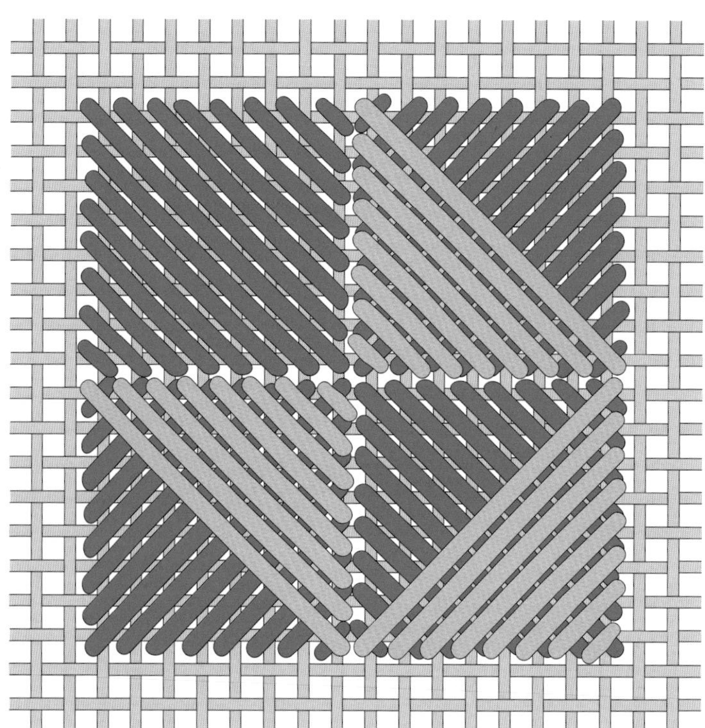

Fig 2.22 *Placement of stitches to work the corner square shown in Fig 2.20 (quarter of design).*

The four corners are overlaid to give a star effect. In this example, the background squares are worked over six threads but they could be worked over four threads to give a smaller star or greater number of threads to give a larger one.

The centre of the next sample, in Fig 2.23, shows another pattern that can be formed with overlay stitches. Here the original set of four squares (there are nine sets in this pattern) are worked with the threads in the opposite direction – across the corner rather than pointing to the centre. The central square is worked in deep mauve, pale mauve and cerise. The outer points of the design are worked in mixed colour threads (cerise and pale mauve) and only overlaid with single gold stitches. Again, the background squares show how the colour (pale mauve) changes with the direction in which the stitches are made. The four corner squares, in deep mauve, show a windmill pattern. (*See* Figs 2.24, 2.25 and 2.26.)

Another variation of cushion stitch is to surround each square with a single row of tent stitches; when this is done, it is given the name 'Moorish stitch'.

***Fig 2.23** In this cushion stitch sample the placement of the overlay stitches is altered to produce different patterns.*

***Fig 2.24** Placement of stitches to work the central panel shown in Fig 2.23.*

Fig 2.25 *Placement of stitches to work the side panels shown in Fig 2.23.*

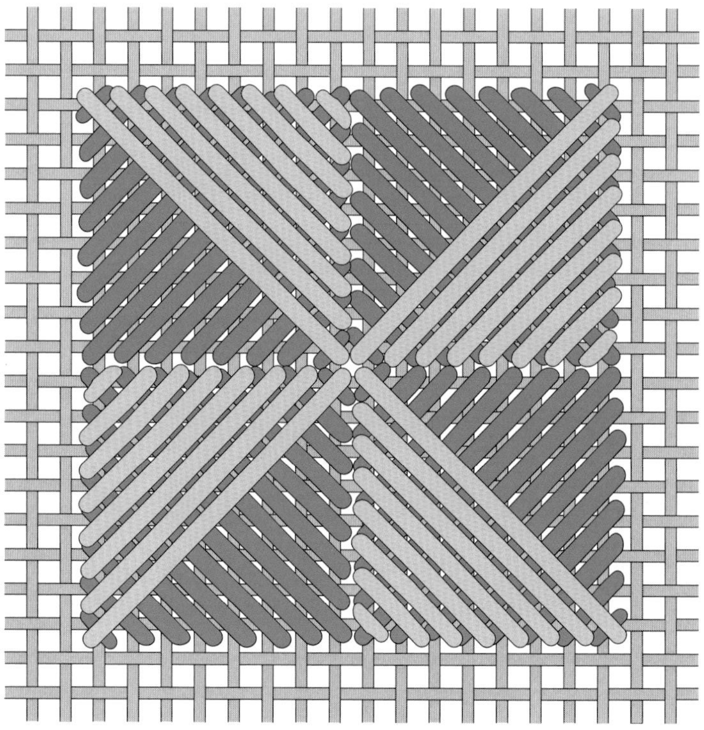

Fig 2.26 *Placement of stitches to work the corner squares shown in Fig 2.23.*

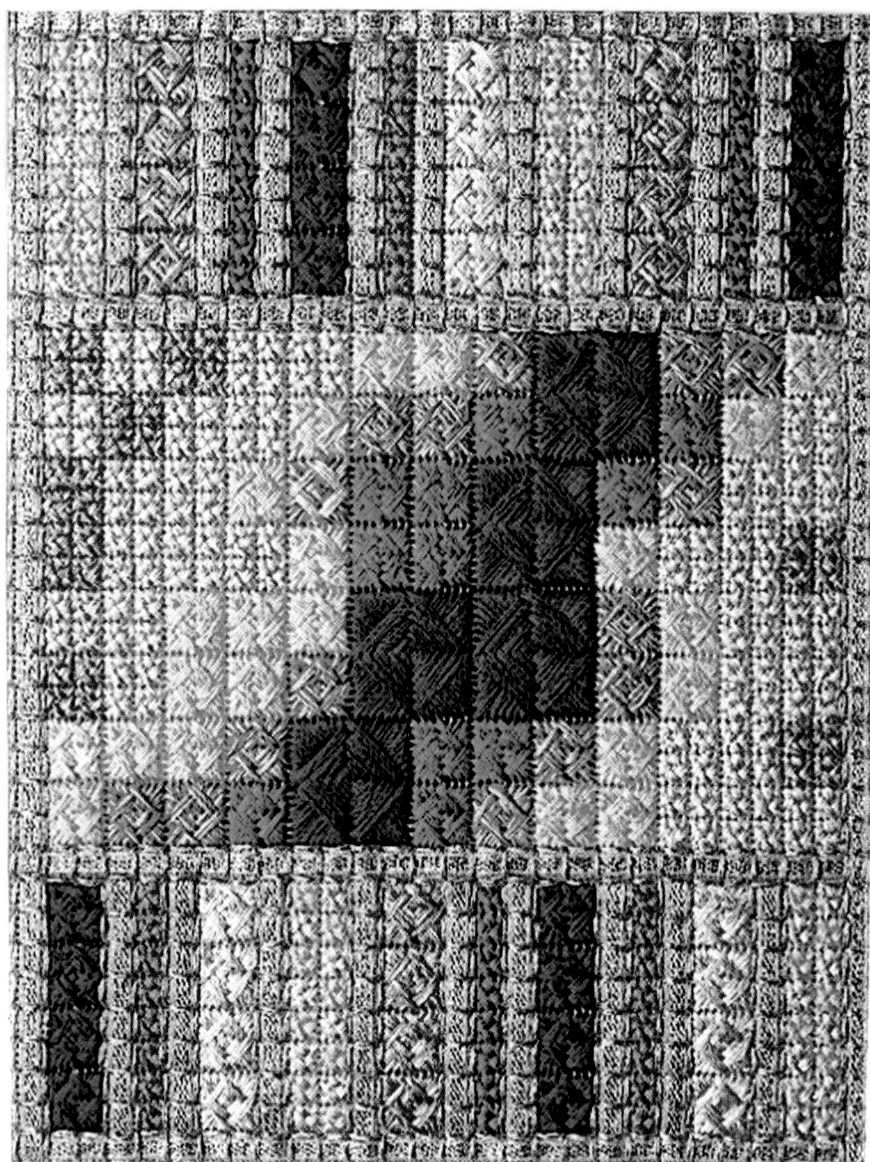

Fig 2.28 Norwich stitch worked over different numbers of threads, in a single colour and with two-colour combinations.

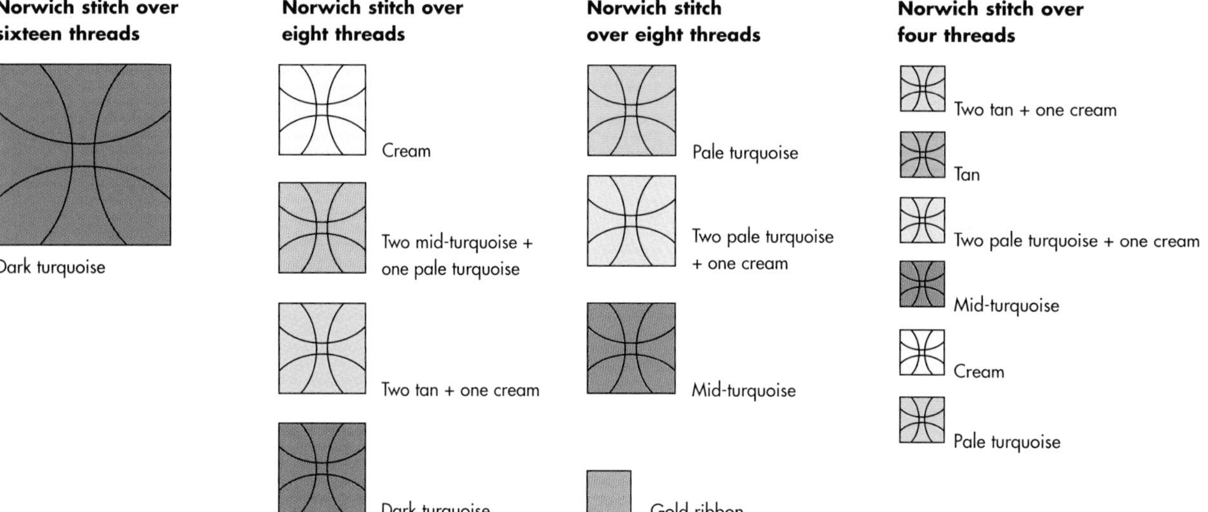

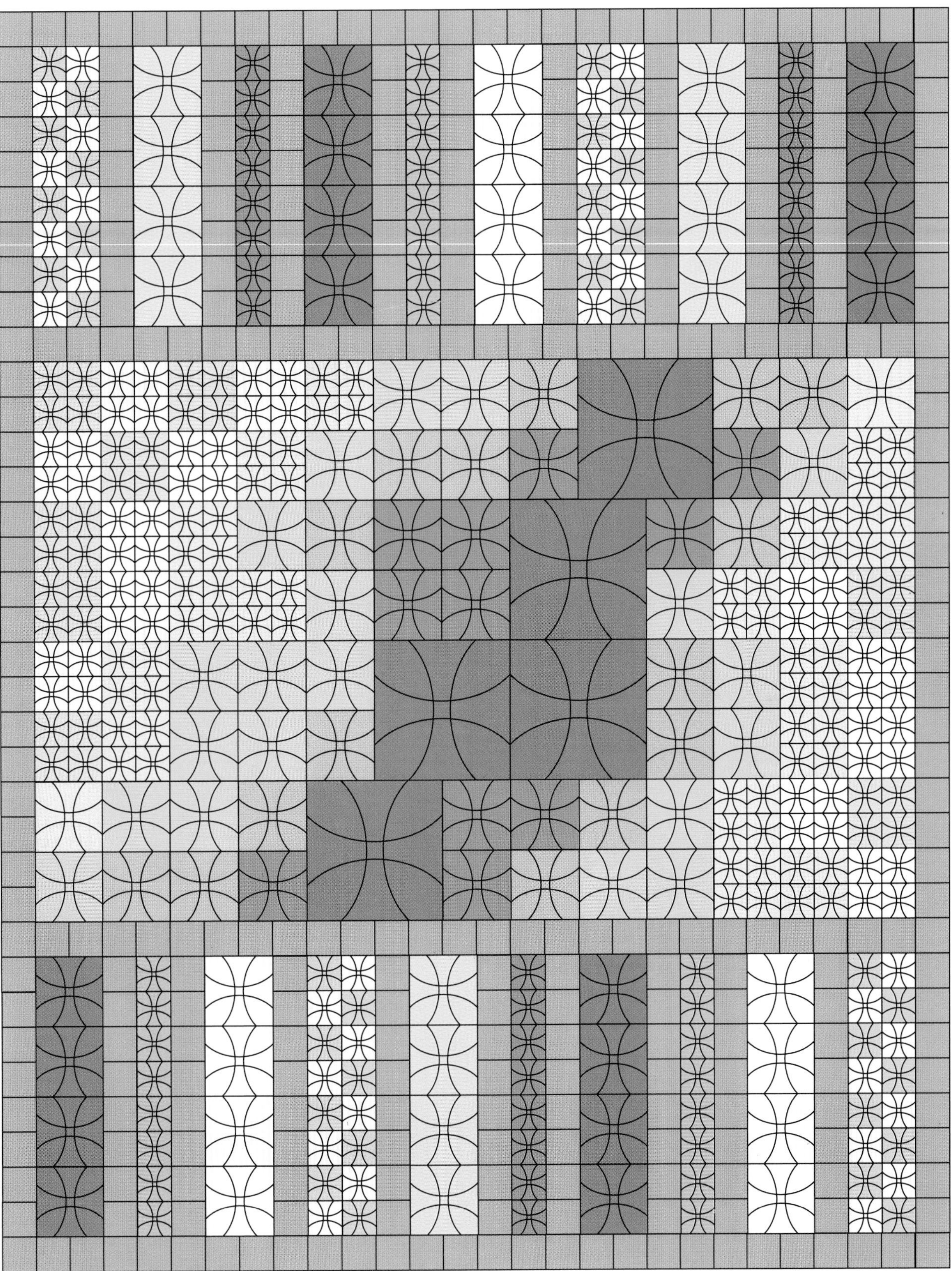

***Fig 2.29** Stitch chart for the design shown in Fig 2.28.*

The sample in Fig 2.30, shows an all-round border in one colour – cream. Across the top and bottom of the design, the squares are worked over 16 threads, in five colours, to give a multicoloured border. Worked in this way, squares of pale and mid turquoise appear. Very effective under-patterns are created by working square blocks of four Norwich stitches together.

***Fig 2.30** Different patterns can be created with multi-coloured Norwich stitches.*

The side borders in Fig 2.30 are worked in two colours – tan and pale turquoise – and the golden grid shown on page 48 is used for the centre panel. The grid is filled with Norwich stitches and the half squares that are left are filled with eyelet stitches in the appropriate colours.

Fig 2.31 Stitch chart for the design shown in Fig 2.30.

Norwich stitch over 16 threads

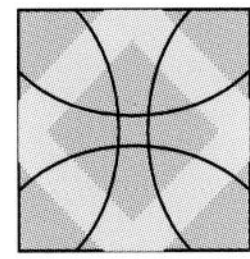

Middle cross and three rounds tan; square finished with pale turquoise

Middle cross and one round pale turquoise; two rounds mid-turquoise; one round tan; one round cream; square finished with deep turquoise

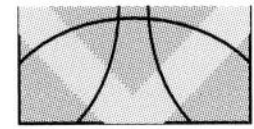

Half Norwich stitch over 16 threads: middle cross and three rounds tan; finished with pale turquoise

Golden grid

Norwich stitch over eight threads

Two tan + one pale turquoise

Tan

One tan + two pale turquoise

Cream

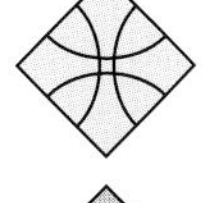

Pale turquoise

Mid-turquoise

Two mid-turquoise + one dark turquoise

Eyelet stitch with 16-thread base in two tan + one cream

Eyelet stitch with 12-thread base

Tan

One tan + two pale turquoise

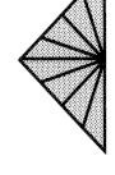

Mid-turquoise

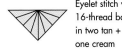

Two mid-turquoise + one dark turquoise

In the final Norwich stitch sample, the squares are worked diagonally to give yet another effect (*see* Fig 2.32). Some are worked in just one colour, some in two colours, some in four and even some in five colours. Between the Norwich stitches, the pattern is broken with lines of cushion stitch. These are worked over eight threads, the gold having eight stitches and the mid-turquoise only seven stitches. (*See* Fig 2.33.)

Fig 2.32 *Working Norwich stitches to give a diagonal pattern.*

Norwich stitch over 16 threads

Centre cross and two rounds dark turquoise; two rounds tan; two rounds pale turquoise; one round metallic gold

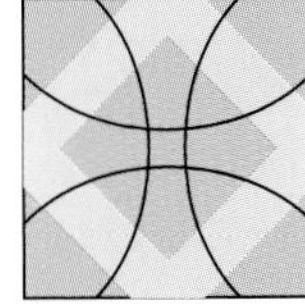

Centre cross and three rounds tan; four rounds pale turquoise

Centre cross and one round pale turquoise; two rounds mid-turquoise; one round tan; one round cream; two rounds dark turquoise

Fig 2.33 Stitch chart for the design shown in Fig 2.32.

Norwich stitch over eight threads

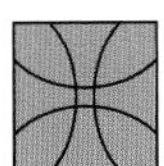

Mid-turquoise

Cream

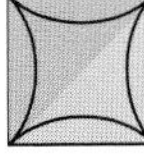

Two half cushion stitches over eight threads, one mid-turquoise, one metallic gold (note alternate versions)

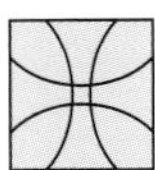

Pale turquoise

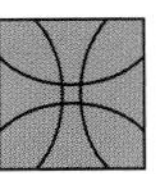

Dark turquoise

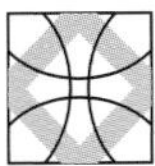

Centre cross and two rounds cream; one round tan

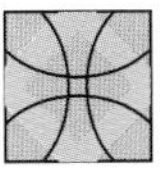

Centre cross and one round metallic gold; two rounds tan

DOUBLE-PLAITED CROSS STITCH

This stitch breaks the 'rule of four' as each single stitch goes over seven threads. It is quite a complex variation of cross stitch (*see* Fig 2.34). Although it gives an interesting finish, it is not easy to use. The reason for this is that quite a thick thread has to be employed in order to cover the background fabric and, even then, a stitch has to be added at the corners; a French knot or a small bead helps and adds interest to the finished design. A sprayed background also helps to hide the poor coverage of the stitch.

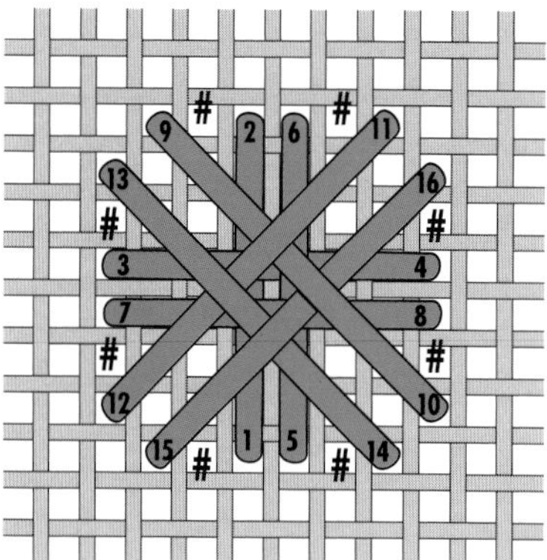

Stitch 15–16 goes under stitch 9–10

Fig 2.34 Working double-plaited cross stitch.

To work a French knot, bring the thread up through the fabric at the point where the knot is required. Loop the needle around the thread once and insert the point into the fabric, right next to the point from which it emerged. Pass the needle through to the back, holding the thread and pulling it carefully into a knot on the upper surface of the fabric. (*See* Fig 2.35.)

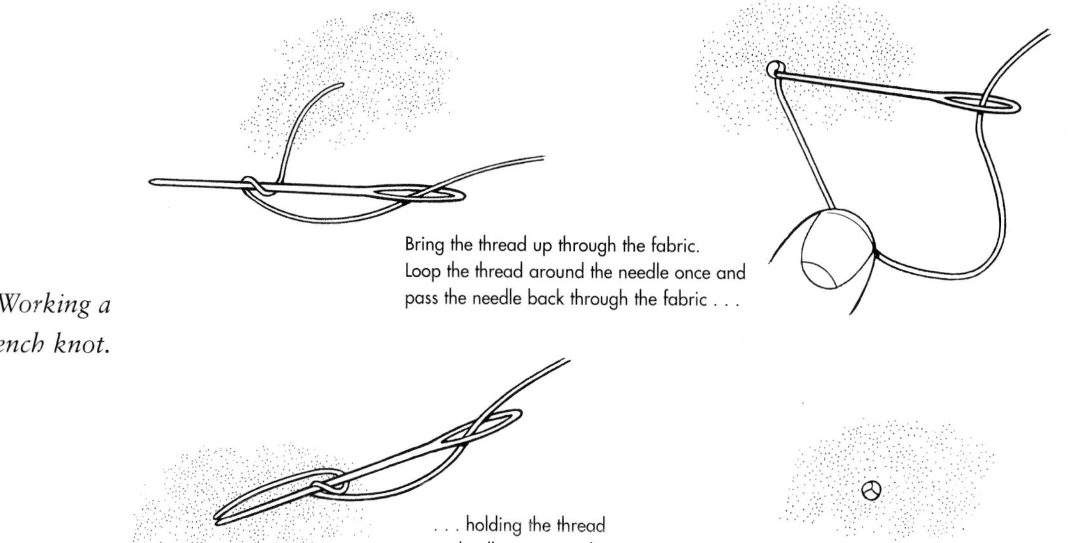

Bring the thread up through the fabric.
Loop the thread around the needle once and pass the needle back through the fabric . . .
. . . holding the thread and pulling it into a knot.
The finished knot.

Fig 2.35 Working a French knot.

VARIATIONS AND SAMPLES

In the sample (*see* Fig 2.36), gold ribbon has been couched into position to enhance the design, to separate the corner sections, and to fill in the spaces which would not divide into seven. Gütermann Dekor threads in maroon (5400), deep pink (5435), hyacinth blue (5900), yellow (1850), and cream (1195), and Madeira metallic gold thread (no. 12, colour 33) were used.

***Fig 2.36** Double-plaited cross stitch sample using couched gold ribbon and beads.*

Fig 2.37 The centre panel of the sample shown in Fig 2.36.

The centre stitches on the sample piece were bordered with a row of single tent stitches in metallic gold thread. Each complete double-plaited cross stitch was worked in a single colour but, at the end, a contrasting thread was used to weave a cross between each of the central diagonal stitches. The vacant hole in each corner was used for this purpose. The central square of 16 complete stitches was then surrounded by couched ribbon.

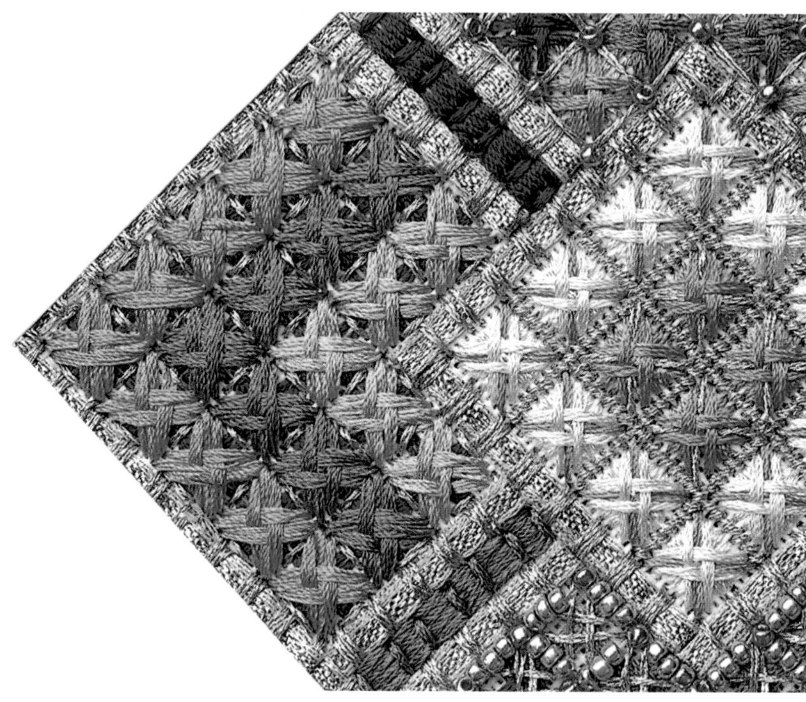

Fig 2.38 The west corner of the design shown in Fig 2.36.

For the west corner, the first four stitches (1–2, 3–4, 5–6 and 7–8) of each square were worked in maroon and the next four in a different colour (9–10, 11–12, 13–14 and 15–16). The outer round of stitches was worked in hyacinth blue, the middle round in pink and the inner in yellow. The final stitch of each round (15–16) is made under stitch 9–10. You will see that there is a vacant hole on each side of the first four stitches. These are marked with a # on the stitch diagram. To finish off this section, a small gold stitch was worked, coming up in the hole to the left of the two stitches and going over the ends of the two threads and into the hole on the right.

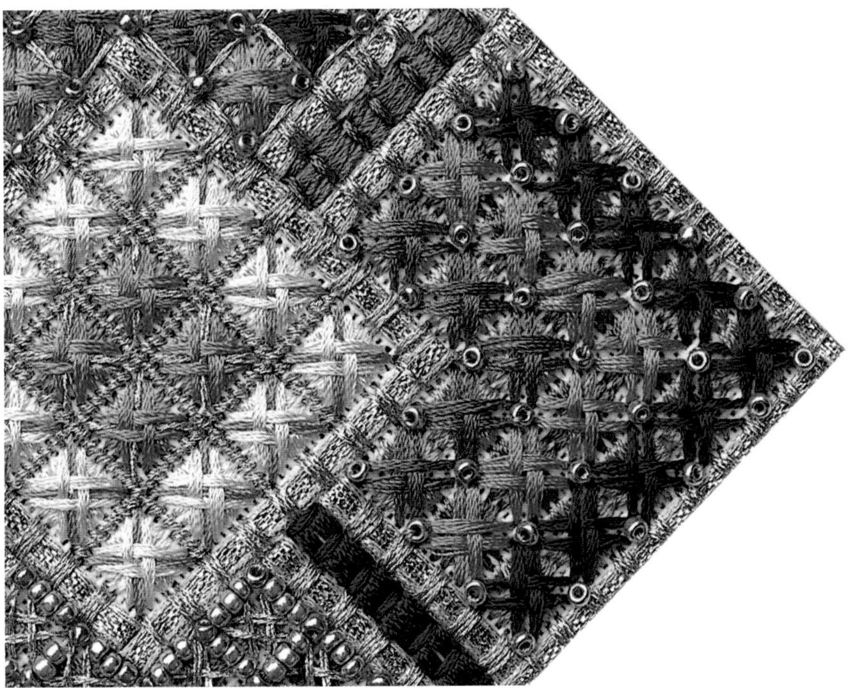

Fig 2.39 *The east corner of the design shown in Fig 2.36.*

For the east corner, starting from the centre, the stitch was begun in yellow and finished with pink. From this point, the top colour of the preceding square became the under colour of the next square. To complete this corner, a single gold bead was added at each stitch intersection.

Fig 2.40 *The north corner of the design shown in Fig 2.36.*

For the north corner, each square was started in metallic gold and the colours were radiated diagonally. Straight metallic gold stitches were then worked to outline each square and a single pink bead added at each intersection.

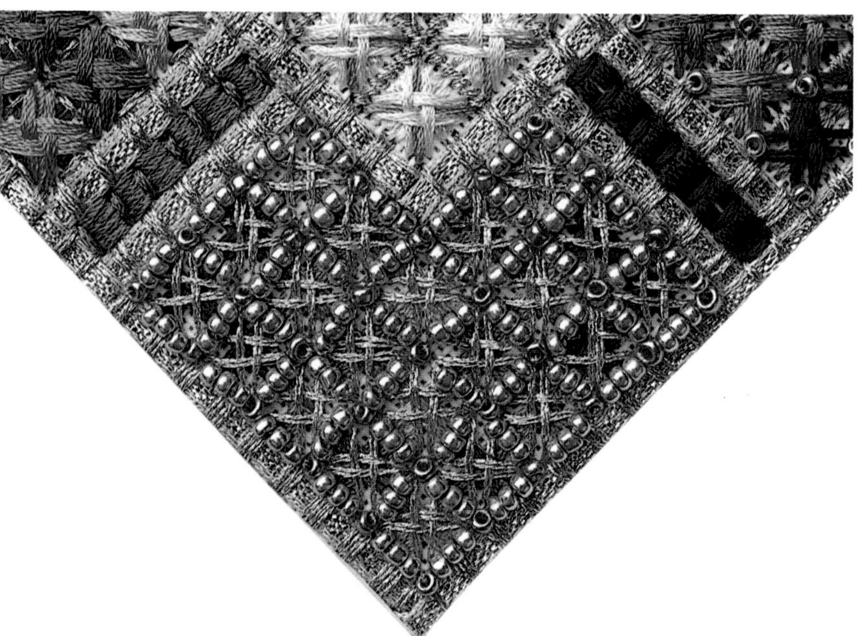

Fig 2.41 *The south corner of the design shown in Fig 2.36.*

In this final section, coloured threads were used to start each cross stitch and metallic gold thread used to complete them. The cross stitches did not cover the background very well, so more beads were added, as shown in Fig 2.41.

ADDITIONAL STITCHES

A number of stitches, other than those which employ the colour through gold technique, can be used to fill in blank areas around designs. Follow the diagrams below for the execution of these stitches.

While they are not used singly, but as part of a larger design, we have highlighted what constitutes a single unit of each stitch, together with the overall pattern they form, for reasons of clarity.

Tent stitch

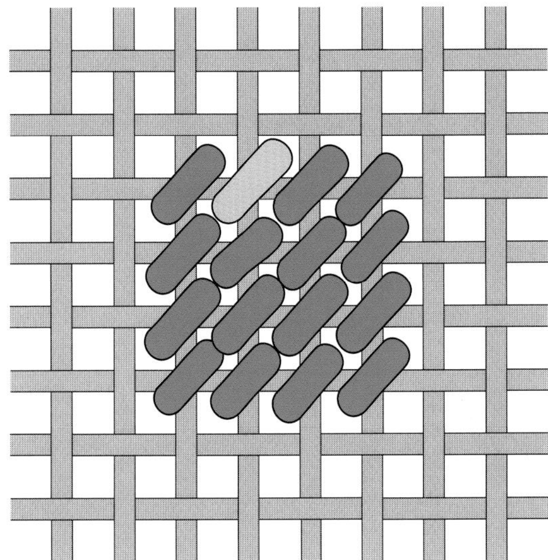

Fig 2.42 *One tent stitch consists of a single diagonal stitch.*

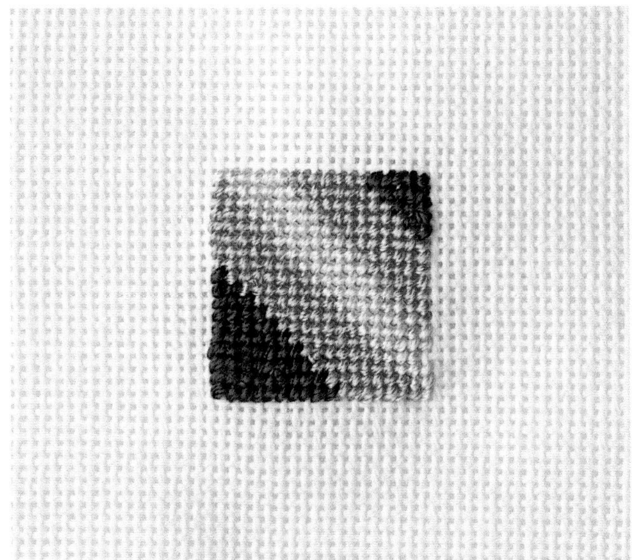

Fig 2.43 *A block of tent stitches worked to give diagonal stripes.*

Cross stitch

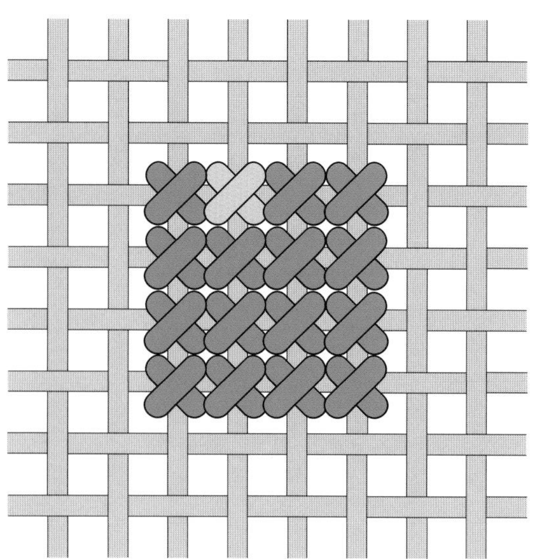

Fig 2.44 A cross stitch consists of two diagonal stitches placed, not surprisingly, to form a cross.

Fig 2.45 A colourful square of cross stitches.

Parisian stitch

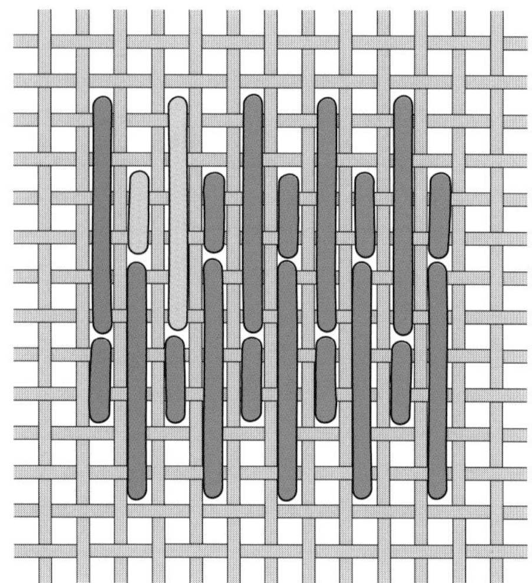

Fig 2.46 A single Parisian stitch consists of one short and one long straight stitch.

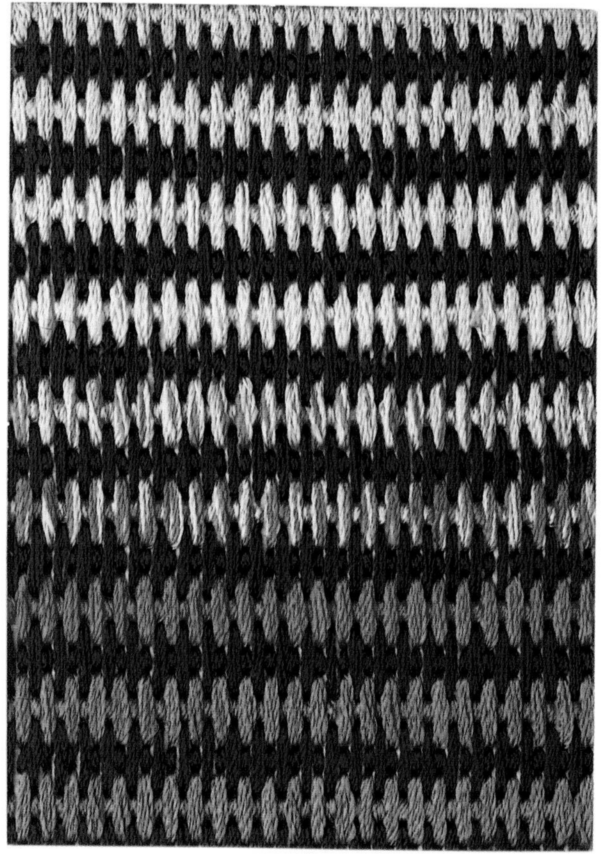

Fig 2.47 Parisian stitch sampler.

HUNGARIAN STITCH

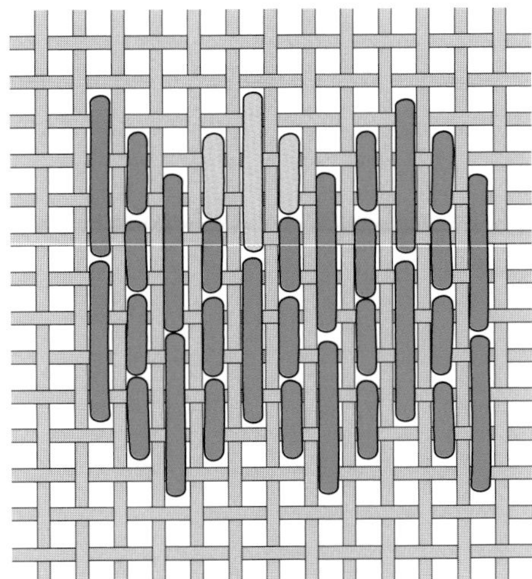

Fig 2.48 *One Hungarian stitch consists of a short, a long and a short stitch, placed as highlighted above.*

Fig 2.49 *Gold thread is used to outline diamonds in this Hungarian stitch sampler.*

HUNGARIAN STITCH VARIATION

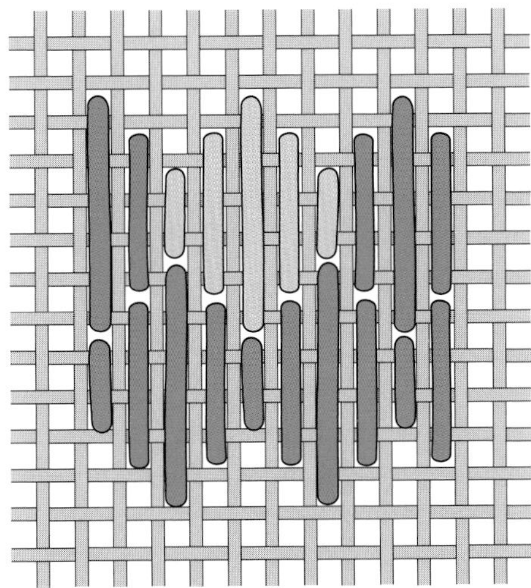

Fig 2.50 *Hungarian stitch can be varied by adding two extra stitches at either side, as shown above.*

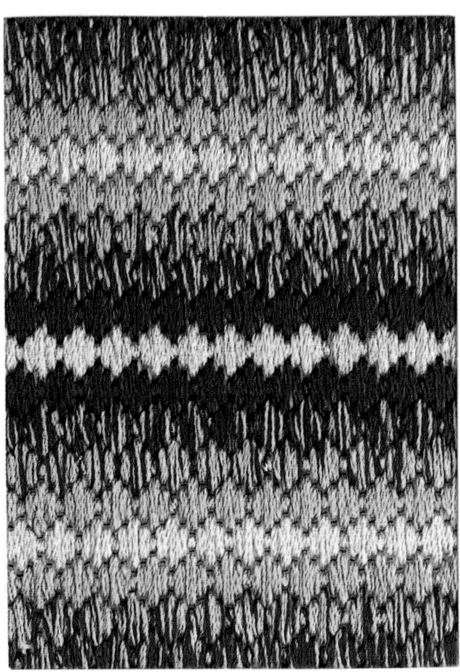

Fig 2.51 *This Hungarian stitch variation gives a more solid-looking design.*

Rice stitch

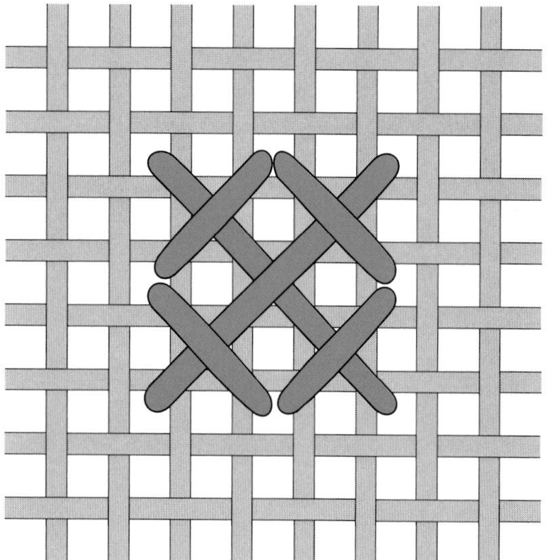

Fig 2.52 *Rice stitch consists of a cross stitch with each of the four arms overlaid with thread of another colour.*

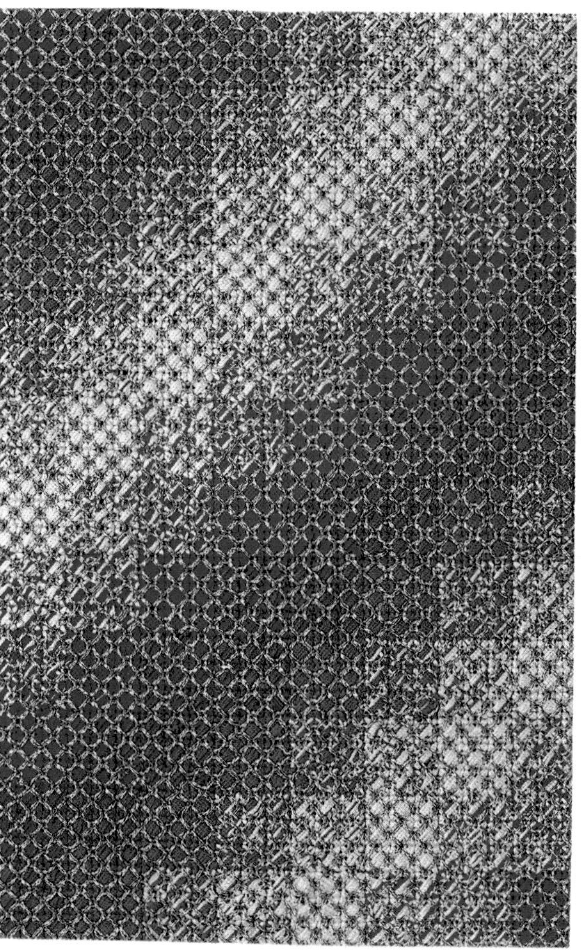

Fig 2.53 *A block of rice stitch gives an interesting woven effect.*

Fig 2.54 *This rice stitch border directs the eye to the central panel of the design.*

Triple rice stitch

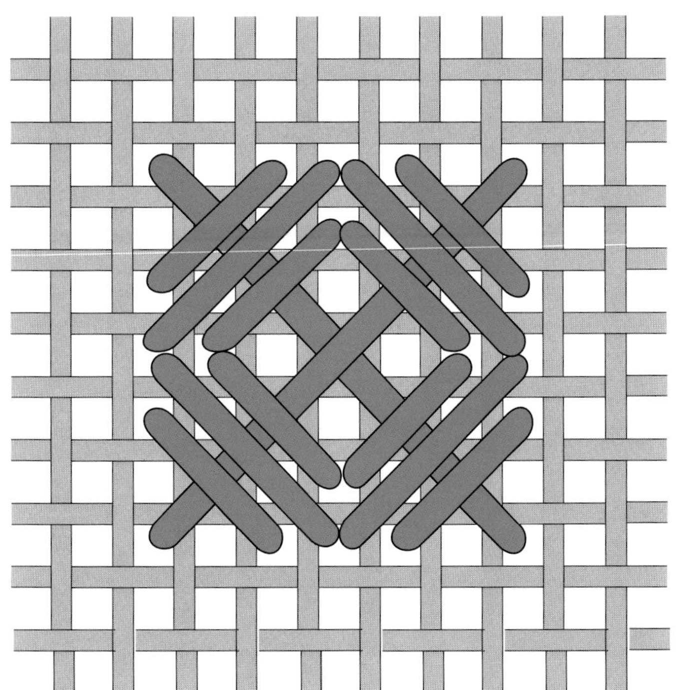

Fig 2.55 Triple rice stitch, as the name suggests, is worked in the same way as rice stitch, but with three overlaid stitches on each of the base cross stitch arms.

Fig 2.56 Triple rice stitch gives the impression of depth.

Pinwheel Milanese

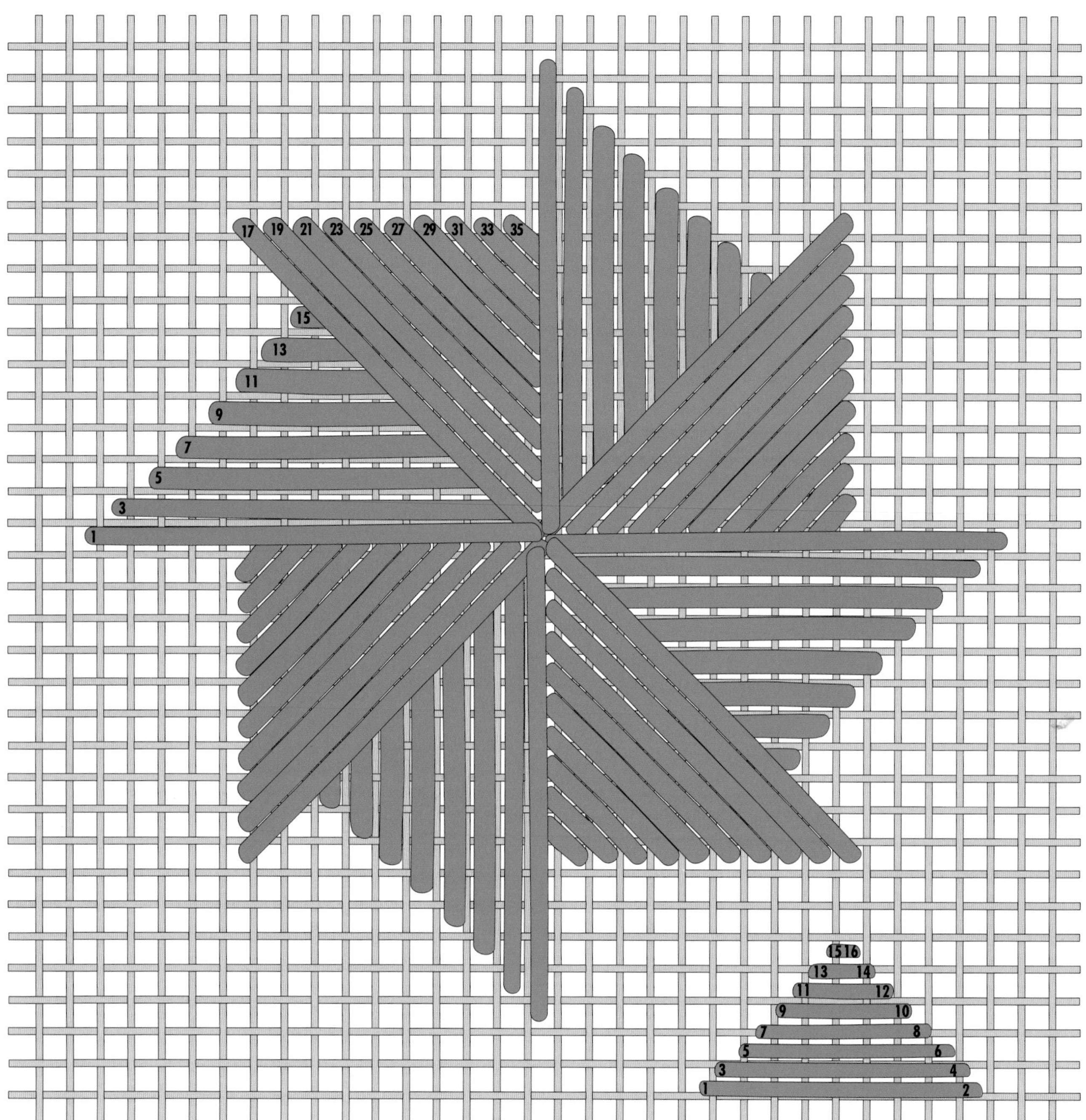

***Fig 2.57** A pinwheel Milanese stitch is made up of eight triangles, with the threads in each placed at an angle of 45° to the previous one. Each triangle consists of eight or ten straight threads with each successive stitch shorter, as shown.*

***Fig 2.58** A single pinwheel Milanese stitch. Notice how the triangles catch the light differently.*

***Fig 2.59** A design based on pinwheel Milanese stitch.*

Mosaic stitch

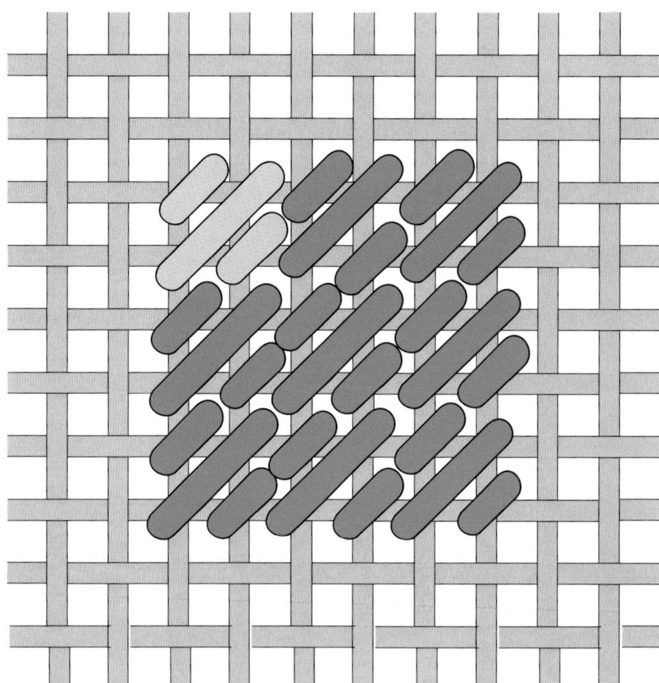

Fig 2.60 *Like Hungarian stitch, a mosaic stitch consists of a short, a long and a short stitch, but for mosaic stitch they are worked diagonally.*

Fig 2.61 *Mosaic stitch gives an interesting texture to the background of this design.*

Eyelet stitch and Straight stitch

Straight stitches, the basic unit of all the preceding stitches, can be used to form eyelet stitches. These are worked in the shape of a triangle, as shown in Fig 2.62.

Straight stitches can also be used on their own, over any number of threads, as in the sample shown in Fig 2.63. Straight stitches may be vertical, horizontal or diagonal.

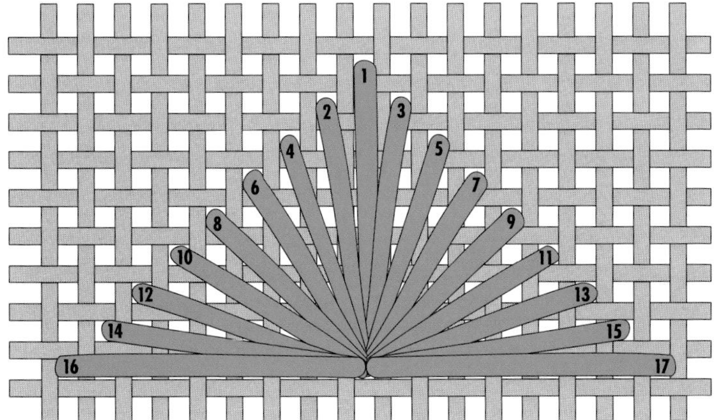

Fig 2.62 *Straight stitches placed to work an eyelet stitch.*

Fig 2.63 *A design made up entirely of straight stitches.*

POINTS TO REMEMBER

Borders

When using colour through gold stitches as a border, always start at the centre and work towards the corners. If the stitches do not fit exactly, it is easier to adapt the corners than to adapt the main band.

Working with multiple threads

It is very useful, when working with multiple threads, to use the middle finger of your left hand (right hand if you are left-handed) to tension the threads from behind your work. This is especially useful if you are working with metallic threads, which have a life of their own and spring about unexpectedly. It also enables you to feel if the threads have become knotted at the back of the work.

Using metallic threads

When working with metallic gold thread, use it double. Thread the needle, pull the two ends level then run your fingers firmly down each thread and let it unwind. Finally, knot the two ends together, avoiding adding any twist to the thread. This should ensure that the thread will remain straight throughout the stitching.

Direction of stitches

With some canvaswork stitches, it is important to keep the frame facing the same way so that the final stitch always lies in the same direction. Rhodes stitch is one example where this is essential and, with Norwich stitch, if the frame does not stay facing the same way, the weaving in the centre of the stitch will not be correct. To be sure which way it is facing, put a small pencil mark on the edge of the frame and keep this facing towards you. (It is so easy to be in the middle of some work, put the frame down when the telephone rings and then pick it up at the end of your conversation and wonder where you should be working!)

CHAPTER 3

Inspiration and Variation

Anywhere you look there may be sources which inspire you to use the colour through gold technique. Photographs, postcards, greetings cards and wrapping paper, floor and wall tiles, flower beds and gardens can all stimulate ideas for colour and design. When borrowing colours from another source, always consider the amount of each colour used in the design and keep the balance the same.

A DESIGN INSPIRED BY TILES

On a visit to Lisbon, Portugal, in the autumn of 1996, we were fascinated by the tiles used to decorate many of the buildings. We photographed several examples as I could see they would make an ideal inspirational source for colour through gold.

The tiles selected for this project, a magazine cover, used mainly blues, as did many of the others, so I kept a blue theme and added gold and cream. I completed the work with Indian rayon threads and outlined the squares in Madeira metallic gold (no. 12, colour 33) with backstitch over four threads.

As I required rectangular shapes, I decided to experiment with Rhodes stitch, stitching rectangles instead of the traditional squares. I stitched in the same way as for the square stitch, starting at the lower left hand corner and finishing with an extra stitch overlaying the first stitch. This worked well (*see* Fig 3.1).

As the top stitches of the larger rectangle turned out quite long and therefore not very practical – they catch too easily – I added a short vertical stitch to hold them in place and to keep them from being caught up when the cover is in use.

Another variation I employed in this design was to work all the side rectangles in the opposite direction from the central rectangles. It is important always to hold the frame facing the same way when working Rhodes stitch in one direction, so that the top threads all lay in the same direction.

Fig 3.1 This design was inspired by typical Portuguese tiles.

ALTERING A STITCH

Most books on canvaswork give very adequate diagrams showing how to work the individual stitches and usually have an accompanying photograph showing a stitched example. However, each stitch tends to be worked in a single colour and, although some books do show various sizes of stitch, little variation is shown.

Here are some suggestions for ways in which stitches can be varied but the list is endless. Play around and you too will come up with new ideas.

- ✦ Changing the size. Stitches can easily be enlarged or reduced.
- ✦ With colour. See what happens when you work composite stitches, changing colour two, three or even four times.
- ✦ Changing the shape. As we have done with Rhodes stitch, traditionally a square stitch, experiment with shape making stitches rectangular, triangular or even octagonal.
- ✦ Stitch with mixed colours in the needle. Changing one thread at a time will result in subtle changes of colour.
- ✦ Take a square stitch and use multiples of it, as well as half-drop repeats (*see* Fig 2.11). A square stitch can also be rotated to form a diamond.
- ✦ Use stitches to form a border. Try working cross-cornered cushion stitch in three colours, side by side: under-patterns will appear.
- ✦ Alter direction. Using cross-cornered cushion stitch as an example, take the two right-hand squares and repeat them in line: the overlay will form an arrowhead border.
- ✦ Alter amounts of overlay.
- ✦ Work square stitches diagonally to give a diagonal striped effect.
- ✦ Work part of a stitch and keep repeating it – half Rhodes stitch is a good example of this.
- ✦ Work stitches with a grid of single tent stitches around each stitch.
- ✦ Work all horizontal stitches in one colour and all vertical stitches in a contrasting shade.
- ✦ Use a backstitch outline. Work a section of stitches and then outline each one in a contrasting colour with backstitch.

CHAPTER 4

Golden Grids

These three basic grids provide an excellent foundation on which to base designs and prove an attractive way to give stitches a gold outline.

A close look at the frontispiece to this book, *The Elephant Thief*, shows a grid – golden grid 1– used to interpret the decoration of the archway. Such grids have been used in several pieces throughout the book.

All the examples in the following illustrations have been worked using metallic gold thread doubled, to work single, long stitches as indicated on the charts.

GOLDEN GRID 1

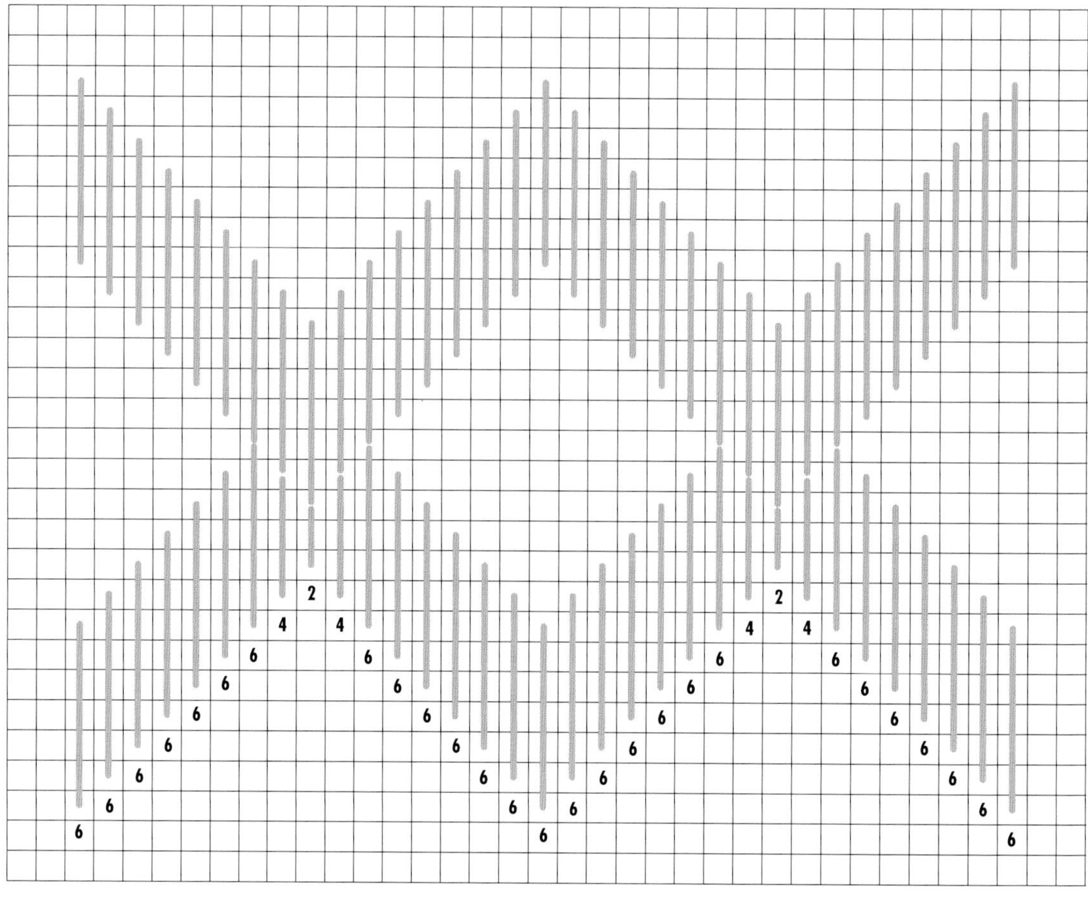

Fig 4.1 Placement of stitches for working Golden Grid 1.

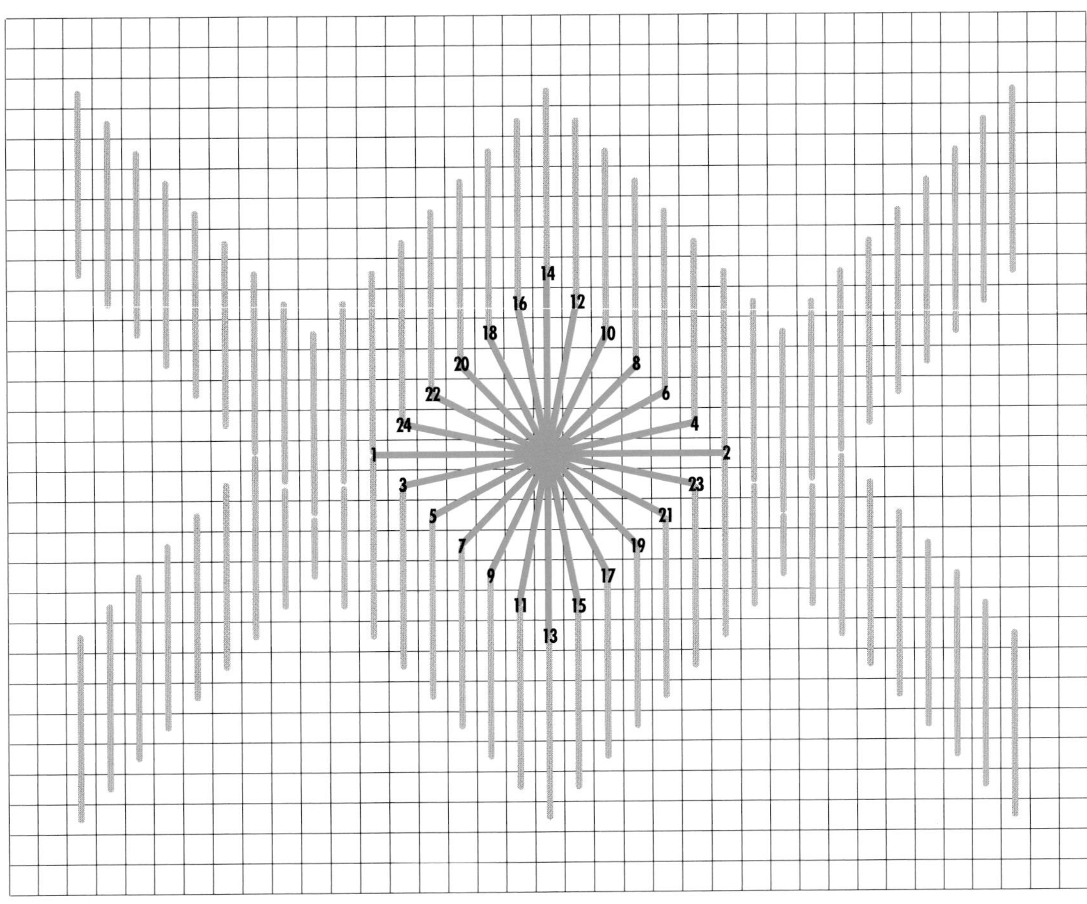

Fig 4.2 *Placement of stitches for working a Rhodes stitch within Golden Grid 1.*

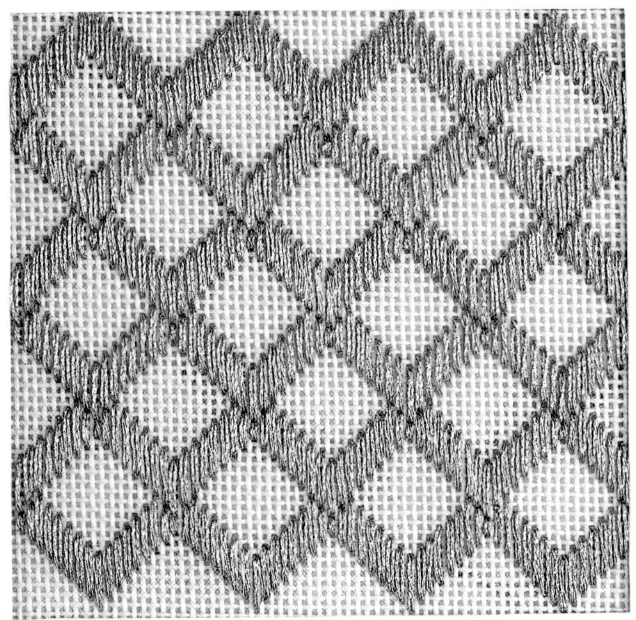

Fig 4.3 *The diamond pattern produced by Golden Grid 1.*

Fig 4.4 *Golden Grid 1 'filled in' with Rhodes stitches.*

GOLDEN GRID 2

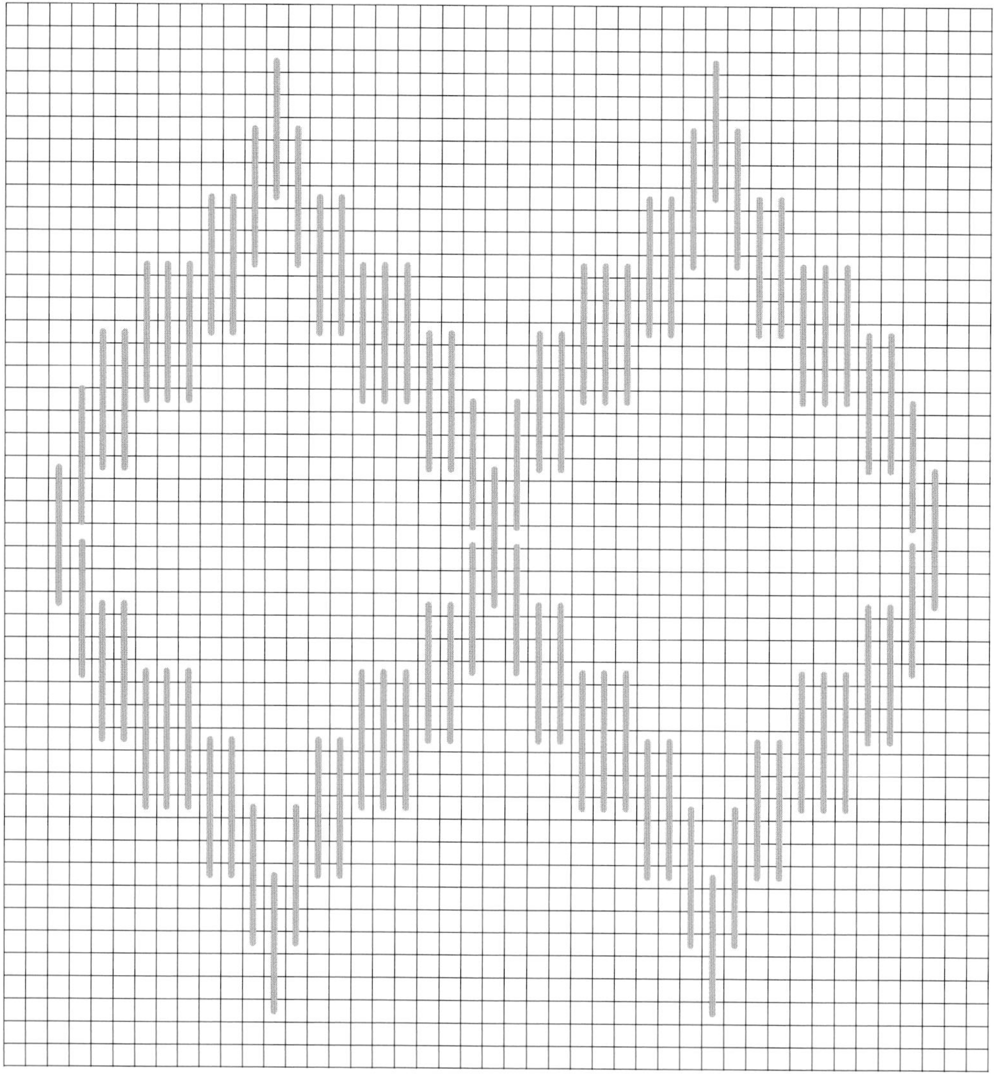

Fig 4.5 Placement of stitches (all over six threads) for working Golden Grid 2.

Fig 4.6 *Golden Grid 2 produces an almond shape.*

Fig 4.7 *Golden Grid 2 used to contain letters on a greetings card.*

GOLDEN GRID 3

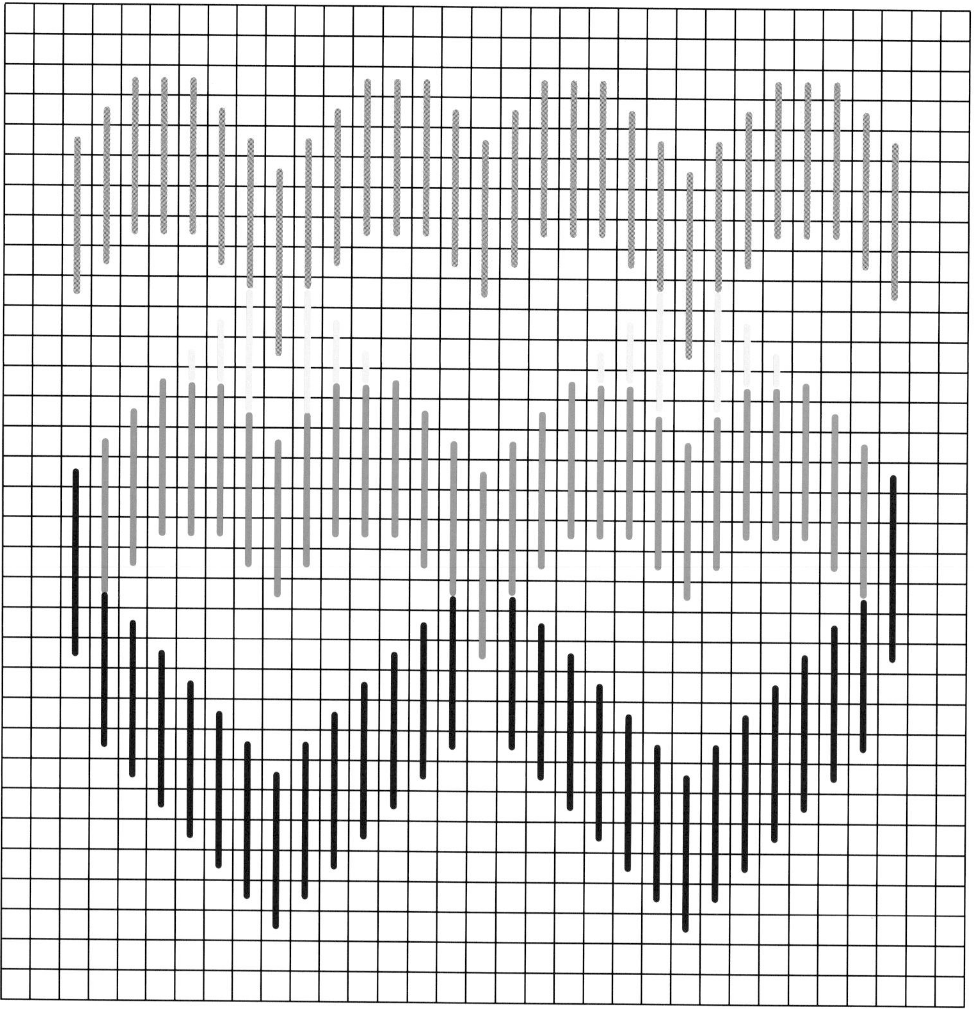

Fig 4.8 Placement of stitches for working Golden Grid 3.

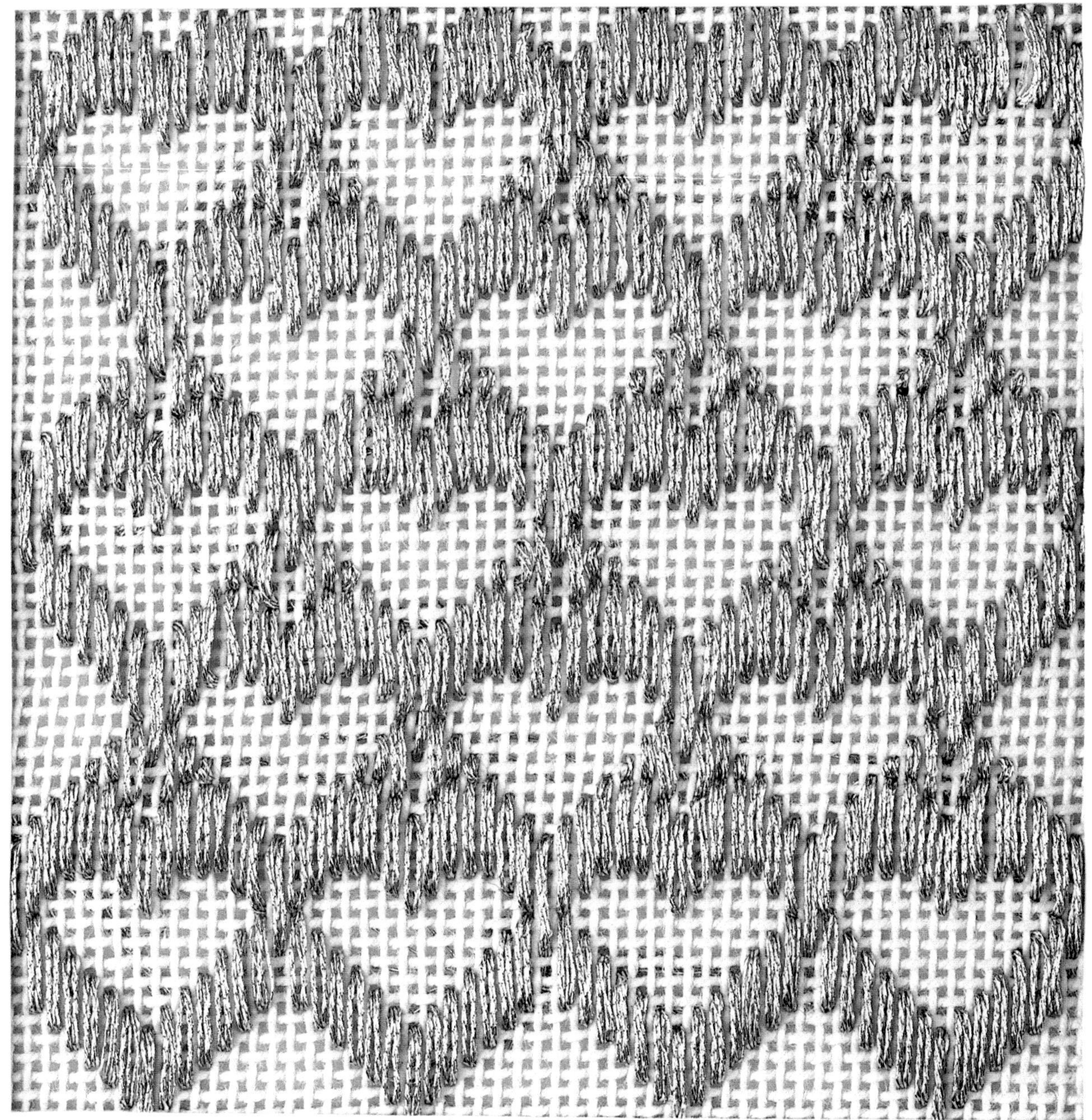

Fig 4.9 *Golden Grid 3 produces a distinctive heart shape.*

Fig 4.10 Golden Grid 3 used as a motif on an anniversary card.

PART TWO

THE PROJECTS

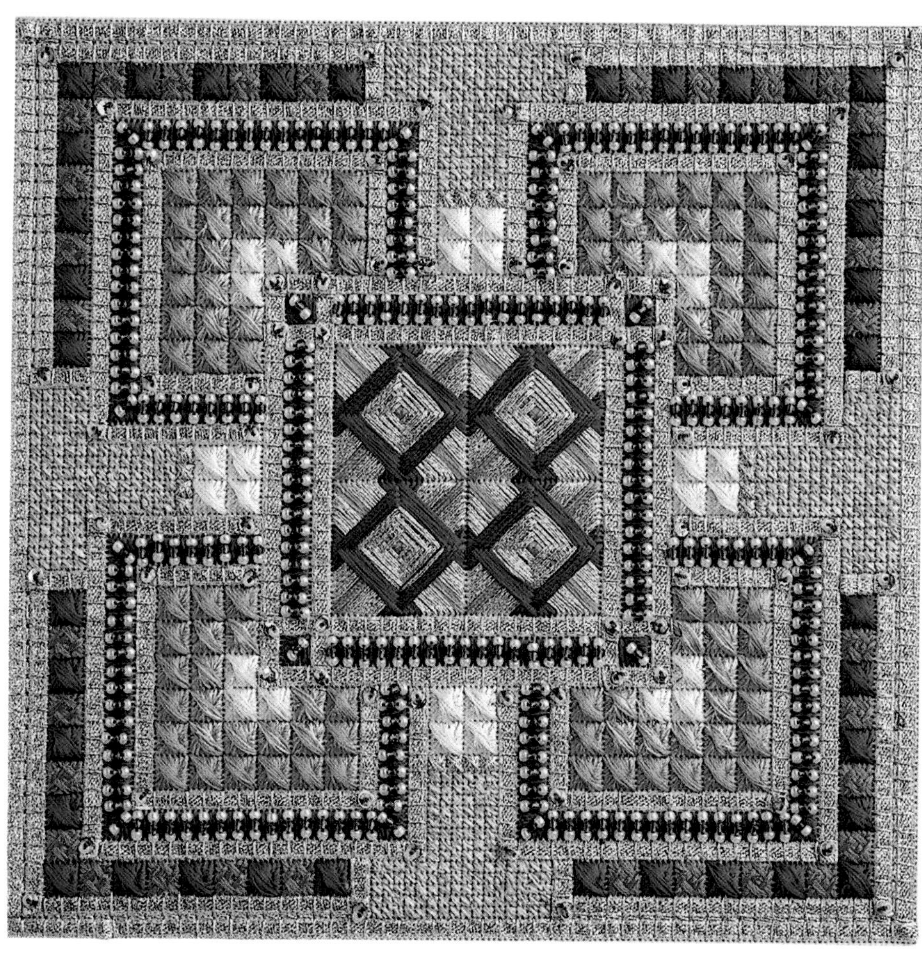

CHAPTER 5

Greetings Card

The perfect 'all purpose' greetings card – a stunning design in glorious colours which must bring a real glow to the eyes of the recipient.

Strongly influenced by Bargello, this simple embroidery uses only straight stitches on a golden grid pattern, relying on the gold and the lustre of the Marlitt threads to make the design come alive.

Include your own message or add a name to give your card a really personal touch. (*See* page 61 for a complete alphabet.)

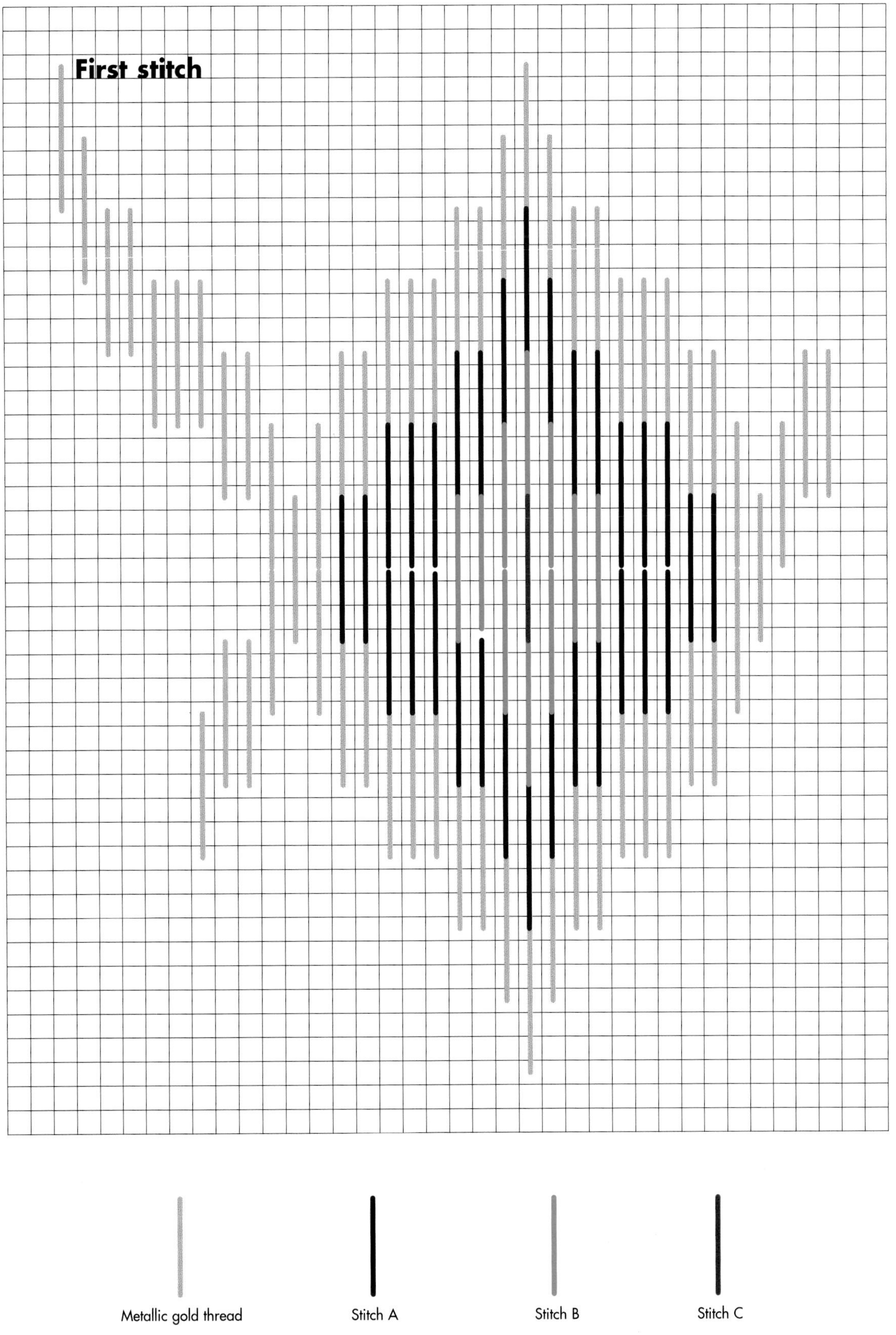

Fig 5.1 Stitch chart for the top-left corner of the embroidery.

THREAD KEY

1 skein each of Anchor Marlitt in:

Peacock	836
Deep turquoise	1055
Pale turquoise	1053
Tan	1079
Yellow	1077
Cream	1036

1 reel of Madeira metallic gold no. 12, colour 33

MATERIALS AND EQUIPMENT

Threads as listed in key
Congress cloth, 8½ x 6in (216 x 152mm)
Wooden frame, 8½ x 6in (216 x 152mm)
Tapestry needle, no. 24
Embroidery scissors
Greetings card with an aperture of 5½ x 3¾in (140 x 95mm)

PREPARATION

Staple or pin the congress cloth to the frame. If drawing pins are used, cover the heads with masking tape to avoid the threads catching. Mark out an area of 141 x 96 threads, by tacking just outside this area.

EMBROIDERY

Use the Marlitt threads in three thicknesses and the metallic gold doubled throughout.

Start by working the golden grid. Each stitch is over six threads and each stitch or group of stitches drops down by half its length (*see* Fig 5.1). Begin with the single metallic gold stitch in the top left-hand corner, then drop down three threads to make the second single stitch. Follow this with a group of two stitches, then three stitches, another two stitches, a single stitch and finally another single stitch, dropping down each time. The final single stitch is the central one, so now repeat the sequence, this time moving up three stitches rather than dropping. This will bring you to the top middle stitch and completes one sequence.

Repeat until seven sequences have been worked across the congress cloth, then work five more rows across until four rows of complete shapes have been formed. You will need to reverse the order of dropping or moving up stitches with each row and you will, of course, have half shapes at the top and bottom. (*See* the photograph of the finished card.)

Fill in the grid as directed below, referring to Fig 5.1 as you work, and leave the letter spaces blank (*see* Figs 5.1 and 5.2). Start in the bottom left-hand corner and work in Rhodes stitch using the following thread combinations:

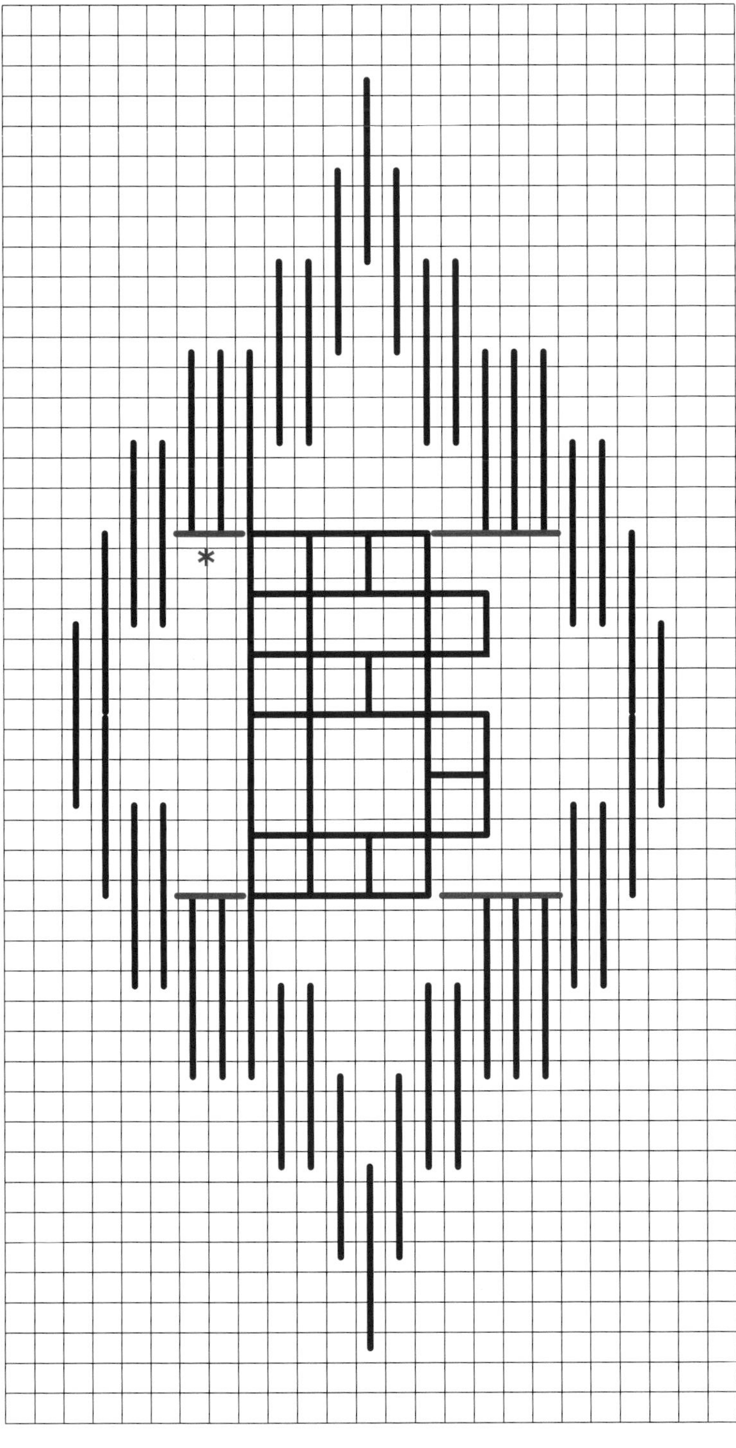
*
The letter W will start one square over

Fig 5.2 *Stitch chart for positioning the letters.*

Row 1 (the lower half row)
A: 3 peacock blue
B: 2 peacock blue + 1 deep turquoise
C: 3 cream

Row 2 (the first row of complete shapes)
A: 3 deep turquoise
B: 2 deep turquoise + 1 pale turquoise
C: 3 yellow

Row 3 (here, in the illustrated card, the letter shapes use all but two half shapes)
A: 3 pale turquoise
B: 2 pale turquoise + 1 tan
C: 3 tan

Row 4 (the last row of complete shapes)
A: 3 tan
B: 2 tan + 1 yellow
C: 3 pale turquoise

Row 5 (four shapes are taken up with letters)
A: 3 yellow
B: 2 yellow + 1 cream
C: 3 deep turquoise

Row 6 (these are only half shapes)
A: 3 cream
B: 2 cream + 1 gold metallic
C: 3 peacock blue

Now work your chosen letters in the empty shapes. (*See* Fig 5.3.) Referring to Fig 5.2, you will see that the top of each letter is level with the base of the groups of three gold metallic stitches in each shape and the bottom of the letter is level with the top of the group of three metallic gold stitches.

Work the letter shapes in mosaic stitch (*see* page 42), using metallic gold thread, and outline each letter with backstitching in peacock blue thread.

Having worked the letters, fill in the remainder of the shapes with pale turquoise vertical stitches, using part stitches where necessary.

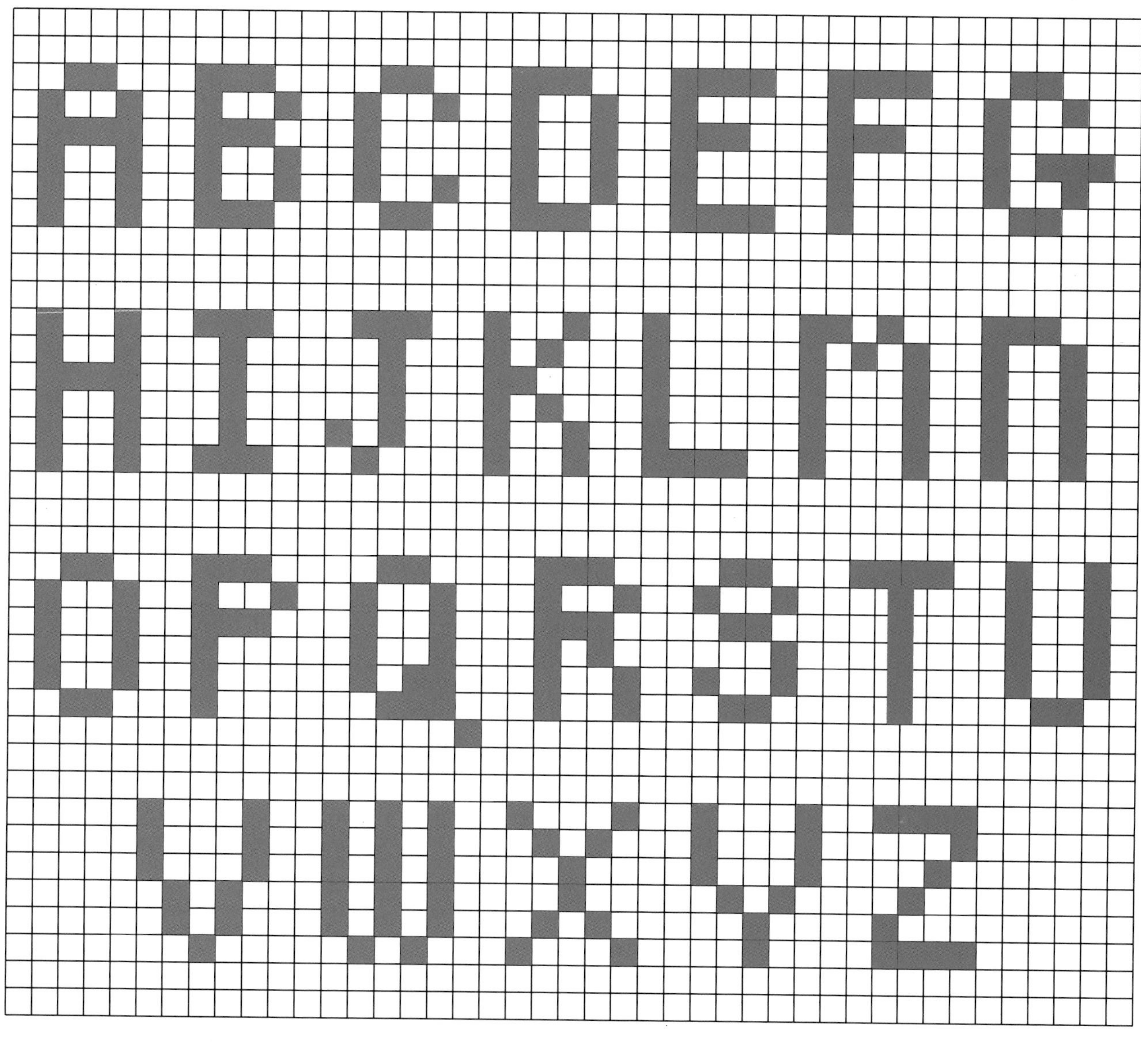

Fig 5.3 Stitch chart for greetings card alphabet.

MAKING UP

The embroidery is now complete and ready to be assembled. (*See* page 160 for advice on mounting and making up the card.)

CHAPTER 6

Golden Wedding Card

Special events deserve celebrating and this attractive card could not be a more beautiful expression of congratulation.

The design shown is for a golden wedding but it can be altered to suit any other anniversary or special event. There are various types of 'church window' aperture cards available which would enable you to make your design unique.

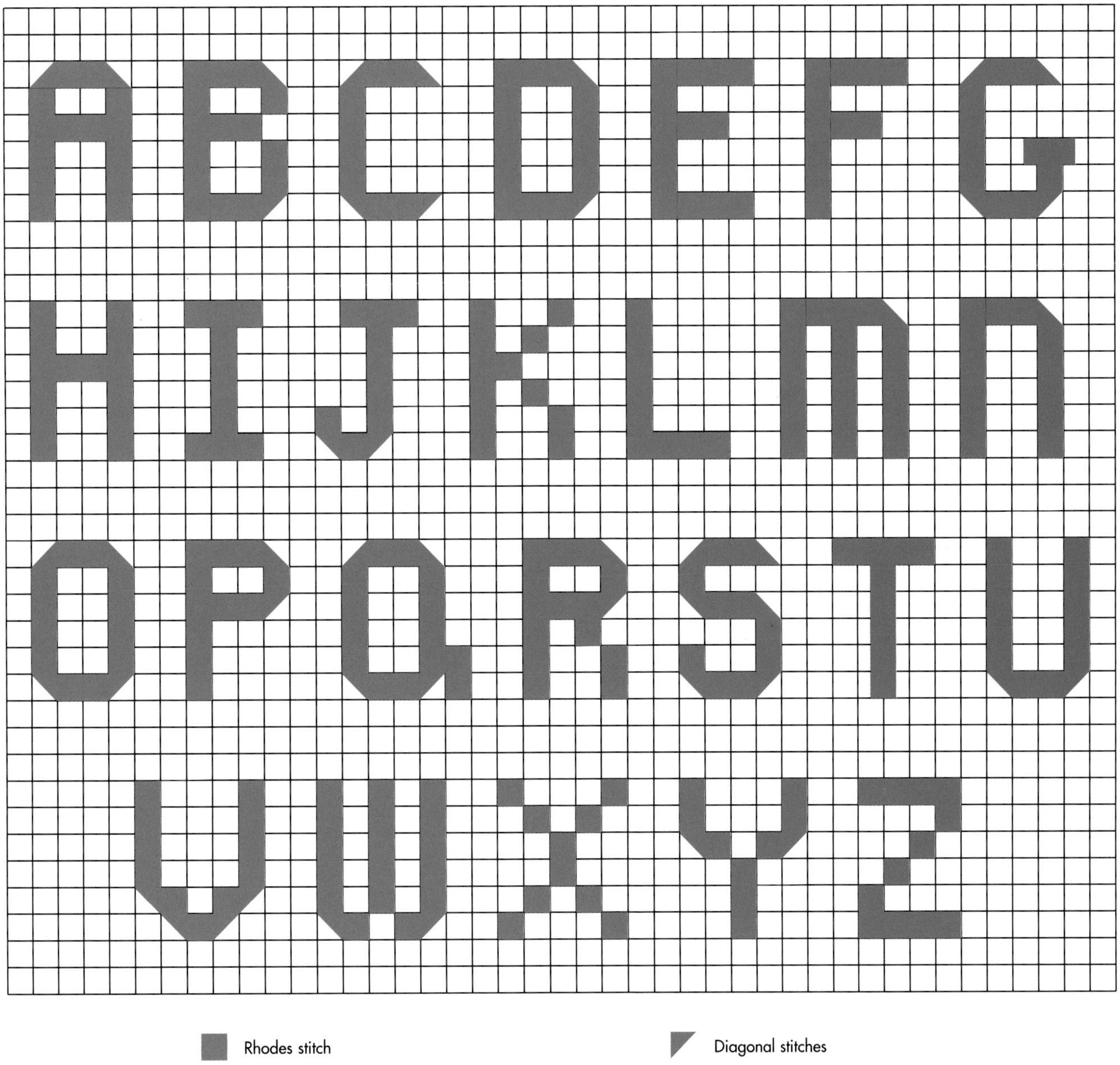

Rhodes stitch

Diagonal stitches

Fig 6.1 Stitch chart for golden wedding card alphabet: capitals.

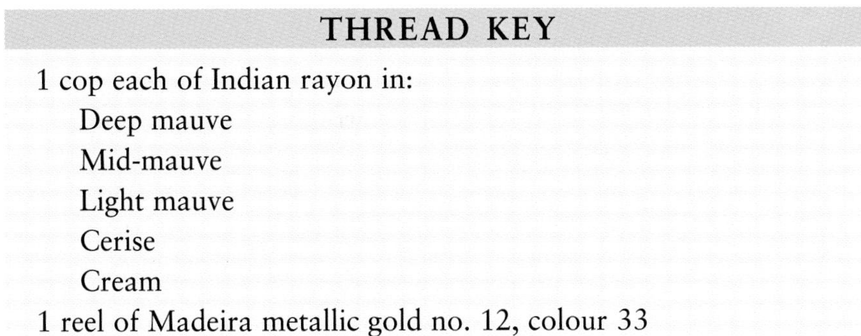

THREAD KEY

1 cop each of Indian rayon in:
- Deep mauve
- Mid-mauve
- Light mauve
- Cerise
- Cream

1 reel of Madeira metallic gold no. 12, colour 33

MATERIALS AND EQUIPMENT

Threads as listed in key
Congress cloth, 8½ x 6in (216 x 152mm)
Wooden frame, 8½ x 6in (216 x 152mm)
Greetings card with church window aperture
Tapestry needle, no. 24
Embroidery scissors

PREPARATION

Staple or pin the congress cloth to the embroidery frame. If drawing pins are used, cover the heads with masking tape to avoid the threads catching. Lay the card over the cloth and, with pencil, carefully mark out the areas to be worked.

EMBROIDERY

Use the Indian rayon threads in six thicknesses and the metallic gold double throughout.

Work the larger letters for the initials in Rhodes stitch, each square over four threads, with the triangular corners to the letters in straight stitches. (*See* Fig 6.1.) Use the darkest shade for this.

Position the initials on the left side, starting the lower letter approximately 14 threads up from the lower edge. Leave six threads between this letter and the word 'and', then leave six more unworked before beginning the top initial. Outline each initial in gold thread.

On the right-hand side, work the number of years being celebrated and any other lettering required, e.g. the date or the range of years, etc. Lower case letters and numbers are all worked in tent stitches (*see* Fig 6.2).

Having completed all the lettering and numbers, work the background in rice stitch. Work each cross over four threads and cross the corners with metallic gold thread. Overlap the lines drawn on the cloth with a complete rice stitch to ensure that no fabric shows.

Where the space doesn't allow rice stitch to be worked, fill in the background with tent stitch.

In the worked example, small areas of each colour were worked randomly, but they could be arranged starting with the lightest at the top and ending with the darkest shade.

MAKING UP

The embroidery is now complete and ready to be assembled. (*See* page 160 for advice on mounting and making up the card.)

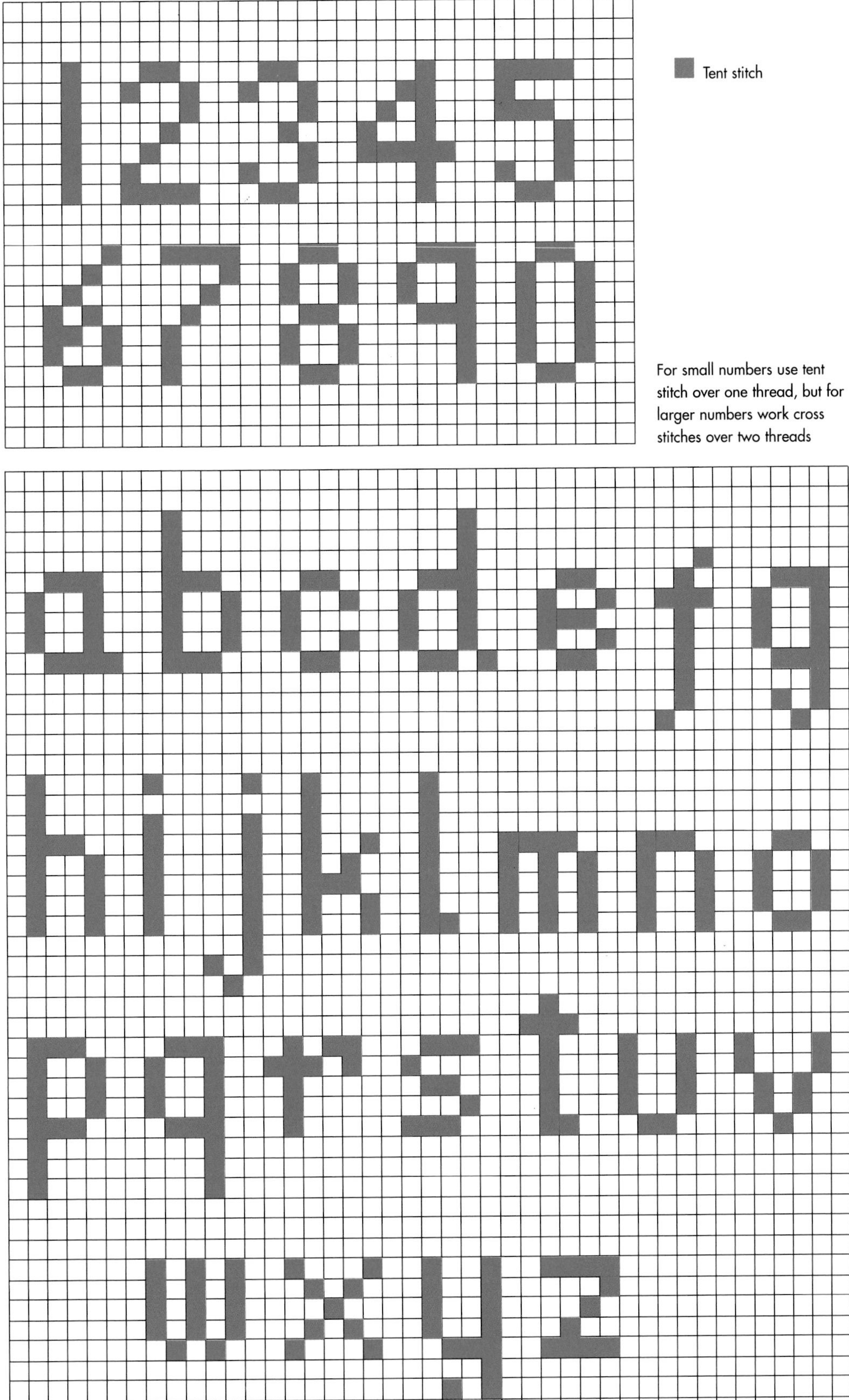

Tent stitch
For small numbers use tent stitch over one thread, but for larger numbers work cross stitches over two threads

***Fig 6.2** Stitch chart for golden wedding card alphabet: lower case letters and numbers.*

CHAPTER 7

DESK SET

This set consists of a blotter, pen holder, notebook cover and letter rack, which all co-ordinate handsomely.

THREAD KEY

1 cop each of Madeira rayon no. 40 in:

Deep orange	1021
Pale orange	1226
Deep green	1052
Turquoise	1292
Deep mauve	1330
Pale mauve	1311

3 reels of Madeira metallic gold no. 12, colour 33

MATERIALS AND EQUIPMENT

For all elements:

Threads as listed in key
Congress cloth, 18in (457mm) square
Co-ordinating cotton fabric, 2m
Matching Gütermann sewing thread
Rectangular embroidery frame, 18in (457mm) square (the individual pieces could be made on smaller frames but more congress cloth would then be required)
Tapestry needle, no. 24
Sewing needle
Curved needle
Embroidery scissors

For blotter:

Thick card, 15 x 21½in (381 x 546mm) x 2
Vilene extra heavy interfacing, 15 x 4in (381 x 102mm) x 2

For letter rack:

Card, ⅛in (2mm) thick x 2 sheets

For pen holder:

Card, ⅛in (2mm) thick x 1 sheet

continued

continued

For notebook cover:
Notebook, 5¾in (146mm) square
Vilene extra heavy interfacing, 12½ x 6in (317 x 152mm)

PREPARATION

Staple or pin the congress cloth to the embroidery frame. If drawing pins are used, cover the heads with masking tape to avoid the embroidery threads catching. Following Fig 7.1, mark out the areas to be embroidered, in pencil, leaving a minimum of 1½in (40mm) between the panels.

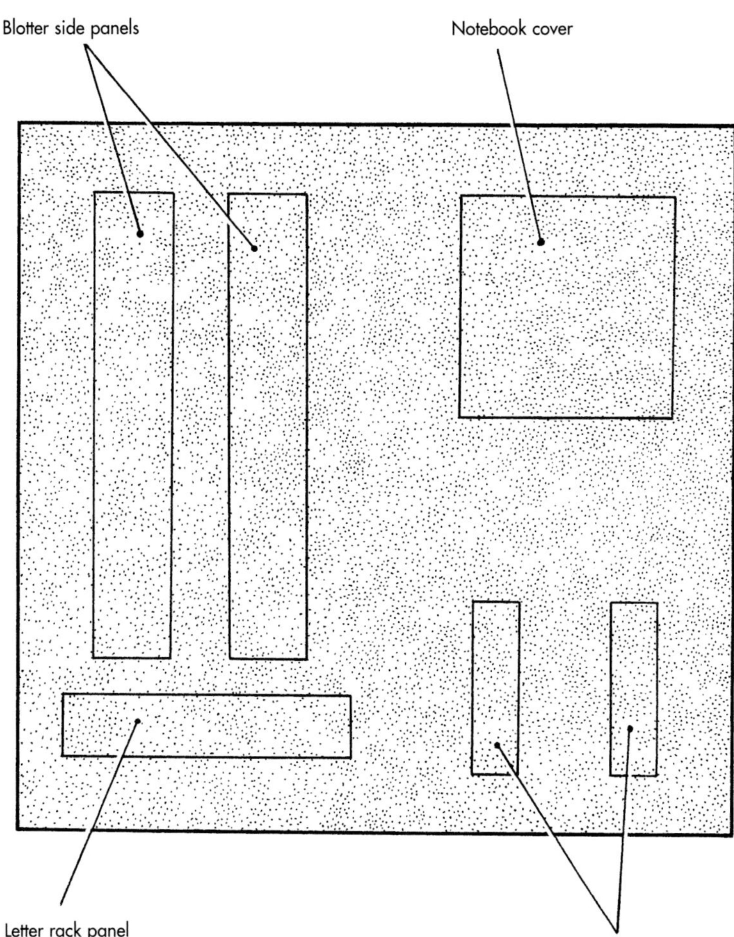

Fig 7.1 Suggested layout for the stitched decorations on the congress cloth.

EMBROIDERY

For each item, all the embroidery is worked in cushion stitch, with the gold overlay at right angles to the coloured threads. Work each stitch in the colours and direction indicated by the charts (*see* Figs 7.2–7.5). Coloured threads are used in six thicknesses and the metallic gold thread double throughout.

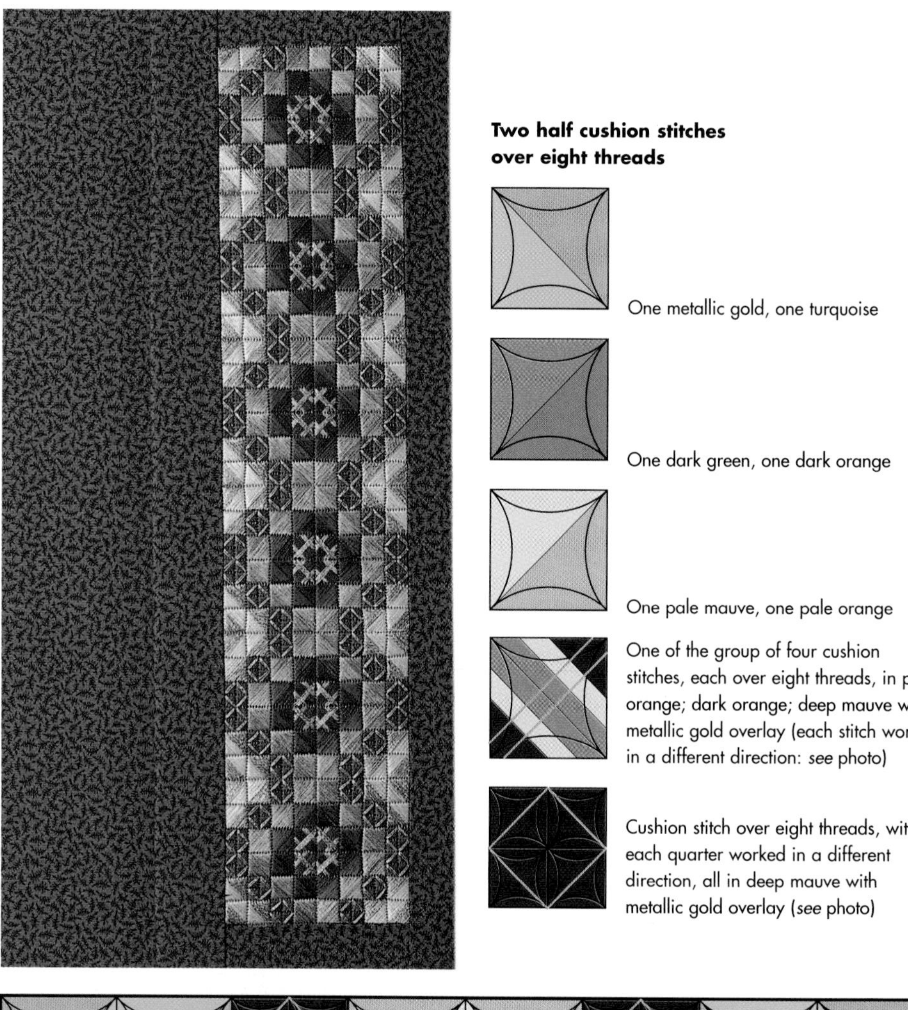

***Fig 7.2** Stitch chart for blotter panels (one-sixth of design).*

Two half cushion stitches over eight threads

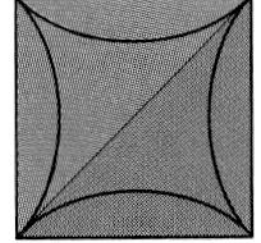

One dark green, one dark orange

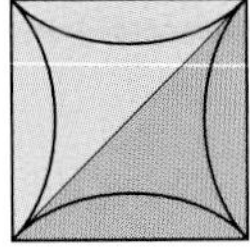

One pale mauve, one pale orange

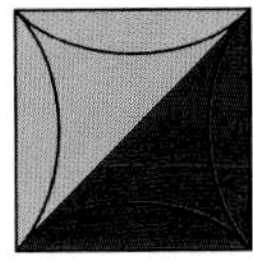

One metallic gold, one deep mauve

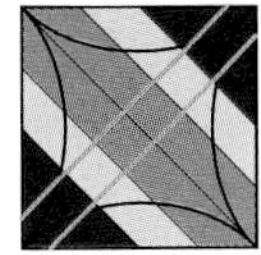

One of the group of four cushion stitches, each over eight threads, in pale orange; dark orange; deep mauve with metallic gold overlay (each stitch worked in a different direction: *see* photo)

Lower half of design is mirror image of top half

Fig 7.3 Stitch chart for pen holder panels (top half of design).

Two half cushion stitches over eight threads

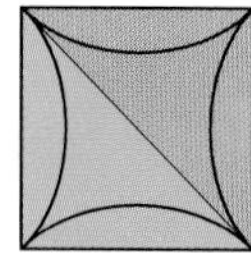
One metallic gold, one turquoise

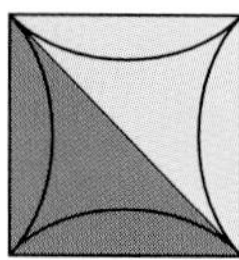
One dark green, one pale orange

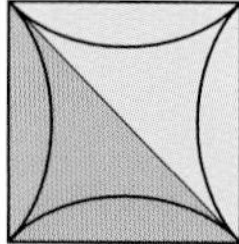
One pale mauve, one pale orange

Cushion stitch over eight threads, with each quarter worked in a different direction, all in deep mauve with metallic gold overlay (*see* photo)

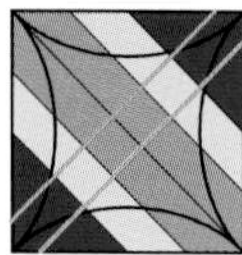
One of a group of four cushion stitches, each over eight threads, in pale orange; dark orange; deep mauve with metallic gold overlay (each stitch worked in a different direction: *see* photo)

Half cushion stitch over eight threads

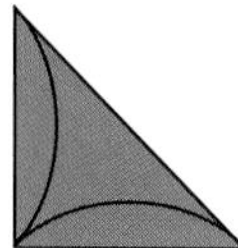
Dark green

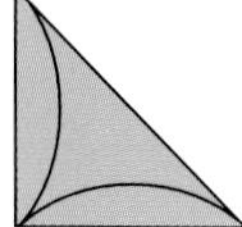
Turquoise

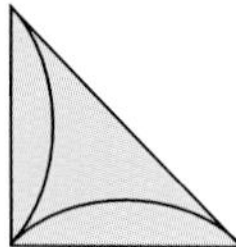
Pale orange

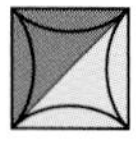
Two half cushion stitches over four threads, one pale orange, one dark green

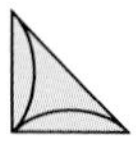
Half cushion stitch over four threads in pale orange

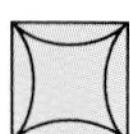
Cushion stitch over four threads in pale orange

***Fig 7.4** Stitch chart for notebook cover (quarter of design).*

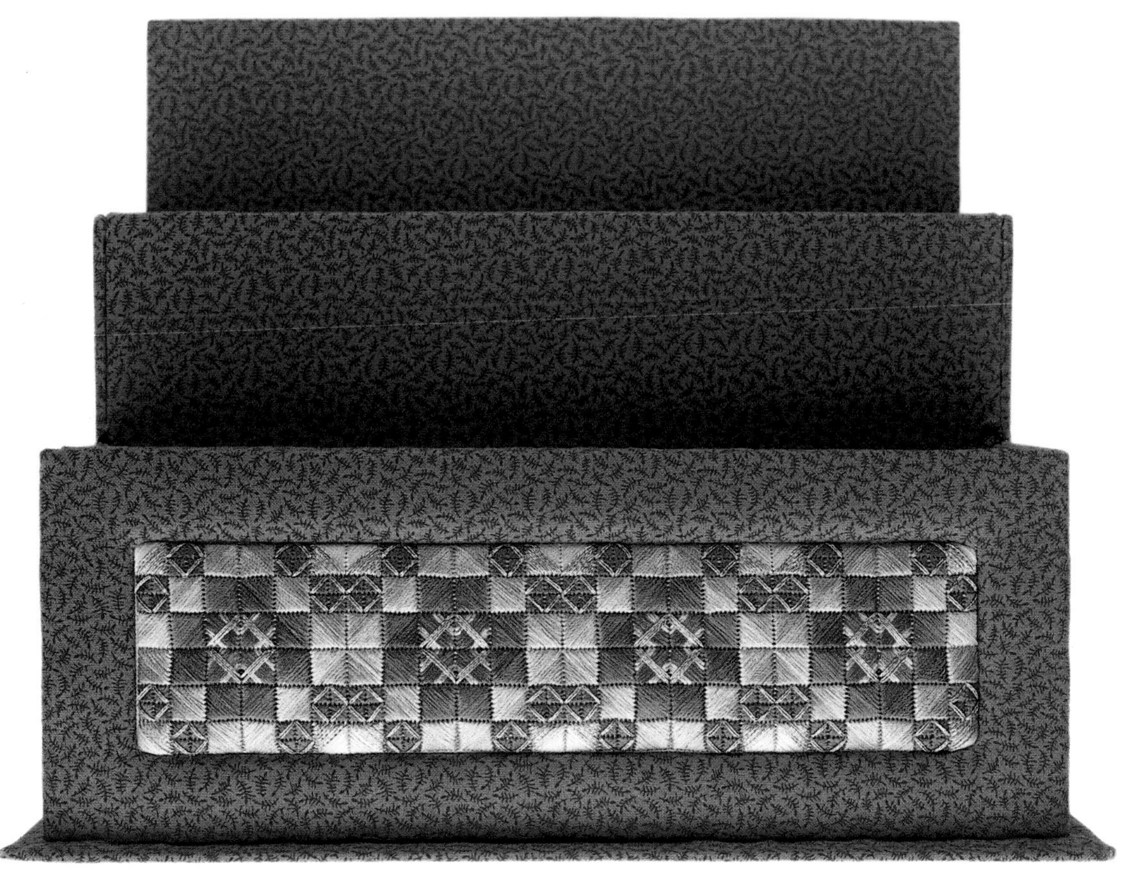

Panel repeat starts here. Whole panel to be repeated three more times.

Two half cushion stitches over eight threads

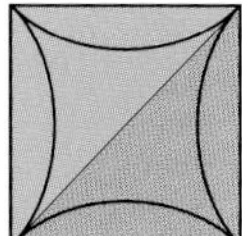

One turquoise, one metallic gold

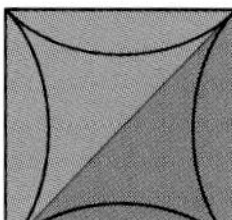

One dark green, one dark orange

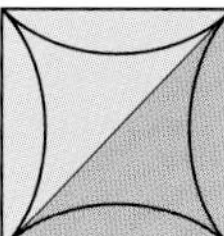

One pale orange, one pale mauve

Cushion stitch over eight threads, with each quarter worked in a different direction, all in deep mauve with metallic gold overlay (*see* photo)

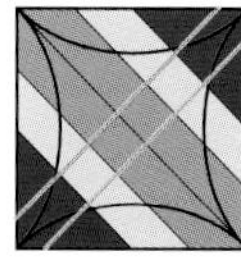

One of a group of four cushion stitches, each over eight threads, in pale orange; dark orange; deep mauve with metallic gold overlay (each stitch worked in a different direction: *see* photo)

Fig 7.5 Stitch chart for letter rack (quarter of design).

Blotter

MAKING UP

Cut two pieces of thick card, each 15 x $21\frac{1}{2}$in (381 x 546mm), and two pieces of cotton fabric, each 18 x $24\frac{1}{2}$in (457 x 622mm). Cover the pieces of card by lacing the edges of the fabric across the card in each direction (*see* page 157 for instructions on lacing fabric over card). With the laced surfaces facing, ladder stitch the two covered cards together on all four edges to form the blotter base.

Cut out the embroidered panels, allowing $\frac{3}{4}$in (20mm) of unstitched cloth all round. To make the first side of the blotter, cut two pieces of fabric, each 4 x 3in (102 x 76mm). Face the top and lower edge of the embroidered panel by placing the right side of the fabric to the stitchery and sewing into the last row of holes used. Fold back and finger press.

Cut two more pieces of fabric, one $16\frac{3}{4}$ x 3in (425 x 76mm) and the other $16\frac{3}{4}$ x 6in (425 x 152mm). Use these pieces to face the longer edges of the embroidered panel.

Now cut a piece of extra heavy interfacing, 15 x 4in (381 x 102mm), and position this centrally over the back of the stitched panel. Fold the top and lower edges over the interfacing and also the narrower of the two side facings, then herringbone stitch these into place.

Fold back the turnings on the three sides of the wider facing and tack them into place, then fold this facing over the back of the panel to form a lining and stitch it into position. Ladder stitch this completed side to one end of the blotter base with the stitched side facing up.

Repeat the process for the second side.

Pen holder

MAKING UP

Read these instructions through before starting to make up the pen holder, checking on the pieces of covered card required and referring to Fig 7.6.

Cut out the embroidered panels from the congress cloth, leaving a $\frac{3}{4}$in (20mm) margin all round. Follow the instructions for 'Stretching the work' given on page 156.

For the front and back of the pen holder cut two pieces of thick card, each 3 x 7in (76 x 178mm) and cut out a panel in the centre of each to the dimensions of the embroidered panel, thus making frames for the embroideries. Follow the instructions for padding the frames and mounting the embroidered panels as given in the section 'Mounting a panel in a padded frame' on page 159.

Cut two pieces of card, each 2¾ x 7in (70 x 178mm), and two pieces of cotton fabric, each 1in (25mm) larger all round than the card, and lace the fabric over the card for the other two outer sides.

Following the arrangement of the pieces of covered card indicated in Fig 7.6, ladder stitch the outer sides together, using a curved needle (*see* page 159). Measure the internal dimensions (allowing for the fabric covering), cut card to fit and lace with fabric. Ladder stitch into place along the top edges using a curved needle.

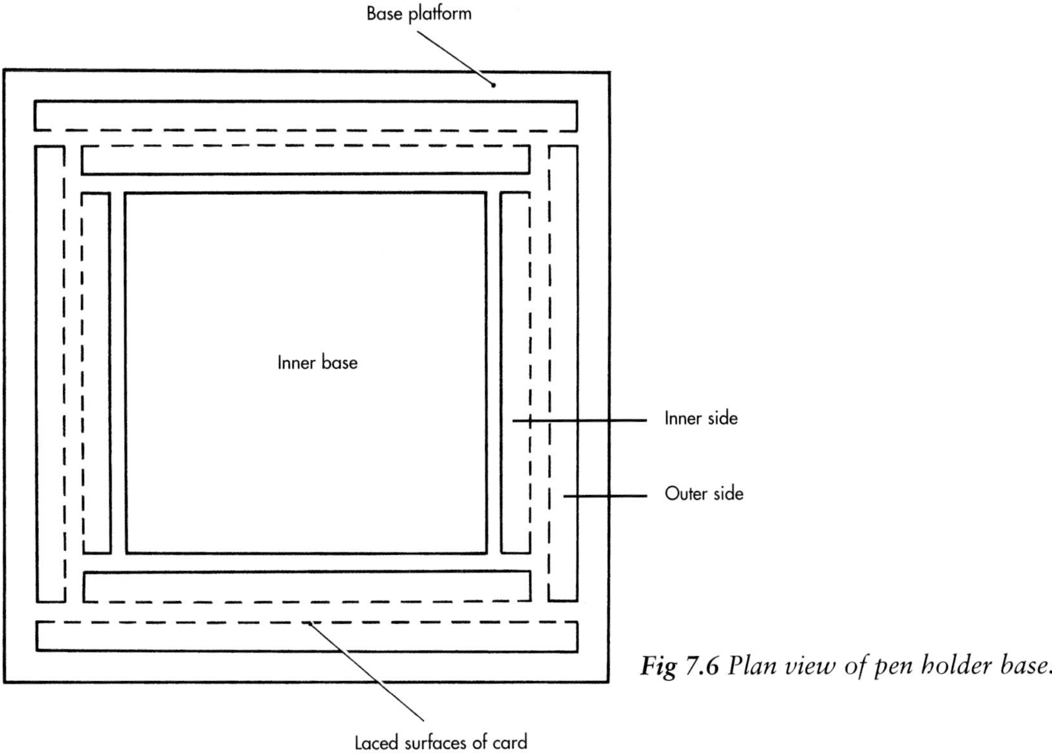

Fig 7.6 *Plan view of pen holder base.*

Cut a piece of card to the dimensions of the inside of the pen holder base and lace with fabric. With the laced surface underneath, push fit into the base.

Finally, cut a piece of card ¾in (20mm) larger than the outside of the pen holder and lace with fabric, ensuring that there is a good margin of fabric outside the lacing stitches. This will serve as a platform base. Position the pen holder on the base, laced surface uppermost and stitch all round into position, using a curved needle.

Notebook cover

MAKING UP

From the cotton fabric cut two pieces of 2¼ x 5¼in (57 x 133mm), one piece of 18½ x 7½in (470 x 190mm) and one piece of 14 x 7½in (356 x 190mm). Face the top and lower edge of the stitched area with the two smaller pieces of fabric. Stitch into the last row of holes used to ensure that none of the congress cloth shows.

Stitch the 18½ x 7½in (470 x 190mm) piece of fabric to the right-hand side of the stitched area and fold back. Stitch the remaining piece of fabric to the other side of the stitched area and fold back. (*See* Fig 7.7.)

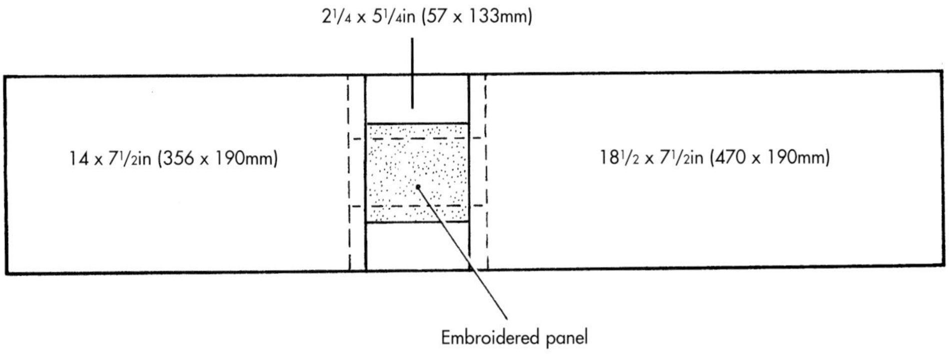

2¼ x 5¼in (57 x 133mm)
14 x 7½in (356 x 190mm)
18½ x 7½in (470 x 190mm)
Embroidered panel

Fig 7.7 Facing the embroidered panel with fabric strips.

Cut a piece of interfacing, 12½ x 6in (317 x 152mm), and place this under the fabric as shown in Fig 7.8. Fold over the seam allowance, ¾in (19mm), on all four sides of the fabric and tack into place. Herringbone stitch into position where the fabric overlaps the interfacing.

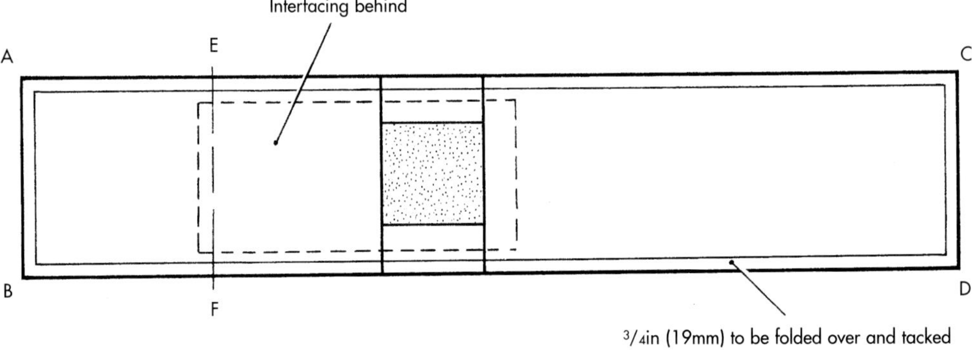

Fig 7.8 Stitching the interfacing in place.

Fold the edge marked C–D over to the line marked E–F, ½in (13mm) inside the edge of the interfacing, and herringbone stitch into place. Now stitch along the open edges.

Fold the edge A–B over just enough to overlap the line E–F and hem the edge down. Again, stitch along the open edges.

There will be an area at each end of the cover without interfacing between the layers of fabric. Fold these in along the edge of the interfacing and ladder stitch at the top and lower edges, to form the flaps into which the notebook can be slipped.

LETTER RACK

MAKING UP

Read these instructions through before starting to make up the letter rack, checking on the pieces of covered card required and referring to the diagrams.

Cut out the embroidered panel from the congress cloth, leaving a $^{3}/_{4}$in (20mm) margin all round. Follow the instructions for 'Stretching the Work' given on page 156.

Cut a piece of thick card $9^{5}/_{8}$ x $3^{9}/_{16}$in (245 x 90mm) and cut out a panel in the centre to the dimensions of the embroidered panel, thus making a frame for the embroidery. Follow the instructions given in Chapter 20 (*see* page 159) for mounting the embroidered panel in a padded frame.

For the shaped side pieces of the rack, cut two pieces of card in accordance with Fig 7.9, then cut two pieces of cotton fabric and two pieces of interfacing, all $5^{7}/_{8}$ x $7^{1}/_{2}$in (150 x 190mm). Iron the interfacing to the fabric pieces, then lace the fabric over the card (*see* page 157).

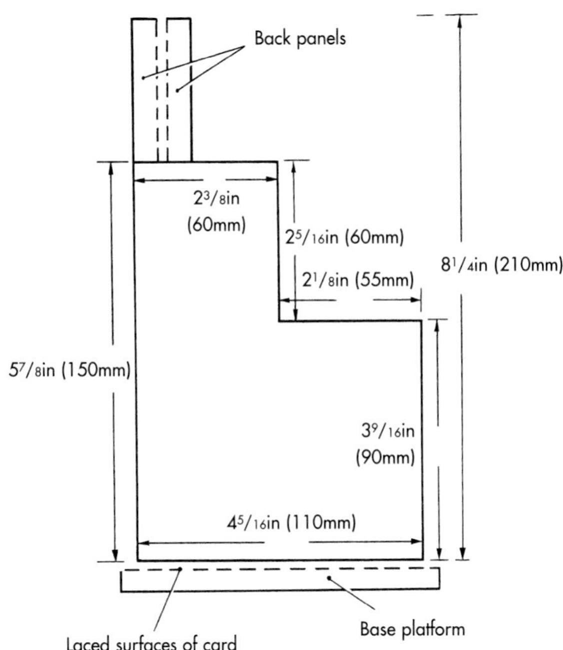

Fig 7.9 Side view of letter rack.

Following the arrangement of the pieces of laced card indicated in Figs 7.10 and 7.11, ladder stitch the three completed outer sides (the two shaped sides and the front panel) together, using a curved needle.

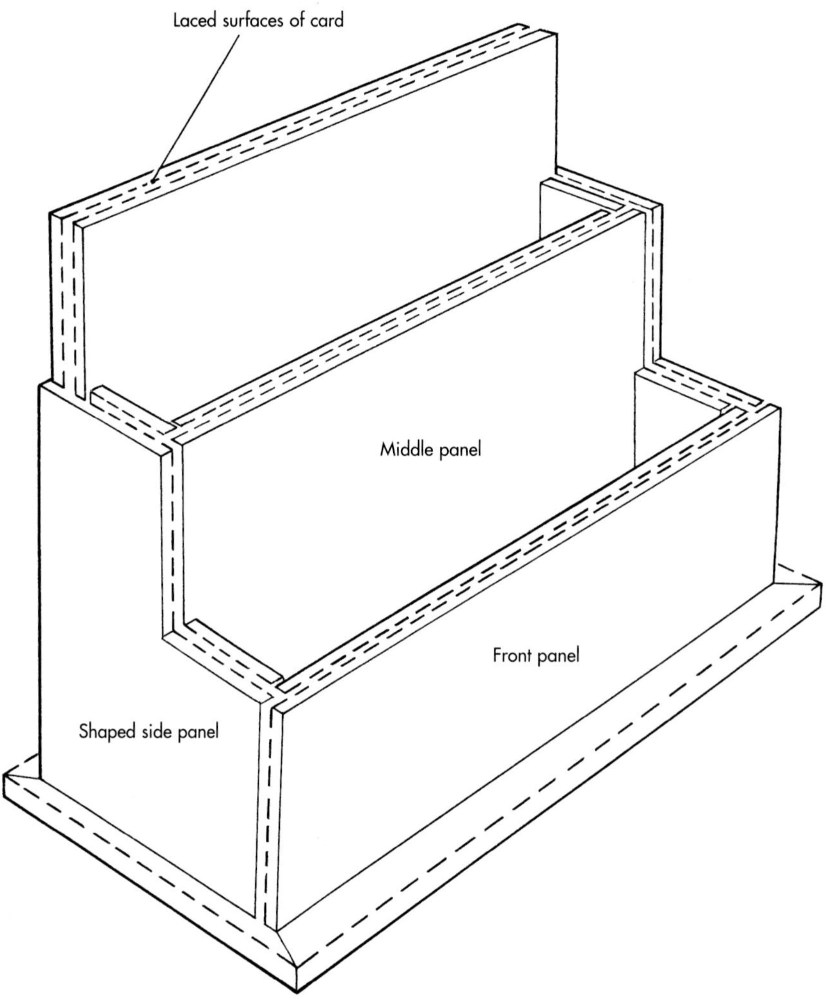

Fig 7.10 Expanded view of letter rack.

There are two identical pieces of card for the back panel of the letter rack; these are laced with fabric individually and ladder stitched together with the laced edges facing. Place these between the side panels at the back and ladder stitch into position using a curved needle.

Cut a card panel for the middle of the rack, $9^{7}/_{16}$ x $5^{7}/_{8}$in (240 x 150mm), and lace with fabric. Ladder stitch the upper part of this card at either end to the top sections of the L-shaped side panels, using a curved needle.

Measure the internal dimensions of the rack (allowing for the fabric covering) then cut card for the inner sides and front, and lace with fabric (*see* Fig 7.11). Ladder stitch into position along the top edges using a curved needle.

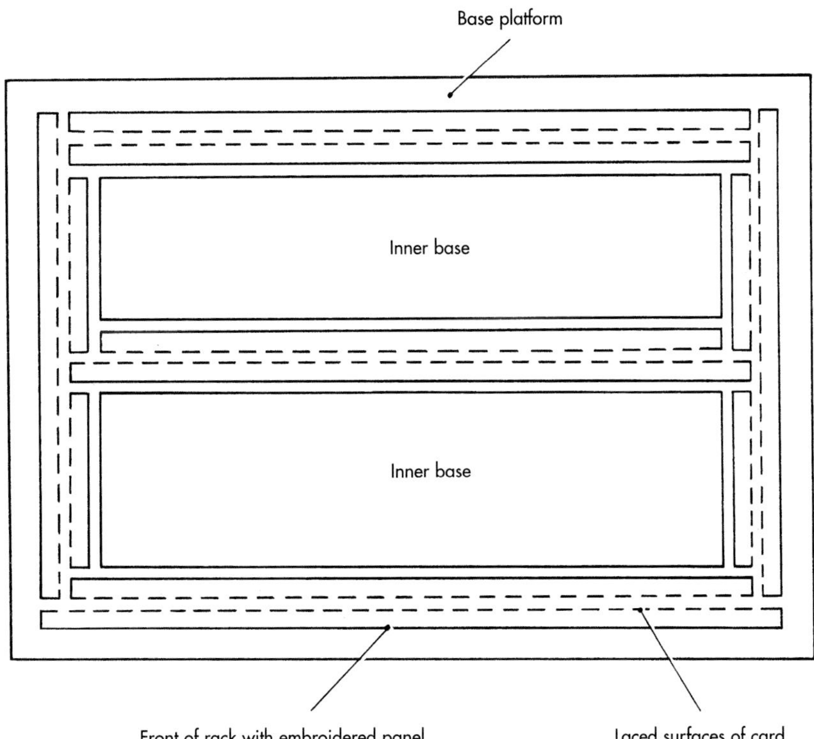

Fig 7.11 Plan view of letter rack.

Next, cut pieces of card to the dimensions of the inside of each of the compartments in the base of the letter rack and lace with fabric. With the laced surfaces underneath, push fit each into the appropriate section of the base.

Finally, cut a piece of card 3/8in (10mm) larger all round than the outside of the letter rack base and lace with fabric, ensuring that there is a good margin of fabric outside the lacing stitches, to use as a platform base. Position the letter rack on the base, laced surface uppermost and stitch into position all round, using a curved needle.

CHAPTER 8

Photo Frame

A glorious combination of colour and stitches, using unstitched areas of congress cloth to produce dramatic black outlines.

THREAD KEY

1 cop each of Indian rayon in:
- Royal blue
- Cerise
- Yellow gold
- Emerald green

2 reels of Madeira metallic gold no. 12, colour 33

MATERIALS AND EQUIPMENT

Threads as listed in key
Congress cloth, black, 14 x 12in (356 x 305mm)
Vilene extra heavy interfacing, 10 x 7in (254 x 178mm)
Lining fabric, black, 12 x 9in (305 x 229mm) *and* 16 x 7in (406 x 178mm)
Narrow ribbon, black, 6in (152mm)
Mount card, 10 x 8in (254 x 203mm) *and* 5 x 7in (127 x 178mm)
Embroidery frame, wooden, 14 x 12in (356 x 305mm)
Tapestry needle, no. 24
Small curved needle
Embroidery scissors
Double-sided tape
Needlework finisher
Small paint brush

PREPARATION

Stretch the congress cloth onto the embroidery frame and secure with staples or drawing pins. If pins are used, cover the heads with masking tape to avoid the threads catching on them.

Mark out an area of 236 x 168 threads with a light coloured thread and then mark out the aperture of 148 x 88 threads. The top border will be narrower than the lower border (*see* Fig 8.1). Mark on the central vertical and horizontal lines: these will serve as guide lines for the changing direction of stitches.

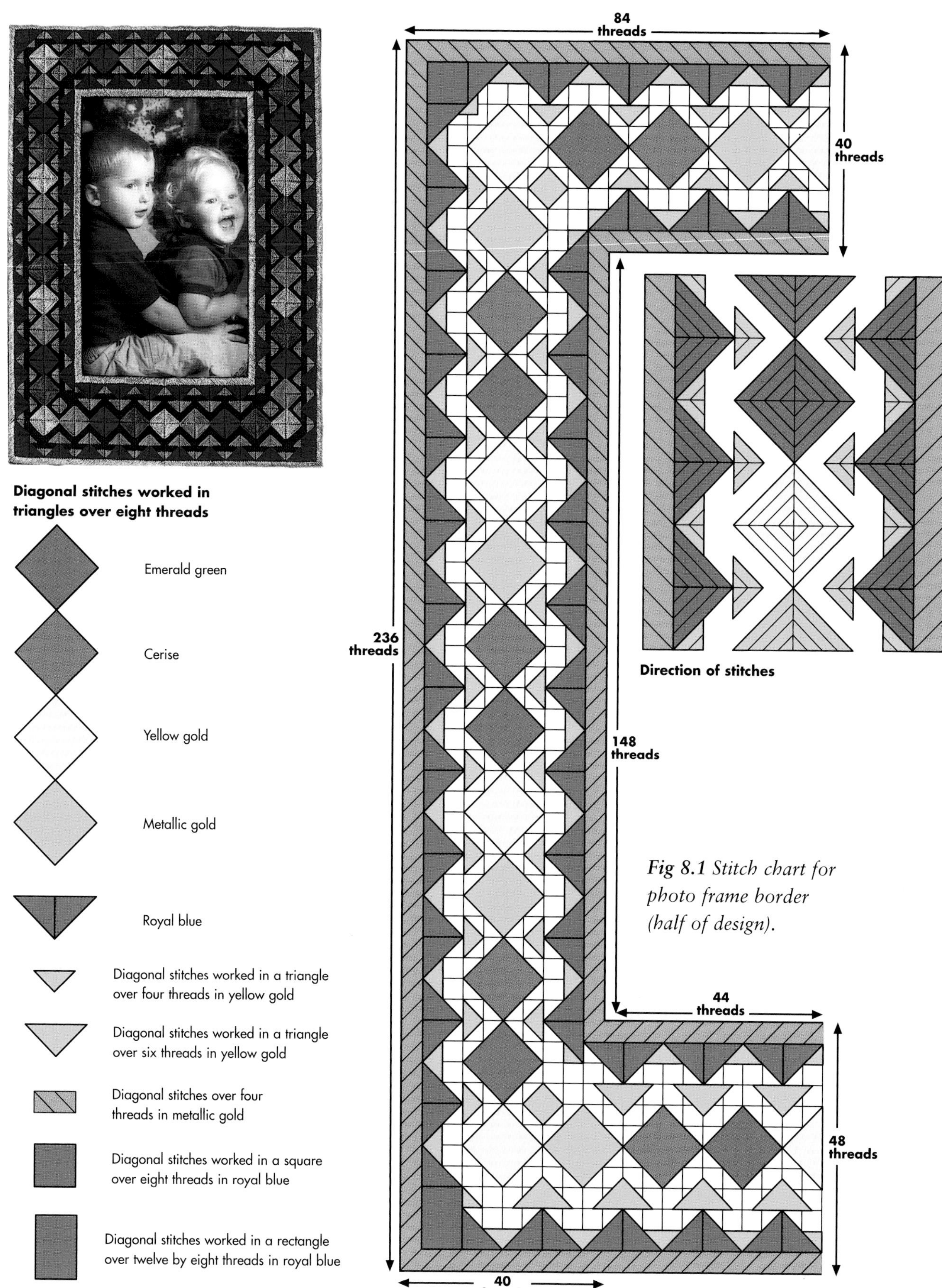
Diagonal stitches worked in triangles over eight threads
Emerald green
Cerise
Yellow gold
Metallic gold
Royal blue
Diagonal stitches worked in a triangle over four threads in yellow gold
Diagonal stitches worked in a triangle over six threads in yellow gold
Diagonal stitches over four threads in metallic gold
Diagonal stitches worked in a square over eight threads in royal blue
Diagonal stitches worked in a rectangle over twelve by eight threads in royal blue
84 threads
40 threads
236 threads
148 threads
44 threads
48 threads
40 threads
Direction of stitches

Fig 8.1 *Stitch chart for photo frame border (half of design).*

EMBROIDERY

Throughout the embroidery, keep referring to Fig 8.1 for the direction and position of the stitches. The coloured rayon threads are used in six thicknesses and the gold thread double throughout. The whole embroidery is worked using diagonal stitches.

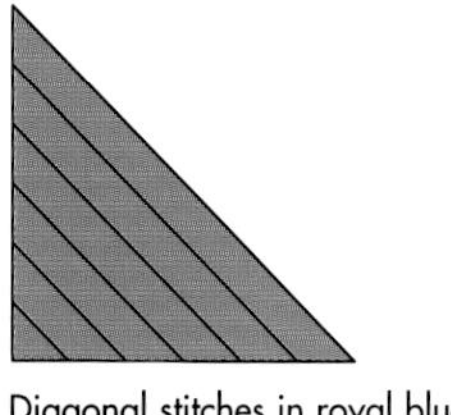
Diagonal stitches in royal blue

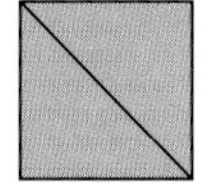
Metallic gold border area

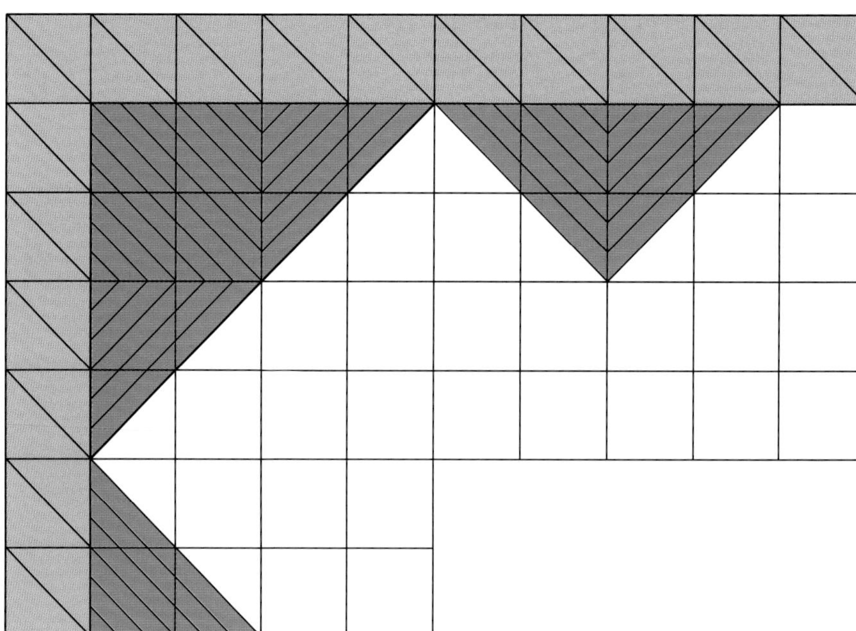

Fig 8.2 Stitch chart for top left corner of photo frame showing blue stitching inside area for metallic gold border.

As it is easier to finish with the metallic gold border stitches, start by working the two top corners, four threads in from the top and side lines. These are worked in blue diagonal stitches over eight threads (*see* Fig 8.2). Then, still in blue, work the two lower corners. These are upright rectangles eight threads wide and 12 threads high.

Starting with a half triangle at each corner, work the blue triangles along the outer borders. Start in whichever direction you choose, but reverse the direction of stitching for each half. Next, work the inner border of blue triangles, starting at the top corners. Note that at the bottom corners, the lower border starts four threads above the lowest point of the side border.

Now stitch the diamonds of colour, starting at the top left corner and working round in a clockwise direction. The colours should be in the following order:

1 metallic gold
2 green
3 cerise
4 yellow

The next step is to work the small yellow triangles, referring to the chart for their position. Note that, in the top and side borders, all the yellow triangles are worked over four threads, but in the lower border some of them are worked over six threads as indicated on the chart.

Finally, work the straight stitches in metallic gold thread at the inner and outer borders, over four threads. Note the change of direction at each central point. The embroidery is now complete.

MAKING UP

Cut a piece of mounting card 1/8in (3mm) smaller all round than the finished embroidered area. Cut the vilene interfacing slightly smaller than the card and use either double-sided tape or glue to attach it to the card.

Using a small paint brush, apply needlework finisher to each corner of the embroidered cloth, both in the aperture and around the outside. Allow this to dry thoroughly before cutting away the canvas to within 3/4in (19mm) of the embroidery, again, in the aperture and around the outside. Cut diagonally into the aperture corners, taking care not to cut the stitching, then lay the embroidery face down and place the vilene-covered mount on top. Stick double-sided tape round the edges of the aperture and pull the canvas edges tightly over the card and onto the tape. Do the same with the outside edges, cutting away some of the excess canvas at the corners. Lace the back of the canvas to hold it in place.

Cut the second piece of card to fit over the back of the frame and cover it with black lining fabric. Position your chosen photograph on this covered card and, using a curved needle, sew the embroidered front and the backing card together.

Now cut a piece of mount card, 5 x 7in (127 x 178mm), and cover both sides with the black lining fabric. This will form the strut. Check that it will stand at the correct angle, then attach it to the backing card. Finally, attach a small piece of ribbon to the backing card and the strut as a stay, to prevent it from opening too far.

CHAPTER 9

CLOCK, TRAY AND MIRROR SET

The 'ultimate' collection to show off your embroidery skills, which will be admired daily by everyone in the home! The basic materials for this co-ordinated set are obtainable by mail order from Framecraft Miniatures Ltd (*see* Suppliers, page 164). Choose your own colour schemes to enhance your room decoration.

THREAD KEY

2 reels each of Gütermann Dekor in:

Maroon	5400
Deep pink	5435
Green	8870
Hyacinth blue	5900
Yellow	1850

4 reels of Madeira metallic gold no. 12, colour 33

MATERIALS AND EQUIPMENT

For all elements:
Threads as listed in key
Beadesign beads x 1 packet of gold no. 72
Tapestry needle, no. 24
Beading needle
Embroidery scissors
Needlework finisher (optional)

For clock:
Congress cloth, 10 x 8in (254 x 203mm)
Rectangular frame, 10 x 8in (254 x 203mm)
'Sudberry House' petite mantel clock kit

For tray:
Congress cloth, 12 x 9in (305 x 229mm)
Rectangular frame, 12 x 9in (305 x 229mm)
'Sudberry House' wooden tray kit

For mirror:
Congress cloth, 10 x 8in (254 x 203mm)
Rectangular frame, 10 x 8in (254 x 203mm)
'Sudberry House' mirror kit

NB: Instructions refer to the above Framecraft products, but can, of course, be adapted to fit other similar kits. (*See* Suppliers, page 164.)

EMBROIDERY

For all the embroidery in this set, use the coloured rayon threads in eight thicknesses for double-plaited cross stitch, as this is a stitch that does not cover the congress cloth well. For mosaic stitch and any straight stitches, use the rayon threads in six thicknesses. Use the metallic gold thread doubled throughout.

Clock

PREPARATION

Attach the congress cloth to the 10 x 8in (254 x 203mm) embroidery frame, using either staples or drawing pins. If pins are used, cover the heads with masking tape to avoid the threads catching on them. Using the template supplied with the kit, mark out the area to be embroidered and mark on the central vertical and horizontal lines with tacking.

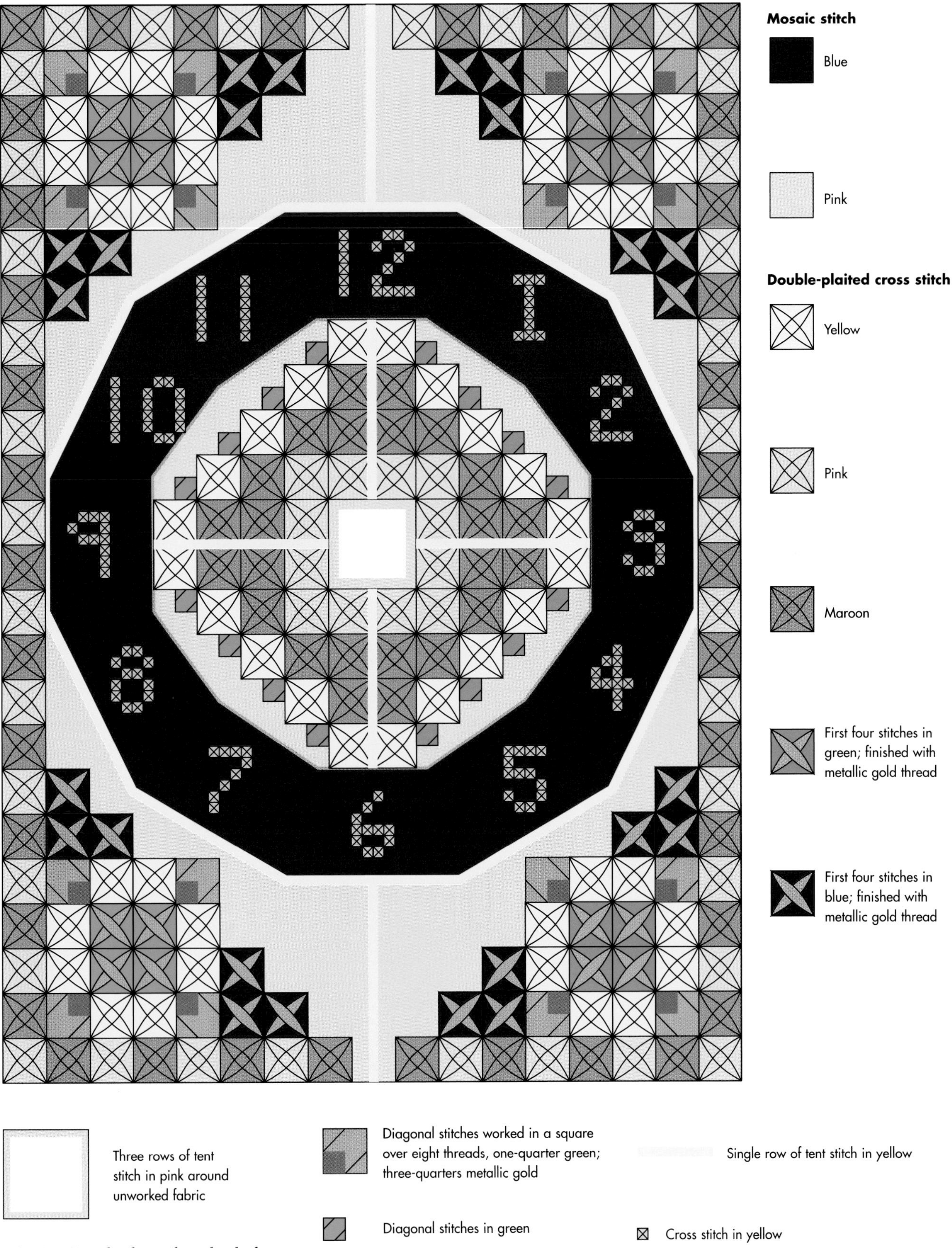
Mosaic stitch
Blue
Pink
Double-plaited cross stitch
Yellow
Pink
Maroon
First four stitches in green; finished with metallic gold thread
First four stitches in blue; finished with metallic gold thread
Three rows of tent stitch in pink around unworked fabric
Diagonal stitches worked in a square over eight threads, one-quarter green; three-quarters metallic gold
Single row of tent stitch in yellow
Diagonal stitches in green
Cross stitch in yellow

Fig 9.1 Stitch chart for clock face.

EMBROIDERY

Start stitching the outer circle 53 holes below the centre mark, working in tent stitch, using yellow thread. Follow the chart in Fig 9.2, which shows only a quarter of the outline. Having completed the outer circle, work the inner circle from the chart using yellow rayon.

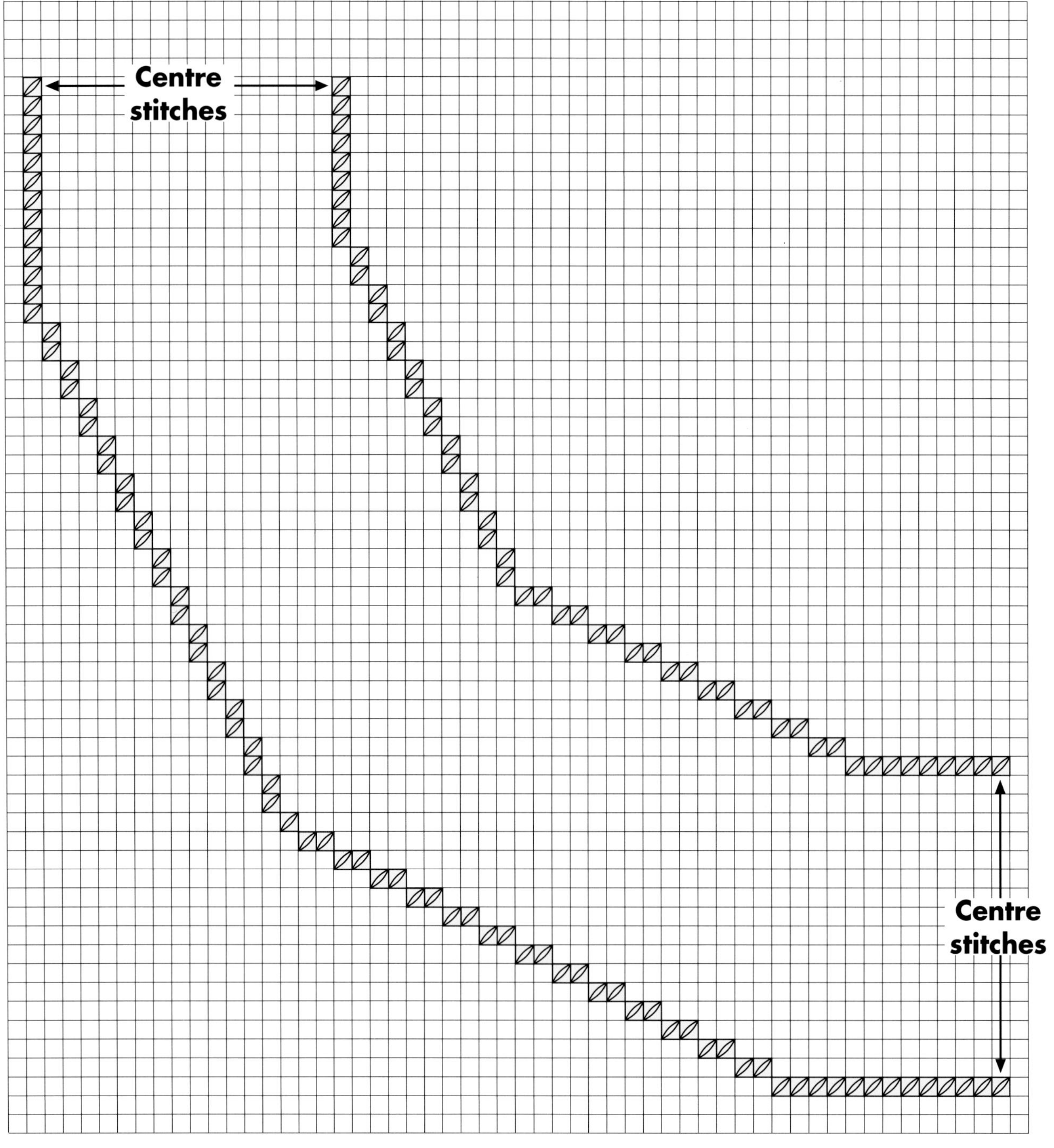

***Fig 9.2** Stitch chart for outline of dial.*

Tent stitch in yellow

With a pencil mark the north, south, east and west points on the clockface (which will be where the centre vertical and horizontal lines cross the outline), then divide the space between each pair of marks into three by marking on two further pencil lines. Position the numbers at these points, working from the chart given in Fig 9.3 and making sure they are evenly spaced. The numbers are all worked in cross stitch, using yellow thread. Once the numbers are completed, work the background to this area in blue mosaic stitch. Work whole stitches where possible and fill any gaps with tent stitches.

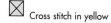

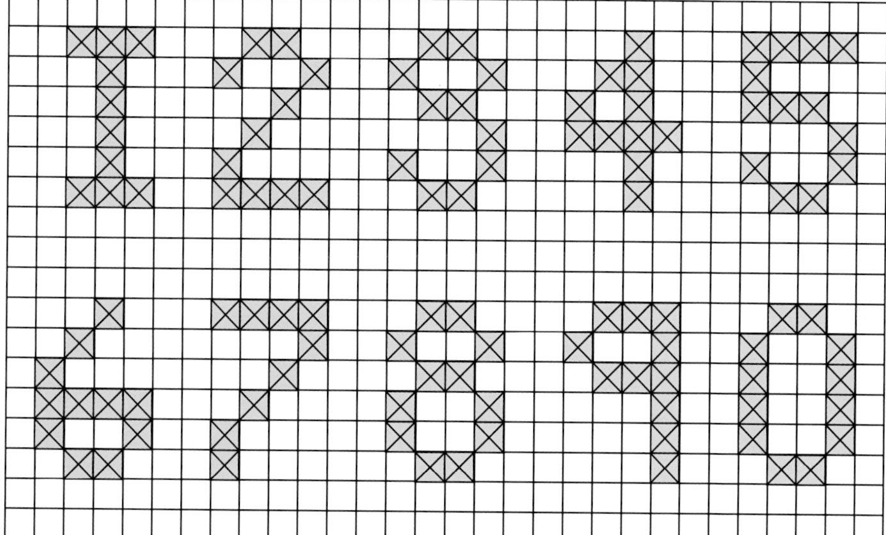

Fig 9.3 Stitch chart for numbers on clock face.

Work a row of single tent stitches to divide the remaining inner and outer areas as shown in Fig 9.1. Mark a square of 15 threads around the centre mark in pencil. Work three rows of tent stitch in pink around the outer edge of this central square, leaving the rest of the square unstitched. (This unstitched area will be removed to fit the clock spindle when finishing the piece.)

Work the outer border in double-plaited cross stitch, using maroon and pink alternately, as shown in Fig 9.1. Note that there is a four-thread gap either side of the central vertical stitch line.

Now return to the area inside the number dial. Work a row of pink double-plaited cross stitches around the central square. Follow Fig 9.1 for the remainder of the squares, which are also worked in double-plaited cross stitch, but in maroon and yellow. On completing this, add the small green squares around the outer edge. These are worked in straight stitches over four threads (*see* Fig 9.3 for the direction of the stitches). Fill in the rest of this area with mosaic stitch in pink.

The next section to work is the area outside the number dial. Start with the lower left-hand corner, working the double-plaited cross stitches first (*see* Fig 9.1). Note that some stitches are worked in two colours: for these, coloured rayon is used for the first four stitches and metallic gold thread for the final four stitches. Each double-plaited cross stitch is made up of eight stitches. There are also four small green squares. When you have worked these, in straight stitches over four threads, fill in with straight stitches in metallic gold thread, as shown in Fig 9.1

Work the other three corners to match. Throughout, keep referring to the photograph of the finished clock to help with the colours and design. All the remaining spaces are filled with pink mosaic stitches as for the inner area. Outline the squares indicated in Fig 9.1 with metallic gold thread.

Finally, work a further border of diagonal stitches in metallic gold around the entire piece, working over three threads on each side but only two threads at the top and bottom. Most of this border will be hidden when the embroidery is mounted but it avoids any of the congress cloth showing.

The embroidery is now complete. As the work will be cut near the stitches, brush on a coating of needlework finisher to prevent possible fraying.

MAKING UP

With a sharp, pointed pair of scissors, cut out the unworked area of the central square, along the first row of unworked holes. This square will now fit over the clock spindle.

Check that the stitched area of the finished piece covers the mounting card provided and cut it out using the next row of unworked holes. The congress cloth cannot be stretched and laced over the edges of the mounting card as it would be too bulky, so use double-sided tape to fasten the work.

Follow the instructions provided with the clock for assembly.

Tray

PREPARATION

Using the 12 x 9in (305 x 229mm) rectangular embroidery frame, stretch the corresponding piece of congress cloth over it and secure with either staples or drawing pins. Using a pencil, mark the vertical and horizontal centre lines on the canvas.

EMBROIDERY

The entire central section of the tray is worked in double-plaited cross stitch. Note that some squares are worked in two colours: coloured rayon is used for the first four stitches and metallic gold thread for the second four.

Follow Fig 9.4 for placing the colours and refer to the photograph of the finished tray to help you. Outline the squares indicated in Fig 9.4 with metallic gold thread, and then outline the remaining squares in the appropriate colour (refer to the photograph of the finished item).

To finish the central panel add the beads in groups of four using the beading needle. Again, refer to the photograph for their position.

Work a diagonal row of metallic gold stitches over five threads along the bottom and top edges of the stitching: note the change of direction at the halfway mark. Having done this, surround the whole design with diagonal green stitches over three threads, again changing direction at the halfway marks. Follow this with a row of diagonal yellow stitches over two threads, working as before.

Next, work a row of double-plaited cross stitch, alternately maroon and pink. Refer to Fig 9.5 and take special note of where the stitches start and finish. Fill in the corner spaces with diagonal stitches in metallic gold thread.

Surround the entire design with a border of diagonal yellow stitches over two threads and a final border of diagonal green stitches over four threads, changing direction at the halfway mark as before.

To ensure that no congress cloth shows, work a further row of green diagonal stitches over four threads along the right- and left-hand sides of the tray – most of this will be covered when the work is mounted.

The embroidery for the tray is now complete.

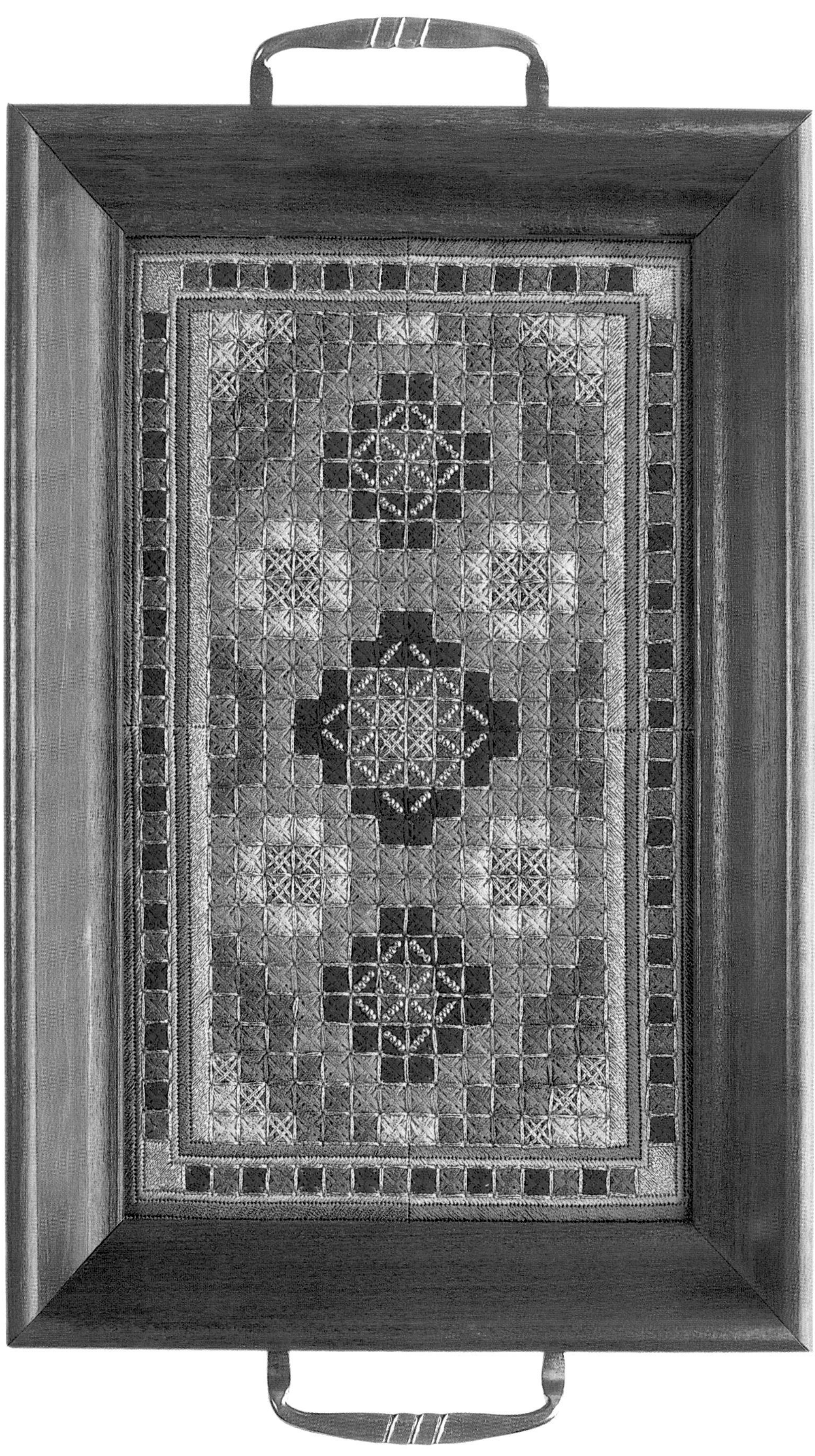

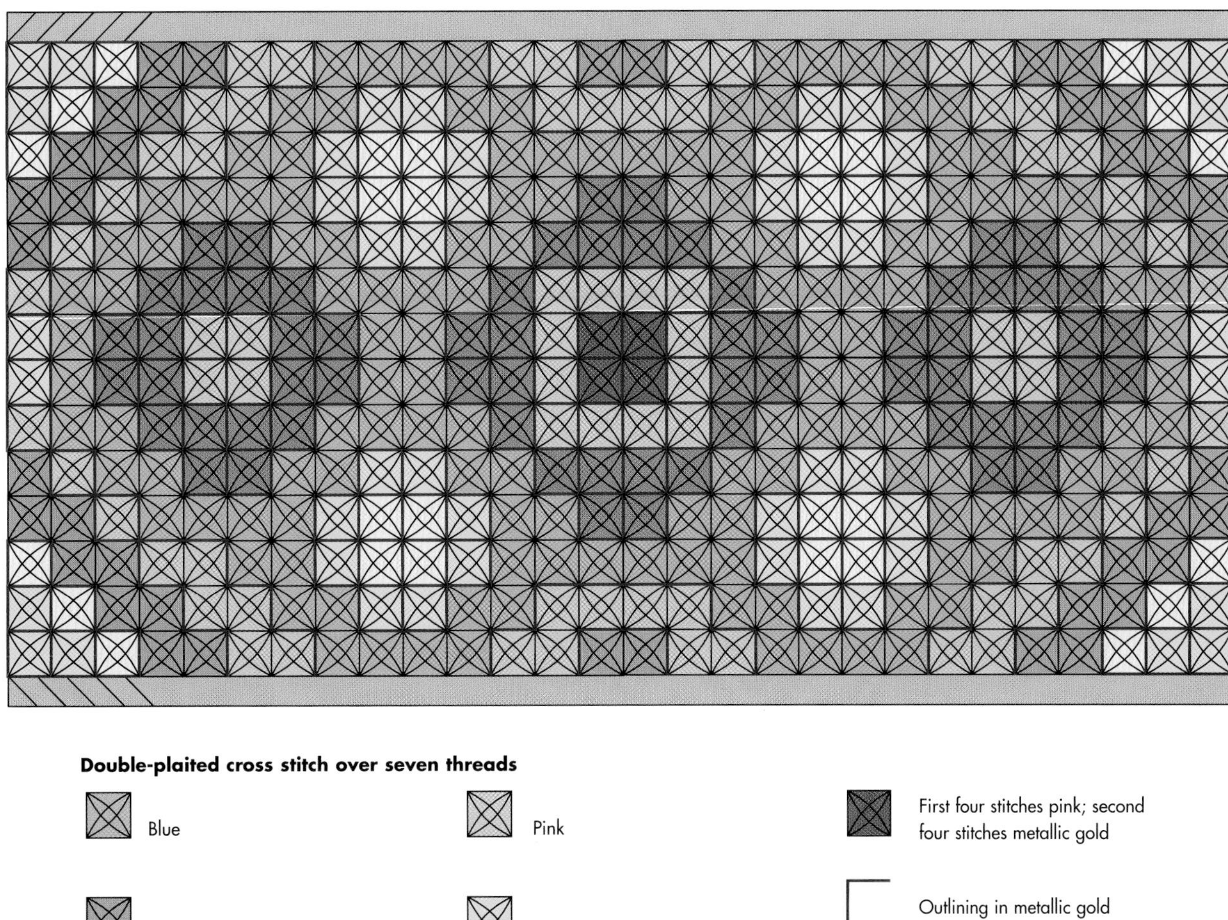

Fig 9.4 Stitch chart for central panel of tray.

MAKING UP

Cut the cloth to fit the tray template, apply needlework finisher to the edges, and assemble the tray following the instructions given in the kit.

Corner of border to be repeated around completed central panel of tray

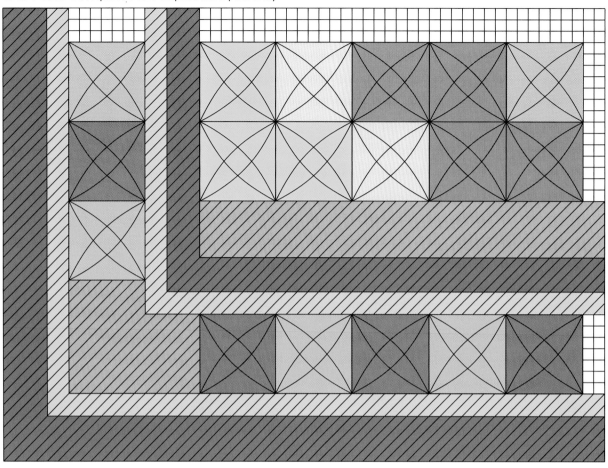

Double-plaited cross stitch over seven threads

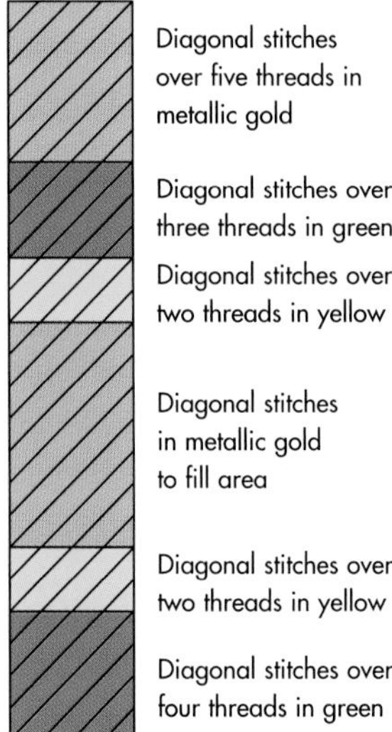

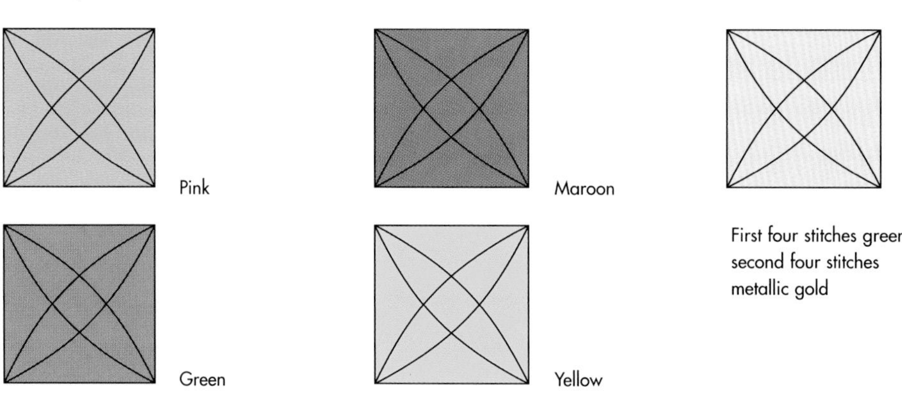

Fig 9.5 Stitch chart for corner of tray border design.

Mirror

PREPARATION

Using the 10 x 8in (254 x 203mm) rectangular embroidery frame, stretch the corresponding piece of congress cloth over it and secure with either staples or drawing pins. Mark on the central vertical and horizontal lines.

EMBROIDERY

The entire central section of the mirror decoration is worked in double-plaited cross stitch. As for the tray, some squares are worked in two colours: coloured rayon is used for the first four stitches and metallic gold thread for the second four. Follow Fig 9.6 for the placing of the colours and refer to the photograph of the finished mirror to help you.

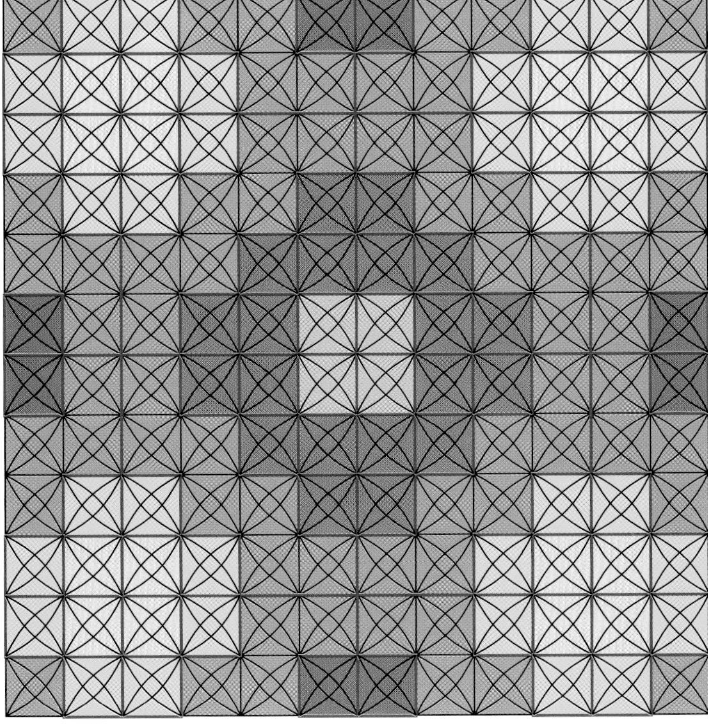

Fig 9.6 Stitch chart for central panel of mirror.

Double-plaited cross stitch over seven threads

First four stitches green; second four stitches metallic gold

Yellow

Pink

Maroon

Green

Blue

Outlining in metallic gold thread

Outline the squares indicated in Fig 9.6 with metallic gold thread and then, in the appropriate colour, outline all those remaining. Refer to the photograph of the finished mirror for guidance. Finally, add the beads in groups, using the beading needle and referring to the photograph for their position.

Work a row of green diagonal stitches over three threads at the top and bottom edge, noting the change of direction at the centre. Follow this with a row of yellow diagonal stitches over two threads.

Next, work a row of double-plaited cross stitch, alternating maroon and pink, and outline each square with metallic gold thread. Finally, repeat the green and yellow border rows as before but in reverse order (*see* Fig 9.7).

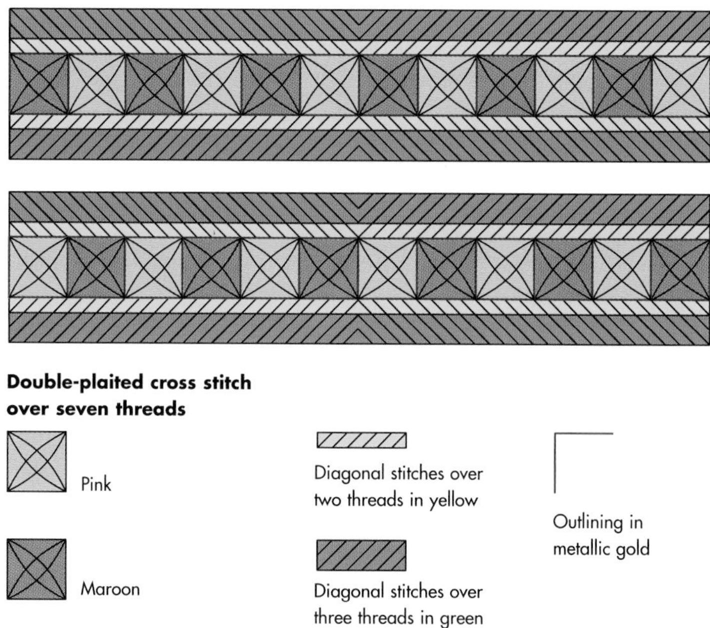

Fig 9.7 Stitch charts for top and bottom borders of mirrors.

To avoid any congress cloth showing, and as the embroidered panel has to be cut out quite close to the stitches, cut the cloth to size and oversew the edges with yellow rayon thread.

MAKING UP

Assemble the mirror according to the instructions which accompany the kit.

CHAPTER 10

JEWELLERY BOX

This 'chest of drawers', chosen to show off triangular Rhodes stitch, will prove useful for the storage of many things: jewellery, needlework threads and equipment, or just knick-knacks.

Choose your colours to tone with the fabrics or vice versa. We started with the lining fabric for the drawers and base platform, imitated the pattern in the embroidered panel, and then chose plain fabrics to complement.

THREAD KEY

1 cop each of Madeira no. 30 in:

Green	1079
Cream	1066
Tan	1221
Maroon	1181
Peach	1254

1 reel of Madeira metallic gold no. 12, colour 33

MATERIALS AND EQUIPMENT

For embroidered panel:

Threads as listed in key
Congress cloth, 9in (229mm) square
Embroidery frame, 9in (229mm) square
Tapestry needle, no. 24
Embroidery scissors

For 'chest of drawers':

Card, 2mm thick
HB pencil
Ruler
Stanley knife
Metal safety ruler
Cutting mat
Fabric A (for drawer linings and base platform), approx. 10in (1/4m)
Fabric B (for drawer casings, sides and back), approx. 10in (1/4m)
Fabric C (for outer casing of box and drawer fronts), approx. 10in (1/4m)

continued

continued

Strong lacing thread
Sewing threads to match fabrics
Usual sewing kit, including large and fine scissors, large-eyed needle, sewing needles and curved needle

PREPARATION

Attach the congress cloth to the frame using either staples or drawing pins. If drawing pins are used, cover the heads with masking tape to avoid the threads catching.

EMBROIDERY

Throughout the design, use the rayon threads in six thicknesses and the metallic gold threads double.

Start to work from the bottom left-hand corner with the green triangular Rhodes stitch (*see* Fig 10.1), leaving ample space for the border to be worked at the end. (The three rows of the border go over 12 threads). The symbols, #, around the outside of the design show where half stitches will need to be worked to complete the design. Complete the central square and then work the border (*see* Figs 10.1 and 10.2).

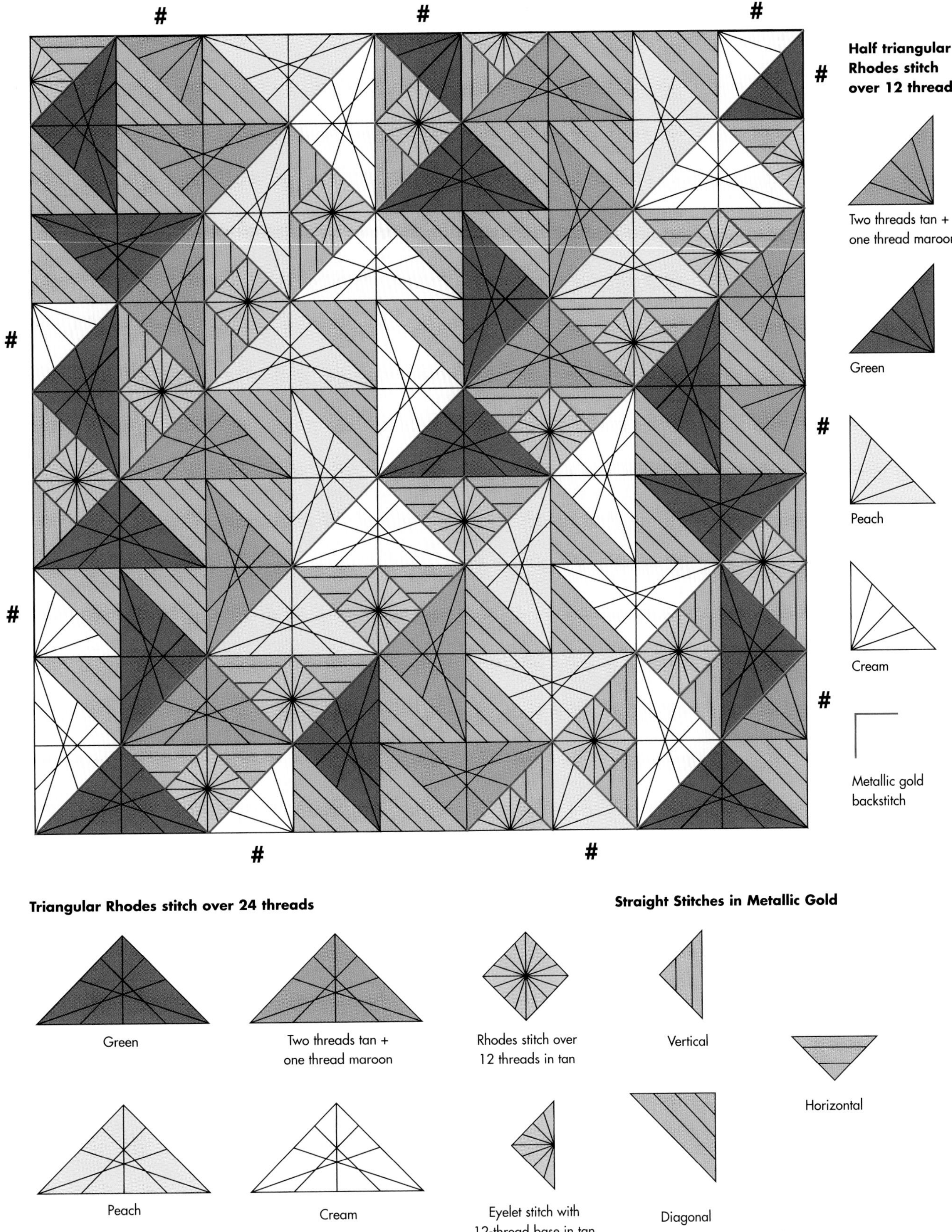

Fig 10.1 Stitch chart for central square of jewellery box design.

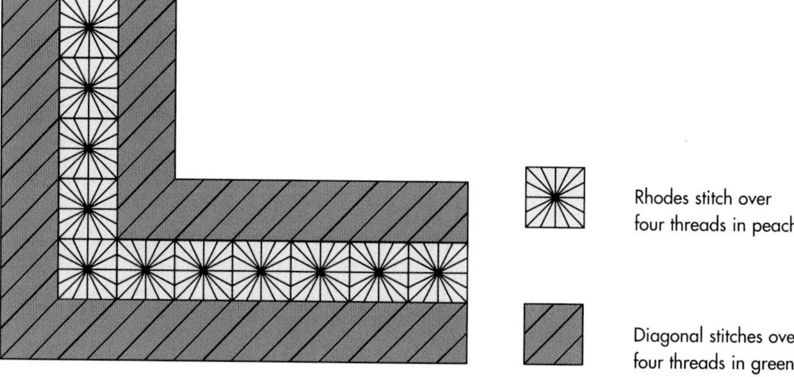

Fig 10.2 Stitch chart for corner of jewellery box border design.

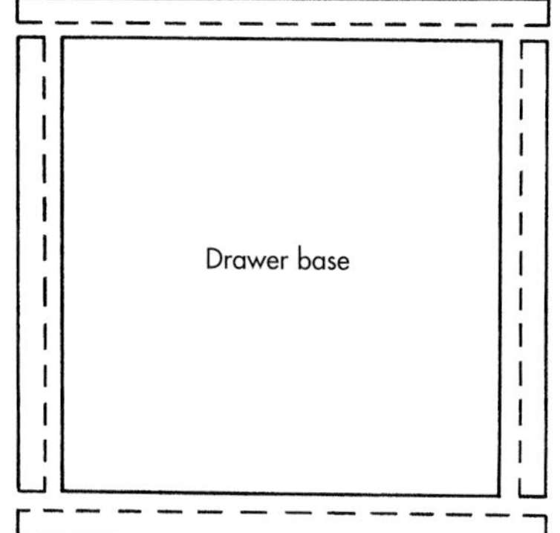

Fig 10.3 Plan view of drawer base.

MAKING UP

Boxes with drawers are built up starting with the construction of the drawers, then the drawer casings and finally the outer casing forming the actual box. It is, therefore, important to decide on the overall maximum dimensions of the box in the design stage and to work backwards with the appropriate calculations to establish the required size for the drawers. In taking measurements and cutting card, always make allowances for the thickness of the fabric, turnings and lacings.

FRONT, BACK AND SIDES

Cut the sides, front and back of the drawer from thick card, so that the front and back lie across the full width of the side panels to give a smooth, unbroken front to the drawer. (*See* Fig 10.3.)

The size of the embroidered panel is $5\frac{5}{16}$in (135mm) square, so we made the finished box top and platform base $7\frac{1}{16}$in (180mm) square and each drawer $1\frac{9}{16}$in (40mm) high. For each drawer, cut the following pieces:

Base: $5\frac{1}{2}$in (140mm) square x 1
Side panels: $5\frac{1}{2}$ x $1\frac{9}{16}$in (140 x 40mm) x 2
Front and back: $5\frac{11}{16}$ x $1\frac{9}{16}$in (145 x 40mm) x 2

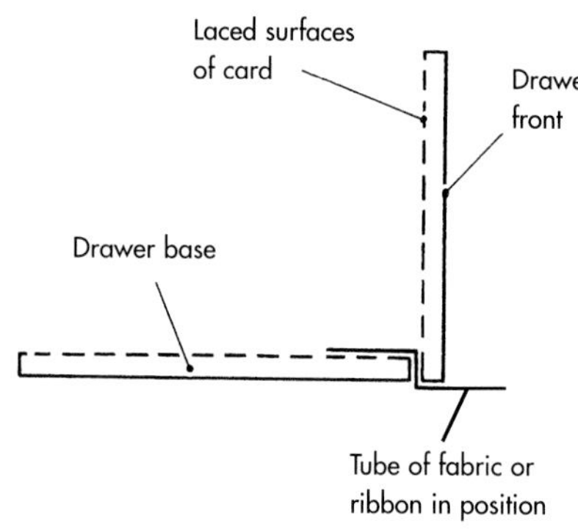

Fig 10.4 Positioning the fabric pull tab.

Cut fabric B to cover the sides, back and base, then cut fabric C to cover the front, allowing for $\frac{5}{8}$in (15mm) turnings all round, and lace these over the appropriate card pieces. (*See* page 157 for instructions on lacing fabric over card.)

Drawer handles

The method to be used for opening the drawers should be decided now, before the front is attached to the drawer: either a pull tab or a knob can be used.

To use a pull tab, make a narrow tube of fabric (or ribbon) and stitch this to the centre of one of the laced edges of the base. It will be sandwiched between the base and the front when the front is stitched into position (*see* Fig 10.4).

For a knob, stitch a button or similar to the drawer front, so that any fastening is at the back, where it will subsequently be hidden by the drawer lining.

Base

Attach the sides, laced edges inwards, to the covered base, laced edge uppermost, with ladder stitch, using a matching sewing thread in a curved needle. (*See* page 159 for instructions on ladder stitch.) Stitch the front and back panels into place in the same way.

Lining

Measure the internal dimensions, including the height, of the outer drawer and, allowing for the fabric, cut card for the lining pieces as indicated so that the covered side, front and back cards will be flush with the top of the drawer when stitched into position. (*See* Fig 10.5.)

Cut fabric A for each of the resulting pieces of card and lace (*see* page 157). Stitch into position along the top edges, laced surfaces together, using a curved needle. Measure and cut card for the inner base, allowing for fabric (*see* Fig 10.5). Lace with lining fabric and push-fit into place. If required, the card surfaces of the outer and inner bases can be lightly glued and pressed together to hold the inner base in position.

Repeat for the second drawer.

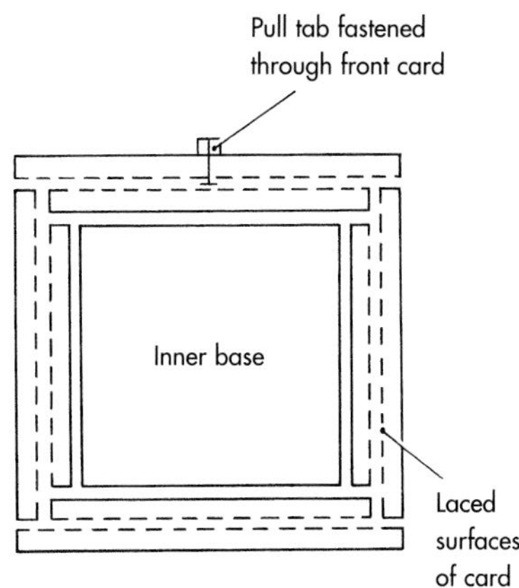

***Fig 10.5** Plan view of drawer, showing inner base.*

Drawer casings

Measure the outer dimensions of the drawer and cut card for the casings (*see* Fig 10.6), allowing for the fabric covering and remembering that the drawer will need to slide in and out from the casing.

When calculating the length of the sides for the casing, add one thickness of card to the length of the drawer to allow for a piece of covered card to be inserted at the back of the casing.

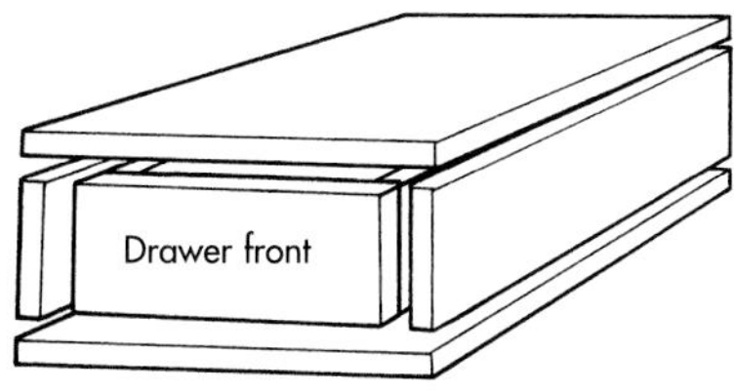

***Fig 10.6** Assembly of card for outer casing.*

Cut card for the casings of the other drawer at the same time – these should be identical. Lace fabric B over these pieces of card and ladder stitch the pieces for each drawer together, laced surfaces outside.

With the drawer in position to stabilize the casing, measure for the back panel insert, allowing for its fabric covering (*see* Fig 10.7). Cut the card, lace with fabric and place in position, flush with the back of the casing, laced surface outside. Ladder stitch into place using a curved needle.

Once both the drawers and their casings have been assembled, ladder stitch the casings securely together (*see* Fig 10.8).

Outer casing

Take measurements and assemble in the same way as for the drawer casings, again, allowing for the insertion of a covered back panel. Cut out the card pieces, lace with fabric C, and stitch the casing together, this time with the laced surfaces on the inside. Position the drawer casings inside the outer casing, and stitch them into place.

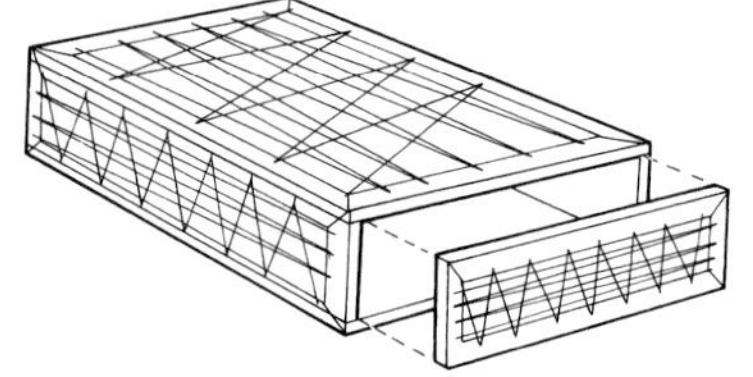

***Fig 10.7** Inserting back panel into casing.*

Platform base

Cut a piece of card 3/8in (10mm) larger all round than the outer casing and cover this with fabric A, keeping the lacing stitches well in from the edges so that they will not show when the casing is in position.

Place the outer casing centrally on this base, pin securely into position, and stitch in place using a curved needle.

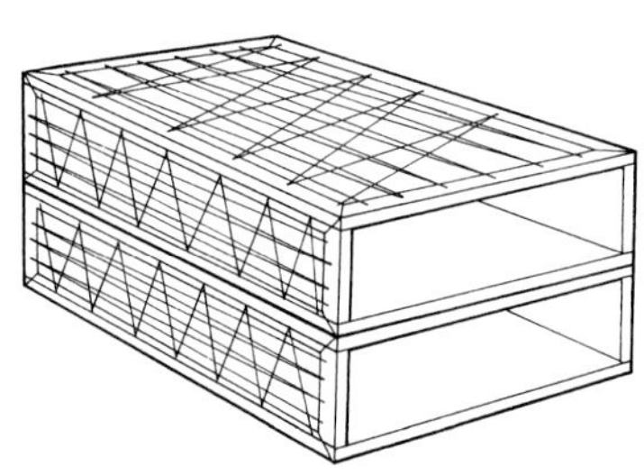

***Fig 10.8** Casings ready to be stitched together.*

Top

Cut a piece of card the same size as the platform base, stretch and mount the embroidery following the instructions on page 156.

Placing the completed top upside down on a soft surface in order to avoid crushing the embroidery – felt or towelling would be suitable – turn the chest of drawers upside down as well and position centrally on the top. Stitch into position with a curved needle. The jewellery box is now complete.

CHAPTER 11

Needlework Set

A practical and attractive sewing set, comprising a scissor weight, needlecase and pin cushion. Each item uses the same fabric as a background and Rhodes, rice and cushion stitches in glorious Gütermann threads.

THREAD KEY	
2 reels each of Gütermann Dekor in:	
Dark blue	5885
Pale blue	6260
Peach	3655
Metallic	24

MATERIALS AND EQUIPMENT

For all elements:

Threads as listed in key
Congress cloth, 10 x 12in (254 x 305mm)
Outer fabric (for needlecase and pincushion)
Sewing thread, to match outer fabric
Vilene extra heavy interfacing, 12in (305mm) square
Wadding
Embroidery frame, 10 x 12in (254 x 305mm) (the individual pieces could be made on smaller frames, but more congress cloth would then be required)
Embroidery scissors
Tapestry needle, no. 24
Sewing needle

For needlecase:

Lining fabric, small amount
Felt to match outer fabric, 10 x 5in (254 x 127mm)

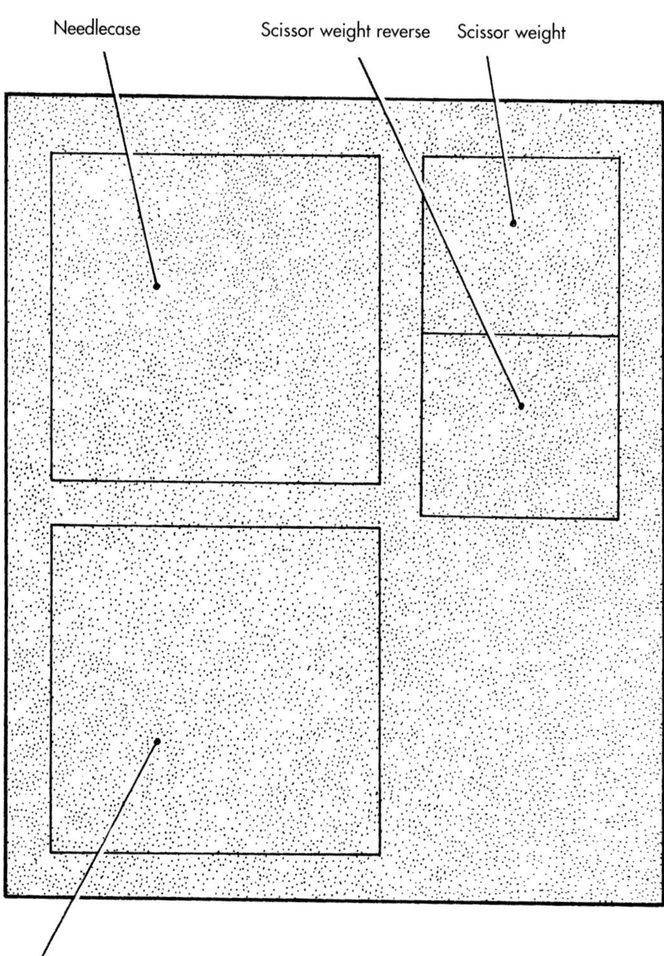

Fig 11.1 Suggested layout for the stitched decorations on the congress cloth.

PREPARATION

Staple or pin the congress cloth to the frame. If pins are used, cover the heads with masking tape to avoid the threads catching. Mark out the areas to be embroidered with tacking (*see* Fig 11.1).

SCISSOR WEIGHT

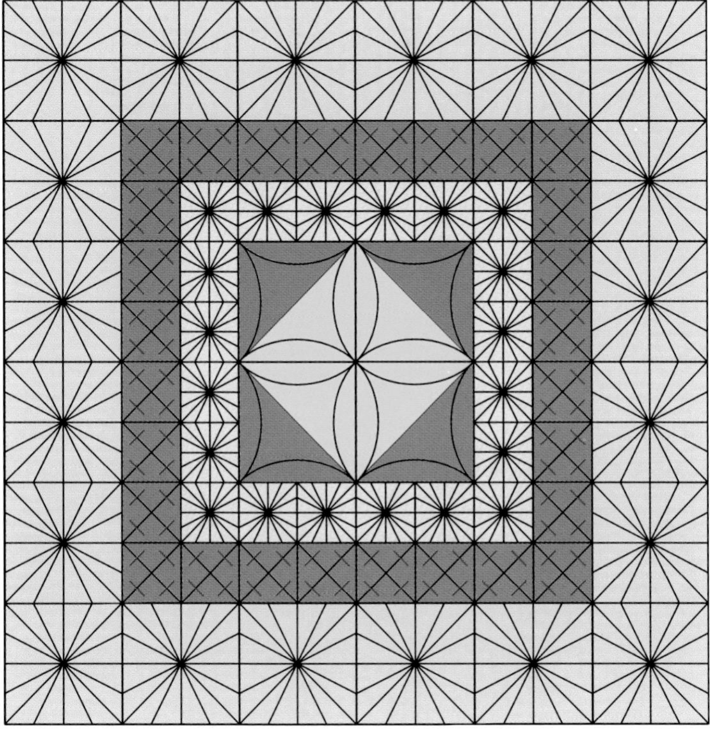

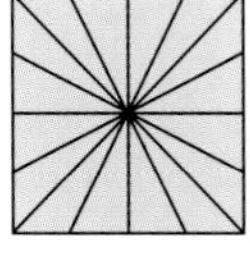

Rhodes stitch over eight threads in pale blue

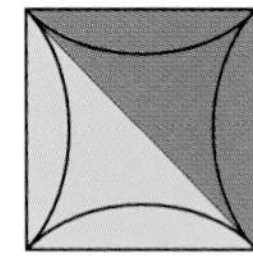

Cushion stitch over eight threads, in dark blue; corner crossed in metallic gold

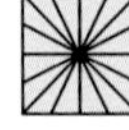

Rhodes stitch over four threads in peach

Rice stitch over four threads in dark blue; arms crossed in metallic gold

***Fig 11.2** Stitch chart for scissor weight design.*

EMBROIDERY

For all the embroidery the coloured and metallic rayon threads are used in six thicknesses. The Gütermann Dekor metallic thread is much finer than the others used in this book, so it is necessary to use six thicknesses.

This is worked in one long strip. Work the centre in dark blue cushion stitch, overlaid with metallic gold, over 16 threads (*see* Fig 11.2). Surround this square with peach Rhodes stitches, each over four threads, and surround these peach stitches with dark blue rice stitches, again over four threads. Outline the whole design with pale blue Rhodes stitches over eight threads to complete one side of the scissor weight.

Repeat the whole sequence to form the reverse of the weight. Take the work from the frame and trim the edges to leave 1/2in (13mm) all round.

MAKING UP

Cut two squares of interfacing, slightly smaller than the stitched area, cut two more slightly smaller than the first, and then a further square, slightly smaller again. Sandwich the smallest square between the middle-sized squares, place the two largest ones on either side and oversew all round.

Encase this small pad with the congress cloth, tuck in the edges and stitch together.

Make a twisted cord (*see* page 154) approximately 28in (711mm) long and attach this to the weight, leaving 2in (51mm) of each end to form a tassel on one corner. Leave the remainder of the cord on the corner diagonally opposite; this will form the loop to which the scissors are attached.

NEEDLECASE

EMBROIDERY

For this piece, use all the threads, including the metallic thread, in six thicknesses. Work the embroidery from Fig 11.3, starting with the centre square of dark blue cushion stitch.

This is over 24 threads and is overlaid with gold. Surround this square with pale blue Rhodes stitches, each over eight threads, and then work five concentric squares of rice stitch, over four threads, in the following colours:

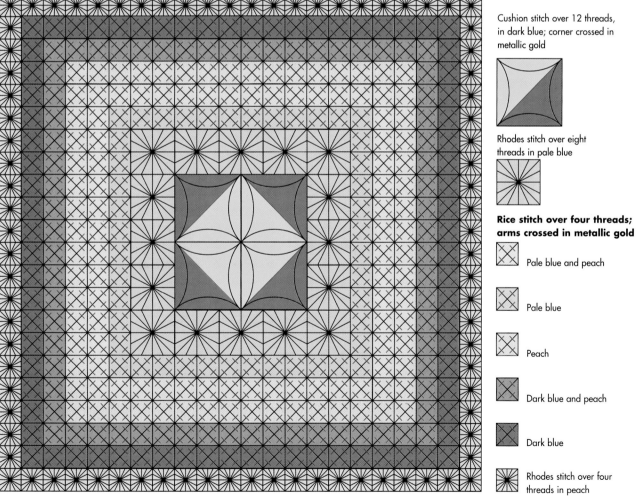

Cushion stitch over 12 threads, in dark blue; corner crossed in metallic gold

Rhodes stitch over eight threads in pale blue

Rice stitch over four threads; arms crossed in metallic gold

Pale blue and peach

Pale blue

Peach

Dark blue and peach

Dark blue

Rhodes stitch over four threads in peach

***Fig 11.3** Stitch chart for needlecase design.*

1 all pale blue;
2 pale blue and peach;
3 all peach;
4 peach and dark blue;
5 all dark blue.

The final square is worked in peach Rhodes stitches, again, over four threads. The embroidery is now complete. Remove it from the frame and trim the edges to leave 1/2in (13mm) all round.

MAKING UP

Cut a piece of interfacing, 10 x 4 3/4in (254 x 121mm), and a piece of outer fabric, 11 1/2 x 6 1/4in (292 x 159mm). Place the interfacing centrally on the wrong side of the outer fabric, turn the edges of the outer fabric over the interfacing and herringbone stitch into place. Place the covered interfacing right side up and mark the central vertical line with a row of pins.

Fig 11.4 Making up the needlecase.

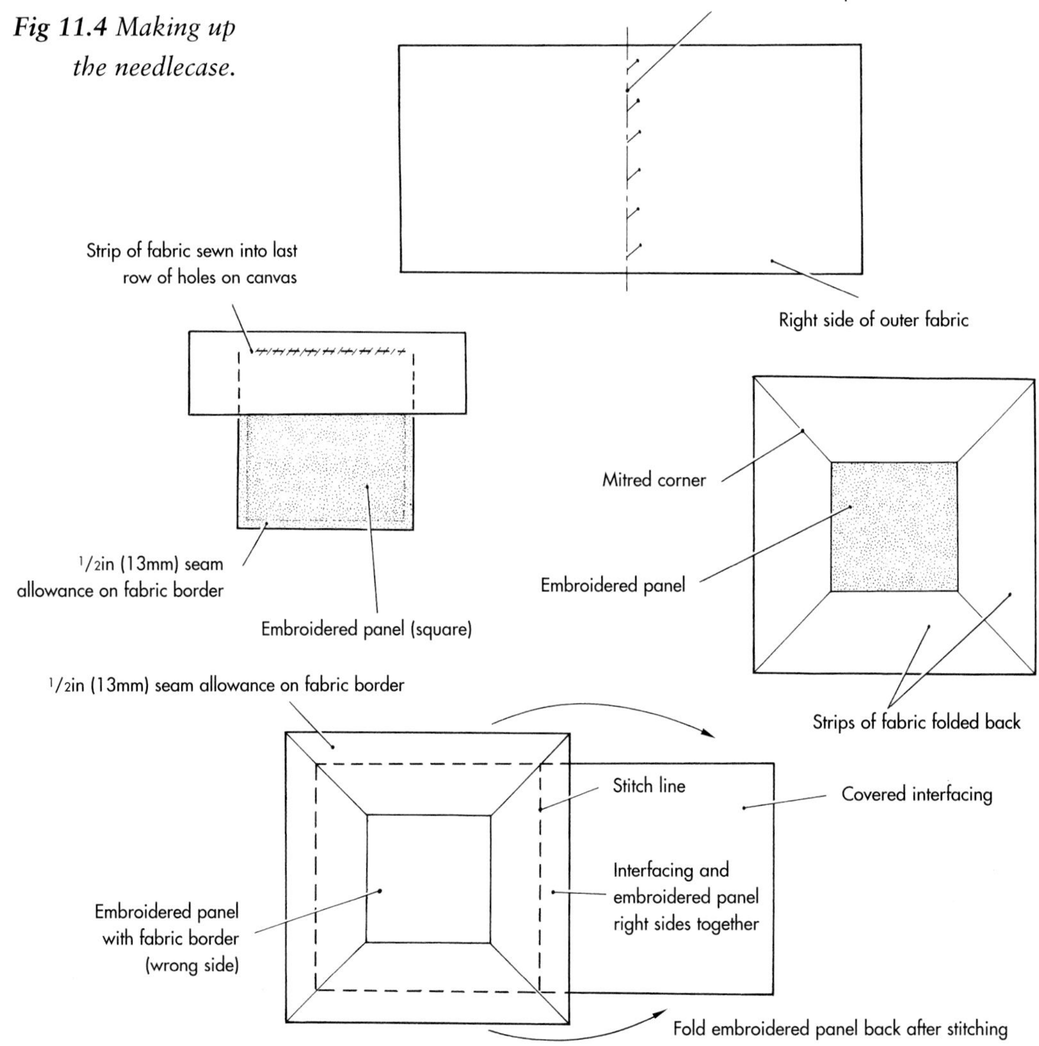

Cut four strips of outer fabric, each 1 3/4 x 6in (44 x 152mm). Sew a strip to each side of the embroidered panel, right sides together, stitching into the last row of holes used on the congress cloth. Fold the strips back, away from the embroidered panel, and mitre the four corners.

Fold over a 1/2in (13mm) seam allowance along one side of the fabric border, and place this fold line over the row of pins marking the centre of the covered interfacing, right sides together. Tack and stitch into place. Now fold the embroidered panel back over this stitched line so that the embroidery can be seen. Fold the raw edges of the outer fabric over to the underside of the interfacing, tack and herringbone stitch into place.

Cut a piece of lining fabric, 1/2in (13mm) larger all round, to cover the inside of the needlecase, tuck the raw edges under and catch into place. Cut a piece of felt to fit and stitch to the centre line of the case.

Make a twisted cord (*see* page 154) to go round the case and leave the ends to form a tassel.

PIN CUSHION

EMBROIDERY

Use all the coloured threads in six thicknesses and the metallic thread double. Leave a square of 32 x 32 holes unworked in the centre: this will be covered by the pad to take the pins.

To start, work a row of pale blue Rhodes stitches, each over 8 threads, round the unworked central square. (*See* Fig 11.5.)

To work the border, begin in one of the corners and work four dark blue cushion stitches, each over eight threads, to make a square covering 16 threads. Overlay this square with metallic gold. For the squares on either side of this corner square, work a pale blue Rhodes stitch over eight threads in the centre, then surround this with rice stitch in peach.

Work these two 16-thread squares alternately round the centre square, then surround the whole design with peach Rhodes stitches, each over 4 threads.

Remove the embroidery from the frame and trim the edges, leaving 1/2in (13mm) all round.

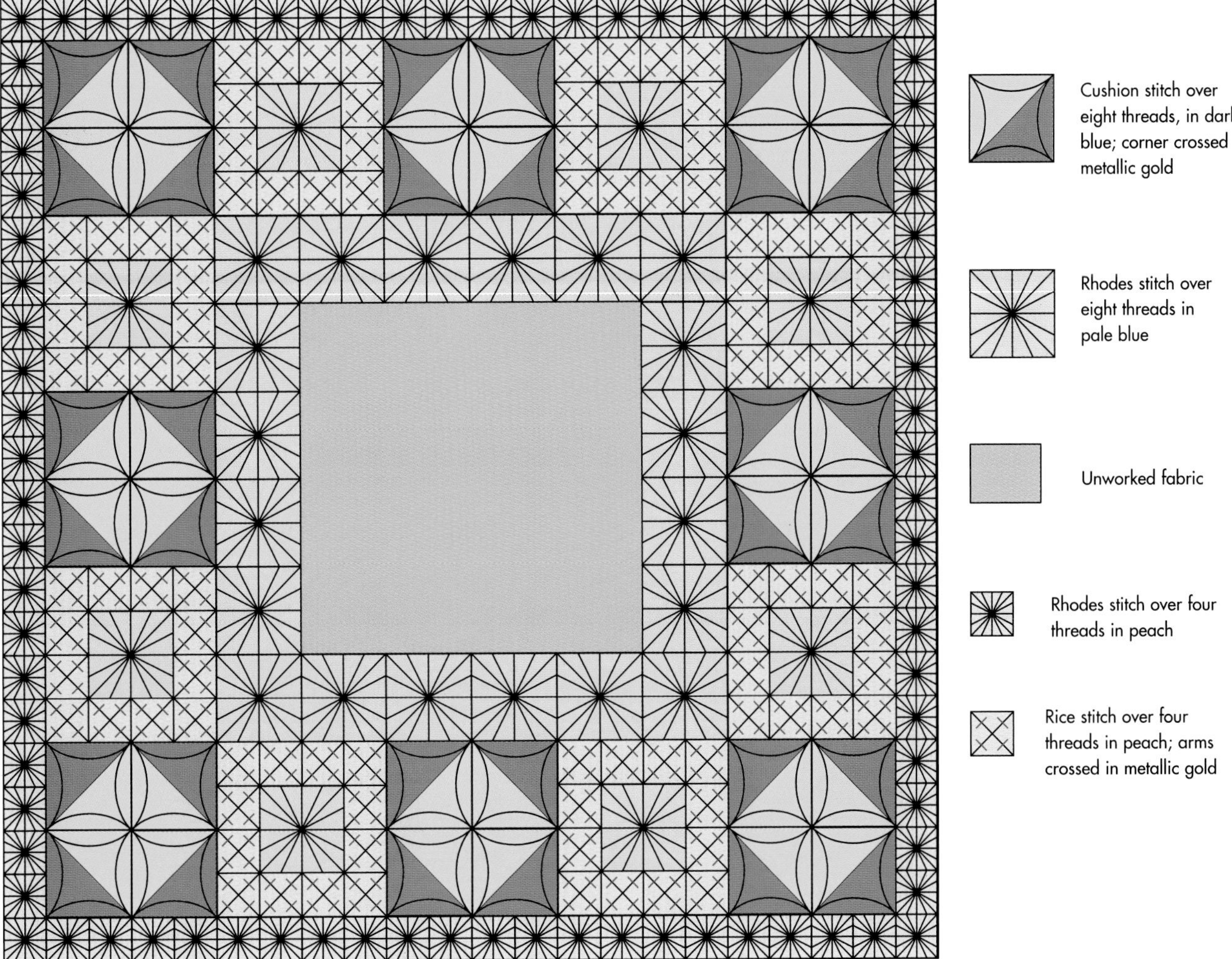

***Fig 11.5** Stitch chart for pin cushion design.*

MAKING UP

Cut a square of interfacing to the exact size of the unworked centre and cover this with the outer fabric. Stitch this firmly into place over the bare congress cloth.

Cut two squares of interfacing, each to the size of the stitched area, and oversew the edges together on three sides. Stuff this with wadding to make a very firm cushion and oversew the open edge.

Now cut a piece of the outer fabric to the size of the stitched area, and centre the cushion on it. Place the embroidery over this and, turning in the congress cloth around its edge, stitch to the outer fabric to make a cover for the pad.

Make a twisted cord (*see* page 154) approximately 24in (610mm) long and sew into place, leaving loops of equal size at each corner. Knot each loop and cut to form a tassel (*see* page 155).

CHAPTER 12

Wooden Pot Lid

This design uses Rhodes stitch in five lovely 'earth' colours of rayon thread. Metallic threads and beads give a rich sparkle to the pot lid, which is neatly finished with a border of green mosaic stitch.

THREAD KEY

1 cop each of Indian rayon in:
- Dark green
- Mid-green
- Light green
- Sand
- Tan

1 reel of Madeira metallic gold no. 12, colour 33

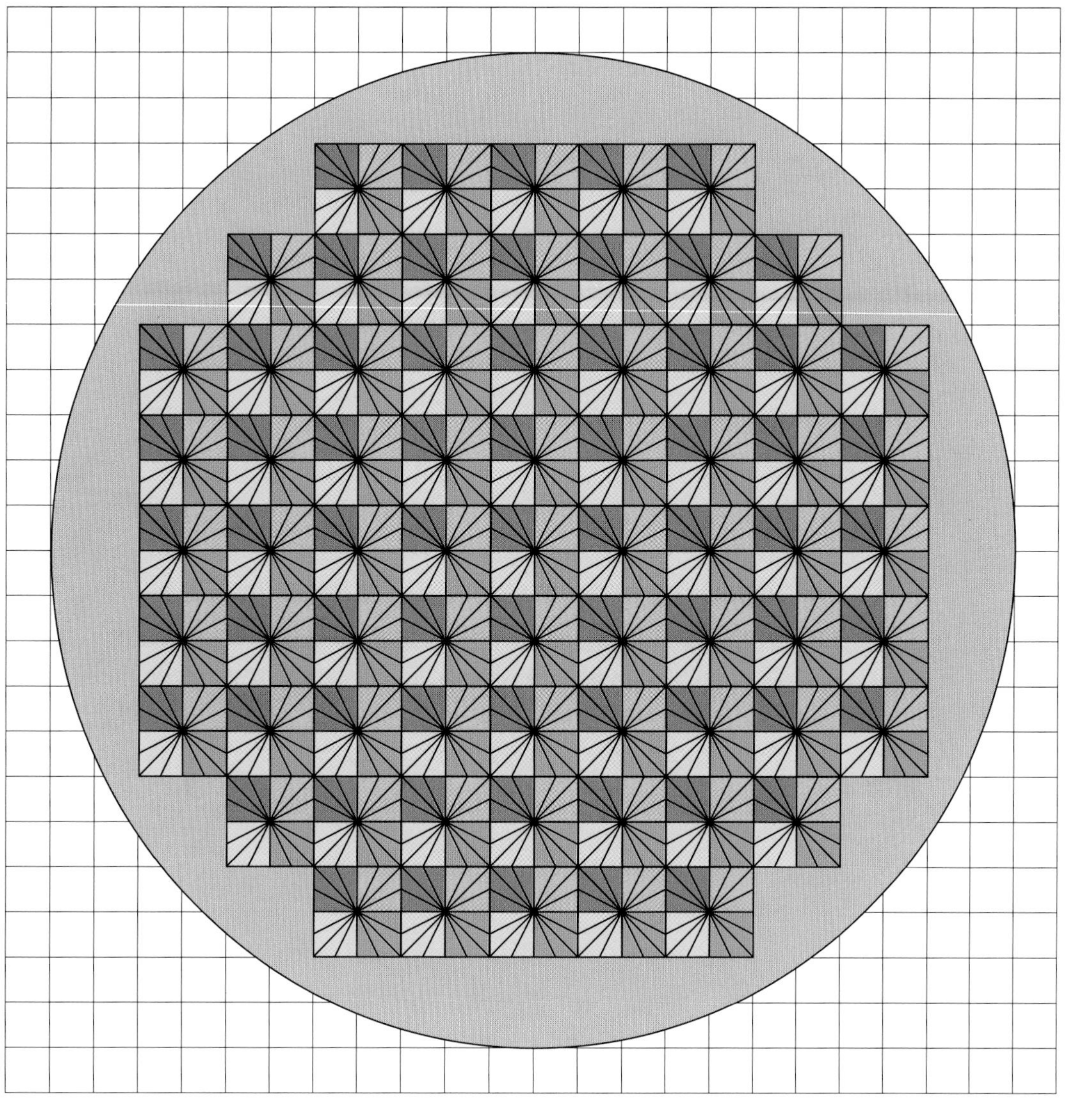

Mosaic stitch in two dark green + one mid-green

Variegated Rhodes stitch over eight threads in dark green; mid-green; light green; sand; tan; metallic gold

Fig 12.1 *Stitch chart for pot lid decoration.*

MATERIALS AND EQUIPMENT

Threads as listed in key
Congress cloth, 8in (203mm) square
Beadesign beads x 1 packet of gold no. 72
Wooden pot with 4in (102mm) diameter lid (available from Kernow Crafts Woodturning: *see* Suppliers, page 164)
Square wooden frame, 8in (203mm)
Tapestry needle, no. 24
Beading needle
Embroidery scissors
Needlework finisher (optional)

PREPARATION

Stretch the congress cloth over the frame and secure with either staples or drawing pins. If pins are used, cover the heads with masking tape to avoid the threads catching on them.

Use the card inset provided with the lid to draw a circle onto the centre of the congress cloth.

EMBROIDERY

All the embroidery is done using six thicknesses for the coloured threads and the metallic thread doubled.

The centre of the design is worked in variegated Rhodes stitch over eight threads, beginning with dark green and working through mid-green, light green, sand and tan. The final two stitches are in metallic gold thread.

Attach the five beads with the last stitch. Centralize them and, in order to keep them in place, secure at each end with a tiny stitch.

Fill the remaining area with mosaic stitch using two dark green and one mid-green thread, doubled over to give the six thicknesses.

The embroidery is now complete. Paint over the outside edge of the embroidery with the needlework finisher and cut the circle out, checking its size against the template.

MAKING UP

Assemble the pot lid according to the instructions given with the kit.

CHAPTER 13

CHRISTMAS CARD

What better way to send your Christmas greetings (and your embroidery skills!) to a special relative or friend than to include them in this unusual Christmas tree card, embroidered in traditional colours. A lasting memento of the Festive Season.

THREAD KEY

1 cop each of Indian rayon in:
- Dark green
- Pale green
- Red

1 reel of Madeira metallic gold no. 12, colour 33

MATERIALS AND EQUIPMENT

Threads as listed in key
Congress cloth, 8in (203mm) square
Beadesign beads x 1 packet each of gold no. 72 and red no. 57
Embroidery frame, 8in (203mm) square
Tapestry needle, no. 24
Quilting needle, no. 10
Vilene extra heavy interfacing, 4½in (114mm)

PREPARATION

Stretch the congress cloth over the frame and secure with either staples or drawing pins. If pins are used, cover the heads with masking tape to avoid the threads catching.

EMBROIDERY

Use the Indian rayon threads in six thicknesses and the metallic gold thread double.

Working from the chart, start either from the top left-hand corner or the lower left-hand corner, with the row of single cushion stitches in alternating gold and red, worked over four threads. Follow this with a row of diagonal gold stitches over two threads.

The section with the Christmas trees uses mosaic stitch, except for the foliage which is worked in dark green Rhodes stitch over four threads. Follow Fig 13.1 which shows the colours used for the mosaic stitches. Having completed the trees section, repeat the row of diagonal gold stitches over two threads and then the single cushion stitches in alternating gold and red, over four threads. This whole section has been labelled 'Section A' on the chart.

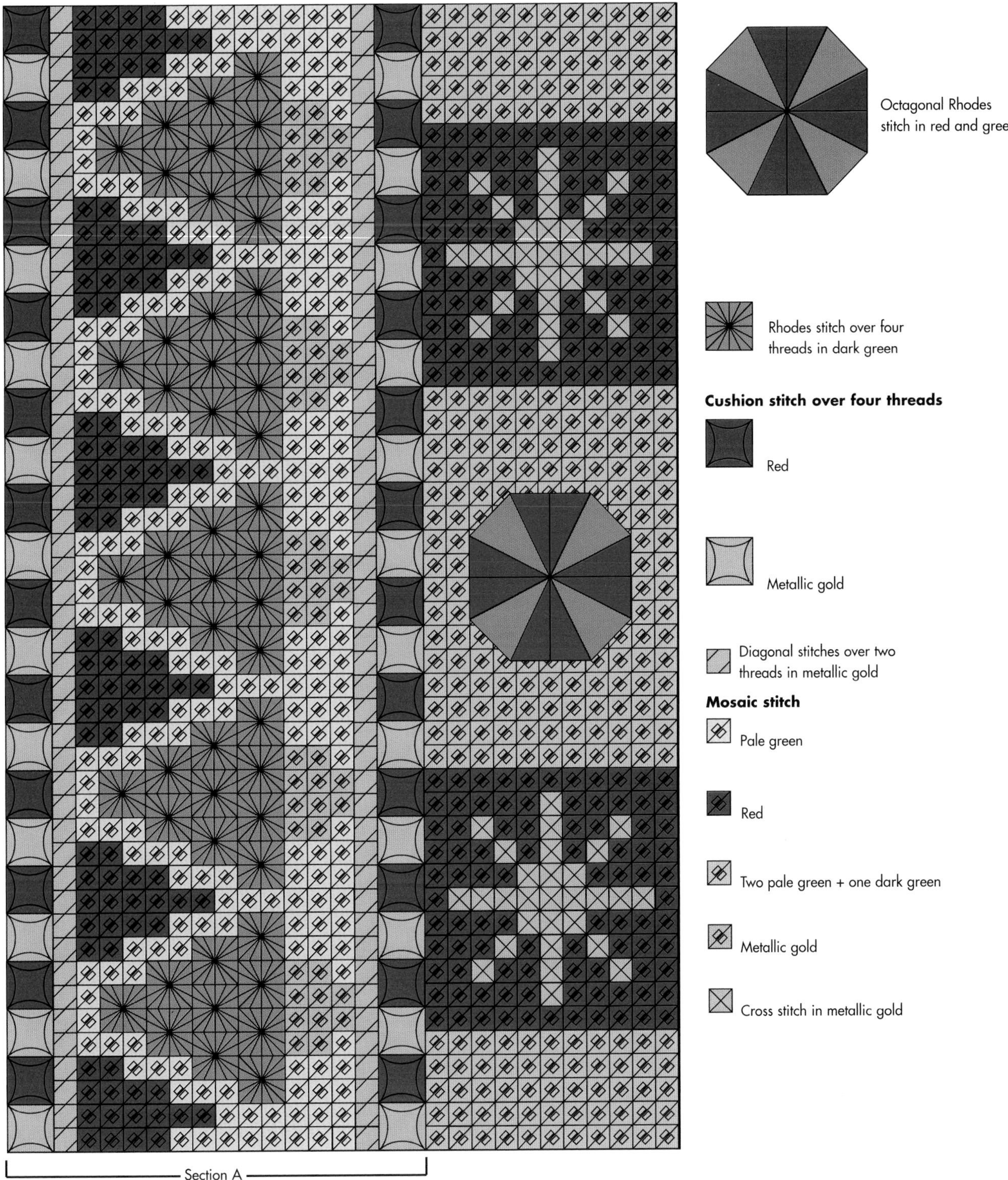

***Fig 13.1** Stitch chart for Christmas card design.*

CHAPTER 14

Christmas Tree Wall Hanging

A truly stunning interpretation of a Christmas tree with which to deck the wall for the Festive Season.

Seven different colour through gold patterns in triangular shapes are framed with gold lamé ribbon and suspended from dowels sprayed with gold. More colour through gold designs are stitched in stripes across the pot. The whole concept is thoroughly original and makes a wonderful Christmas decoration which will surely be a talking point for everyone.

THREAD KEY

1 cop each of Indian rayon in:
- Red
- Green
- Pale yellow
- Deep yellow

5 reels of Madeira metallic gold no. 12, colour 33

MATERIALS AND EQUIPMENT

Threads as listed in key
Congress cloth, black, 10 x 8in (254 x 203mm) x 8 pieces
Panda gold lamé ribbon, 35mm wide, 10 yd (9.14m)
Panda gold lamé ribbon, 3mm wide, 3/4yd (686mm)
Backing fabric, green, 9 x 10in (229 x 254mm) x 8 pieces
Vilene extra heavy interfacing, 15 x 27in (381 x 686mm)
Sewing threads in:
- Green to match the backing fabric
- Black
- Gold to match the ribbon

Dowel, 1/2in (13mm) diameter x 7ft (2.1m)
Spray paint, gold
Rectangular wooden embroidery frame, 10 x 8in (254 x 203mm)
Tapestry needle, no. 24
Embroidery scissors

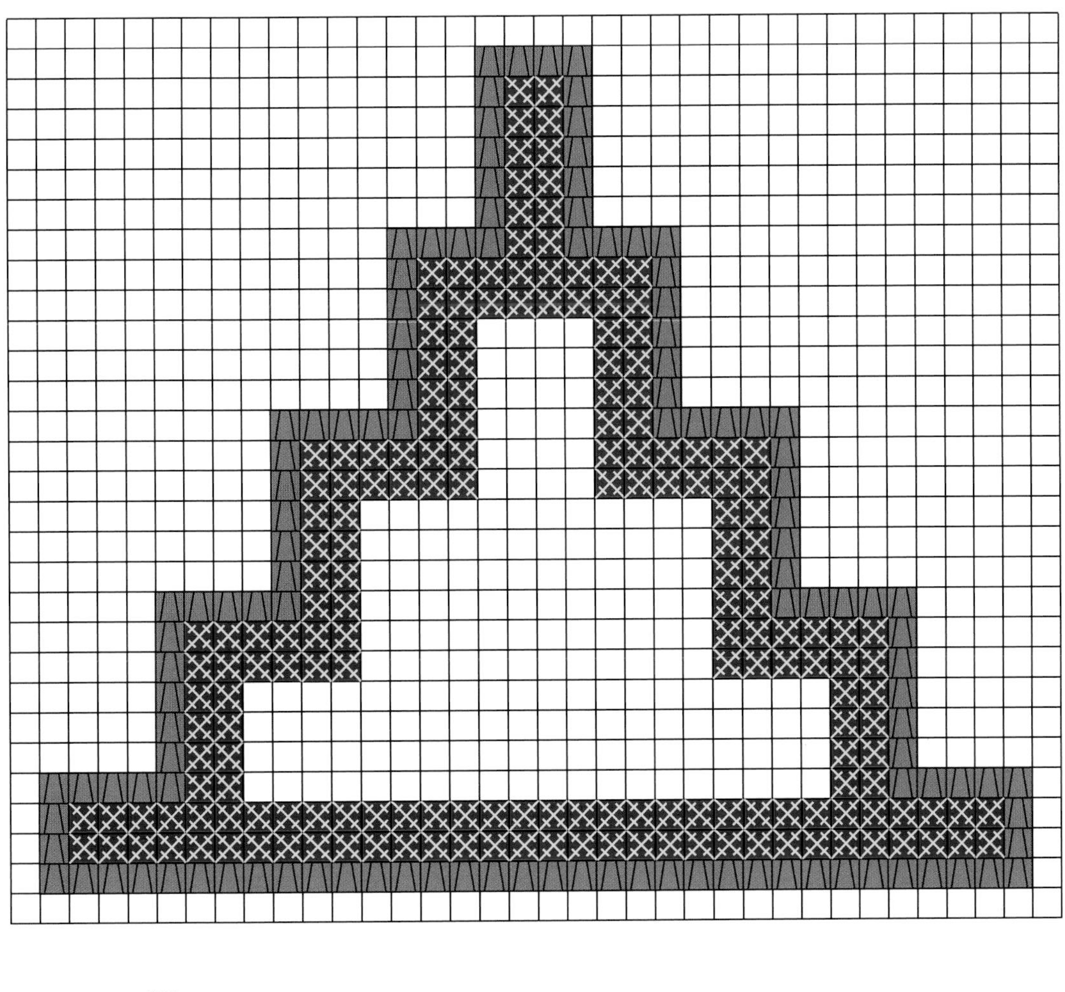

***Fig 14.1** Stitch chart for border of every triangular hanging.*

PREPARATION

The embroidery frame will be used and re-used for each of the eight sections of the wall hanging, so each one must be completed and removed before the next one can be started.

Attach one of the pieces of congress cloth to the frame, using either staples or drawing pins. If pins are used, cover the heads with masking tape to avoid the threads catching on them.

EMBROIDERY

The following instructions are for the seven triangular shapes that form the tree. All the rayon thread is used in six thicknesses and the metallic gold thread is used double. The border design for each is worked in rice stitch and the central designs are all worked with straight stitches.

For the border, start working in the bottom left-hand corner, about 1in (25mm) in from the side and bottom of the frame. Referring to Fig 14.1, work the base crosses of the rice stitch in red thread, each stitch over four threads, and the crossed corners in metallic gold thread.

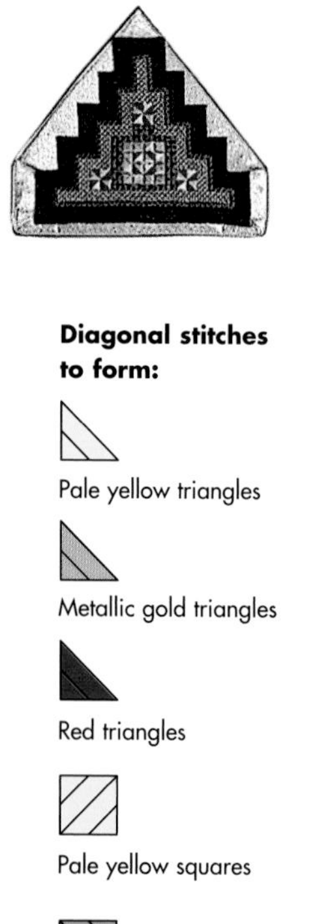

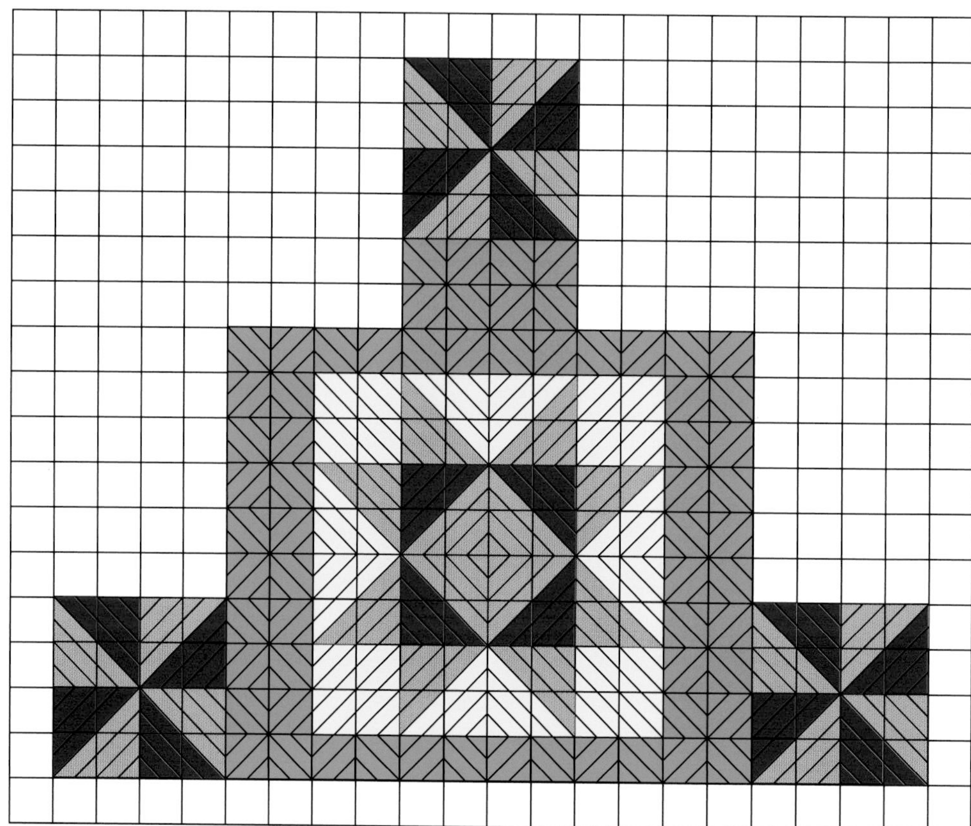

Fig 14.2 *Stitch chart for triangle 1.*

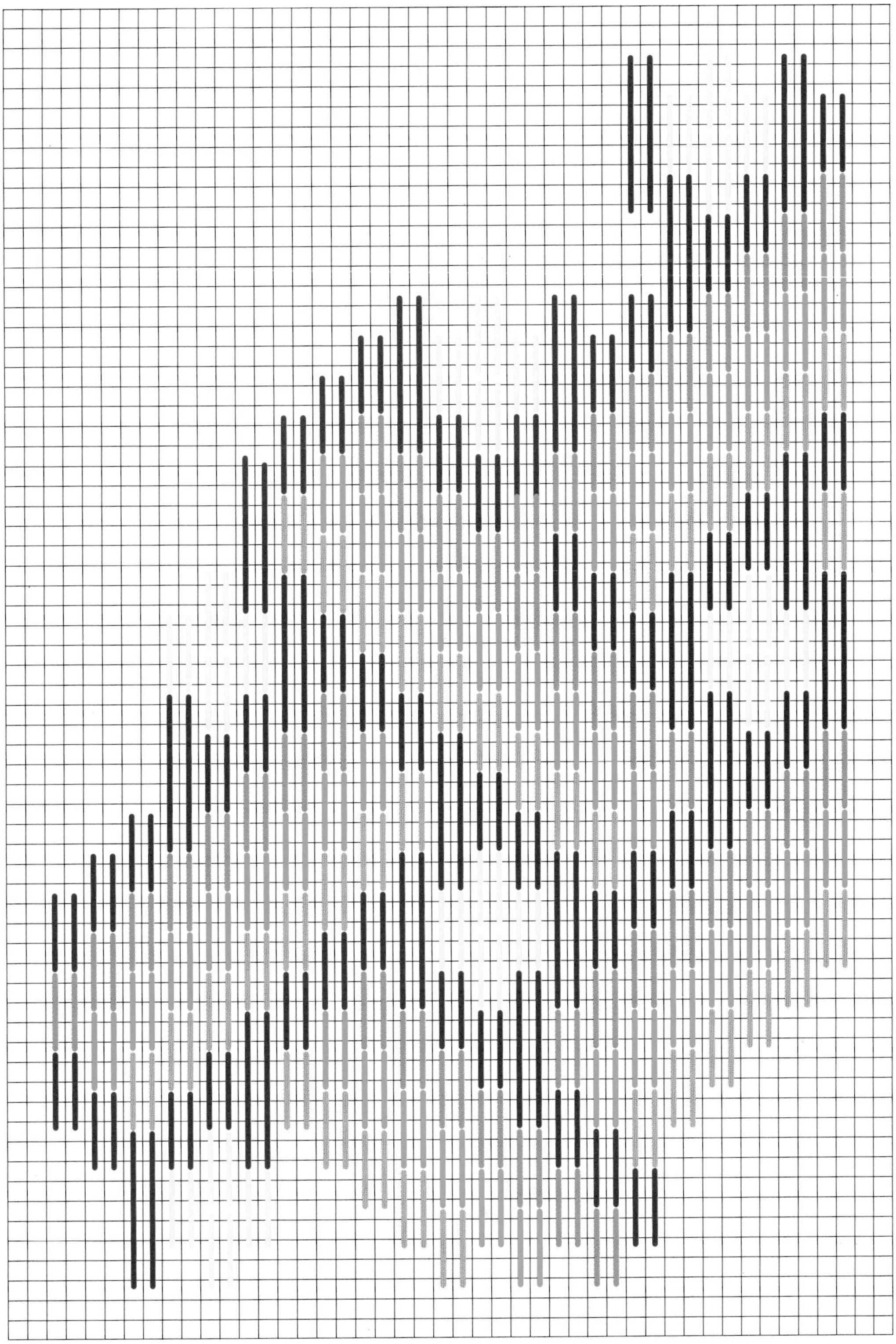

Fig 14.3 Stitch chart for triangle 2.

Straight stitches (vertical)

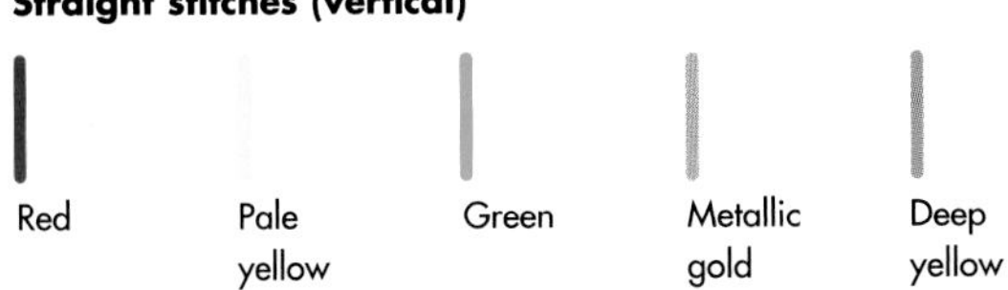

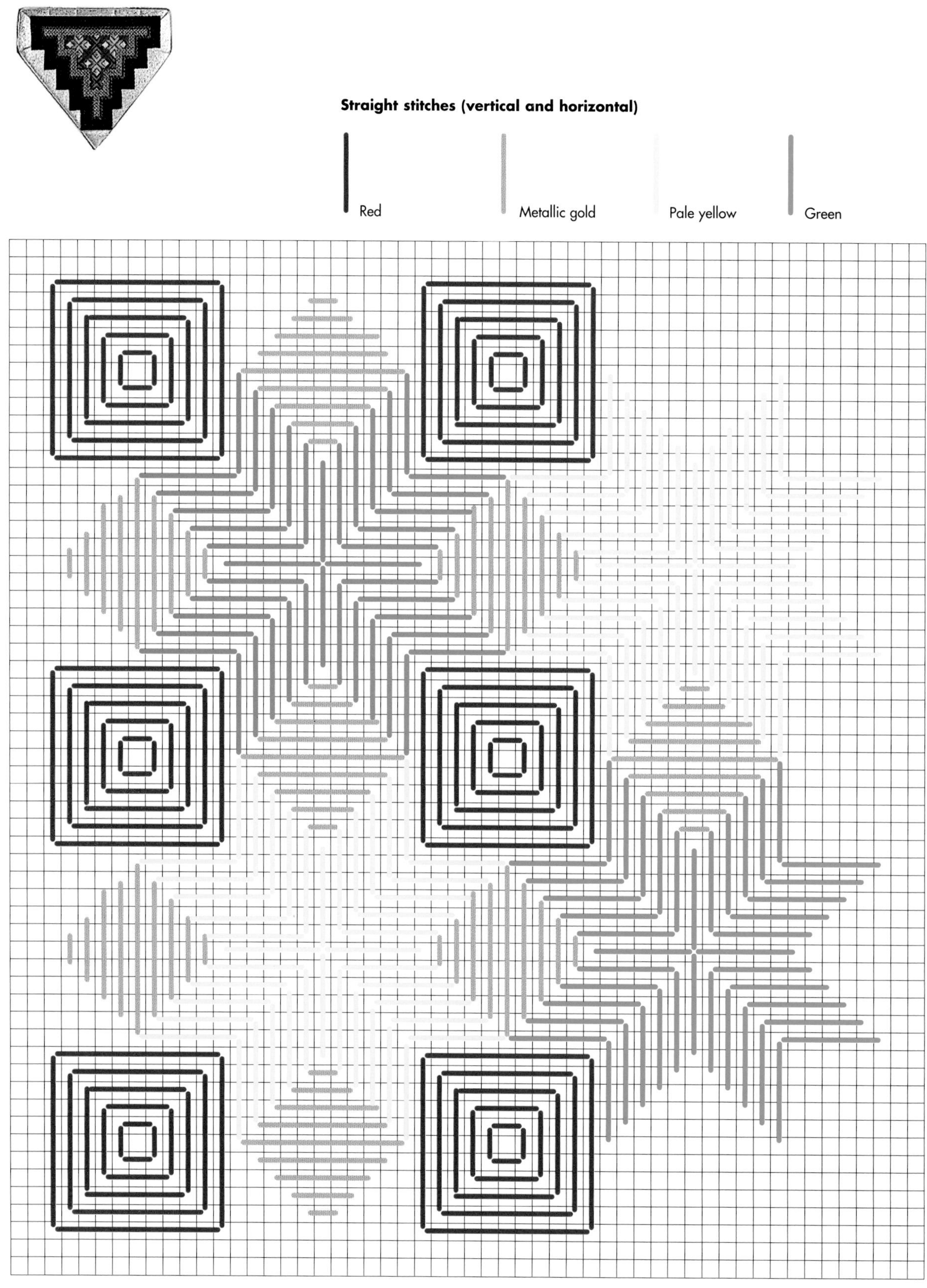

Fig 14.4 Stitch chart for triangle 3.

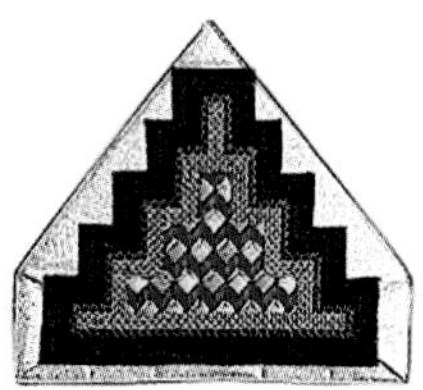

Fig 14.5 Stitch chart for triangle 4.

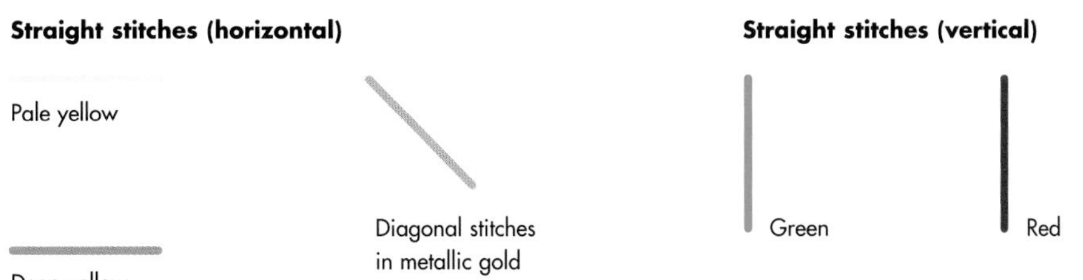

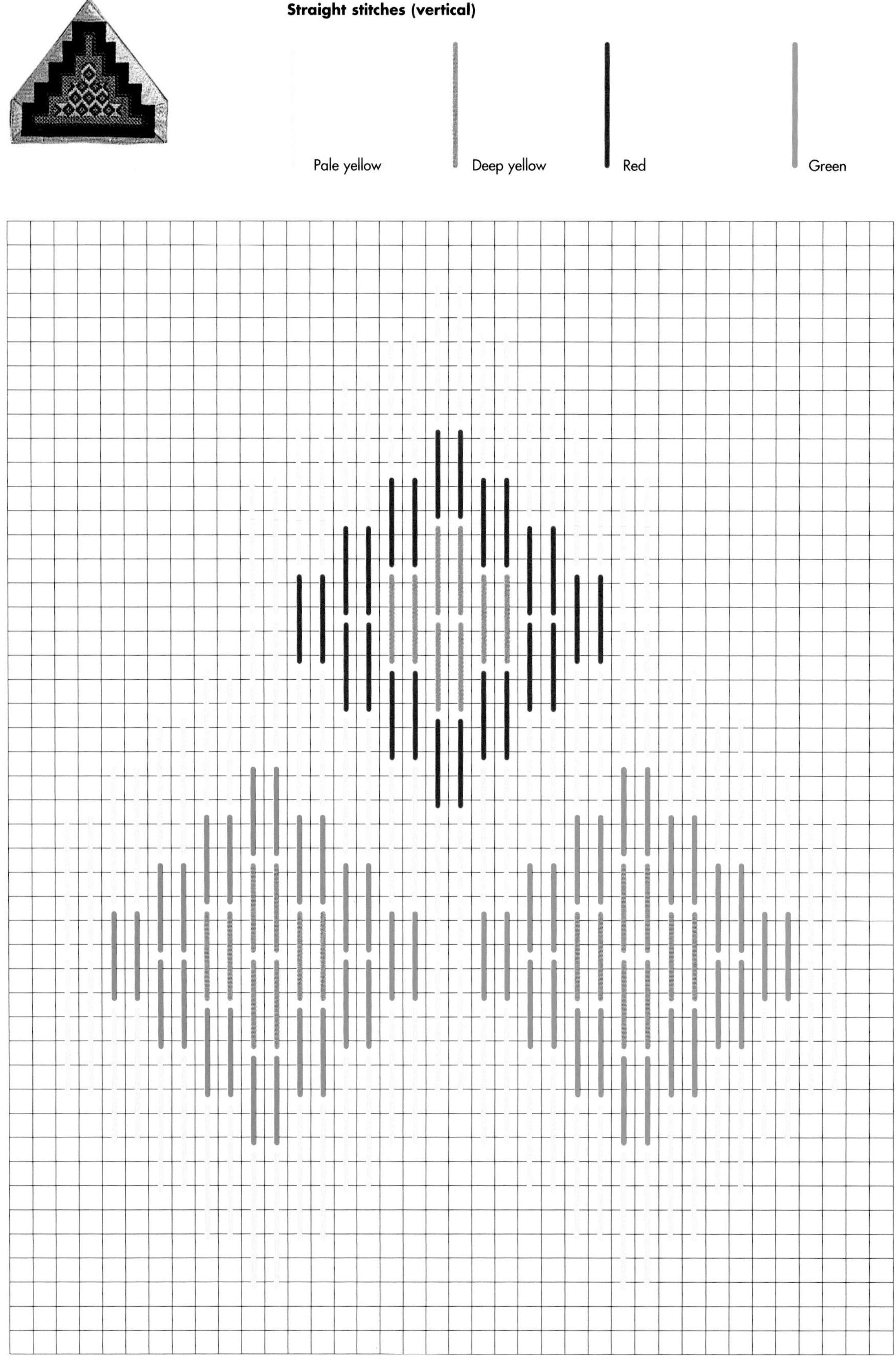

Fig 14.6 Stitch chart for triangle 5.

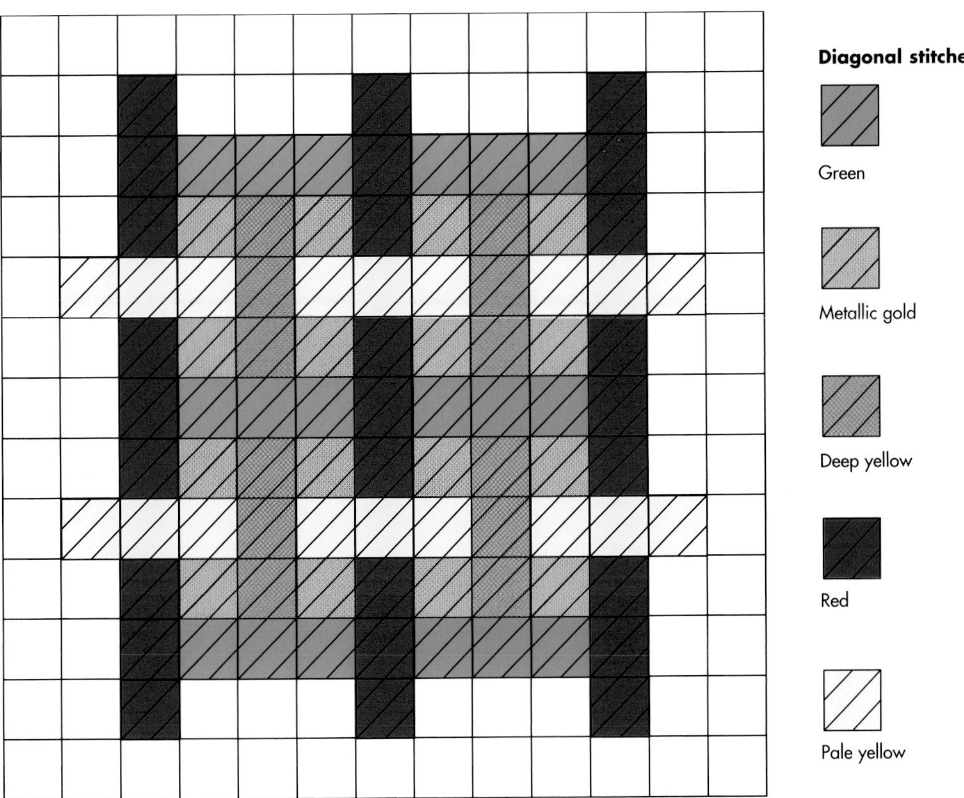

Fig 14.7 Stitch chart for triangle 6.

Fig 14.8 Stitch chart for triangle 7.

Working from each chart in turn (Figs 14.2–14.8), complete the designs within the area outlined by the rice stitches. For each design, start working from the centre of the shape and finish one complete pattern before starting on the part repeats to fill up the rest of the space.

Complete the embroidery by working the straight green stitches round the edge (*see* Fig 14.1).

Straight stitches (vertical) over eight threads in green and metallic gold

Straight stitches (vertical) over five threads in red and metallic gold

Straight stitches (vertical) worked in diamonds, over five threads, in red and deep yellow

Straight stitches (vertical) over six threads in red and pale yellow

Diagonal stitches over four threads in alternate pale yellow and deep yellow

Straight stitches (vertical) over four threads in red

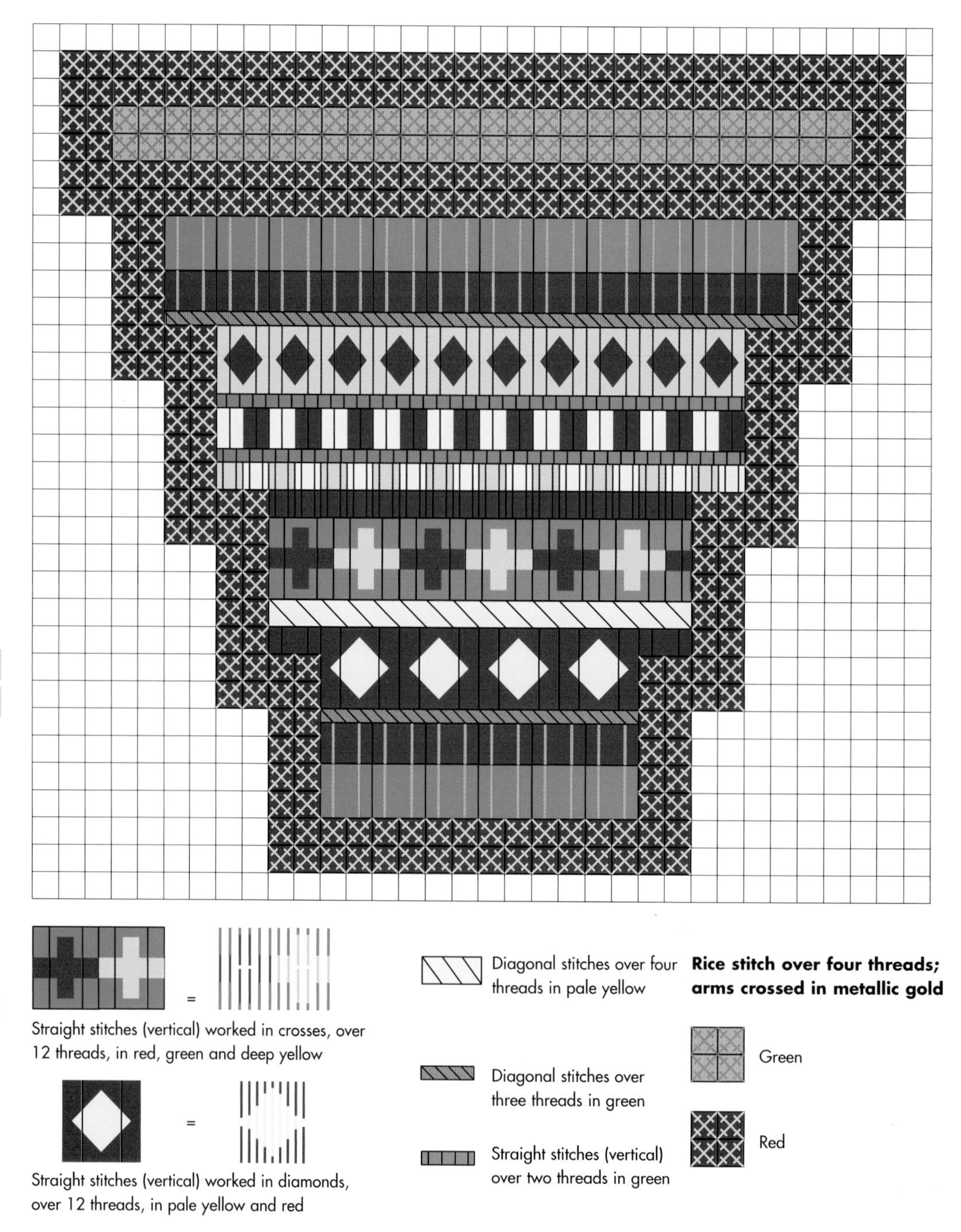

Fig 14.9 Stitch chart for pot.

Referring to the separate chart for the pot (*see* Fig 14.9), work the rice stitch area first. When this is complete, fill in the rest of the stitches, starting at the widest part, the top, and working down to the base.

MAKING UP

Cut the dowel into three 2ft (610mm) pieces and one 1ft (305mm) piece. Smooth them all lightly and spray each one with gold paint.

Using the templates in Figs 14.10 and 14.11, (shown at 50% of their full size), cut out the seven shapes for the tree and the one shape for the pot from vilene extra heavy interfacing. Each piece of embroidery is made up in the same way.

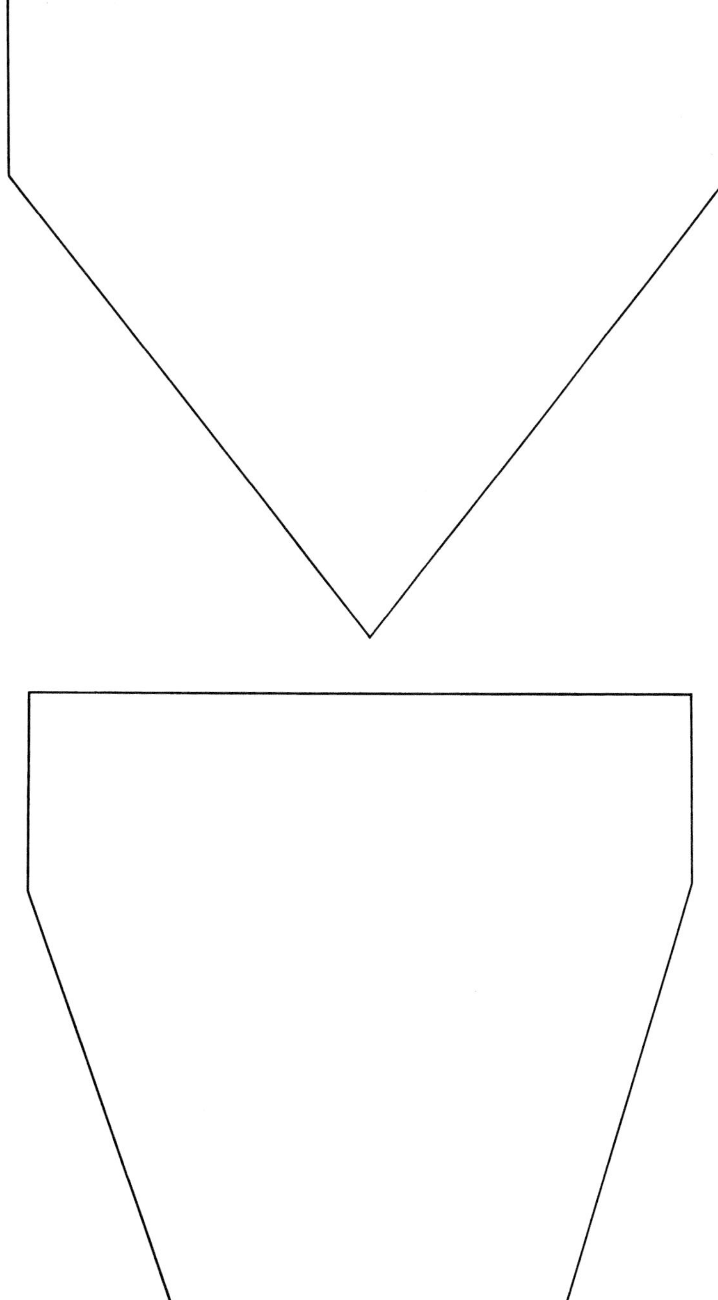

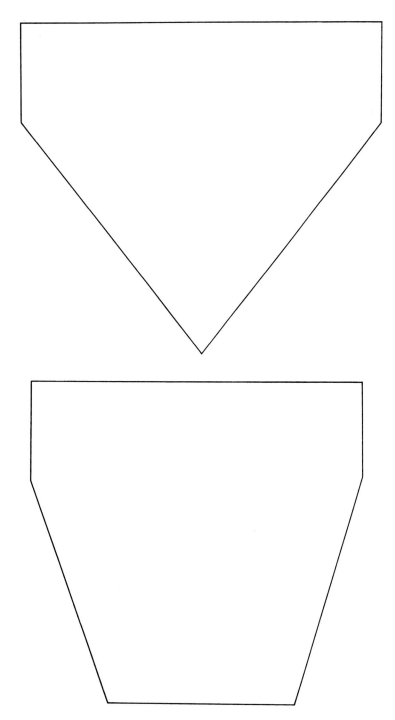

Fig 14.10 *Template for triangles (50% of full size).*

Fig 14.11 *Template for pot (50% of full size).*

Take one piece of the green backing fabric, 9 x 10in (229 x 254mm), place a piece of interfacing on top and, allowing 1in (25mm) of backing fabric all round the interfacing, cut away the excess. Fold the edges of the fabric over to the front and tack into place, pleating the corners neatly. (*See* Fig 14.12).

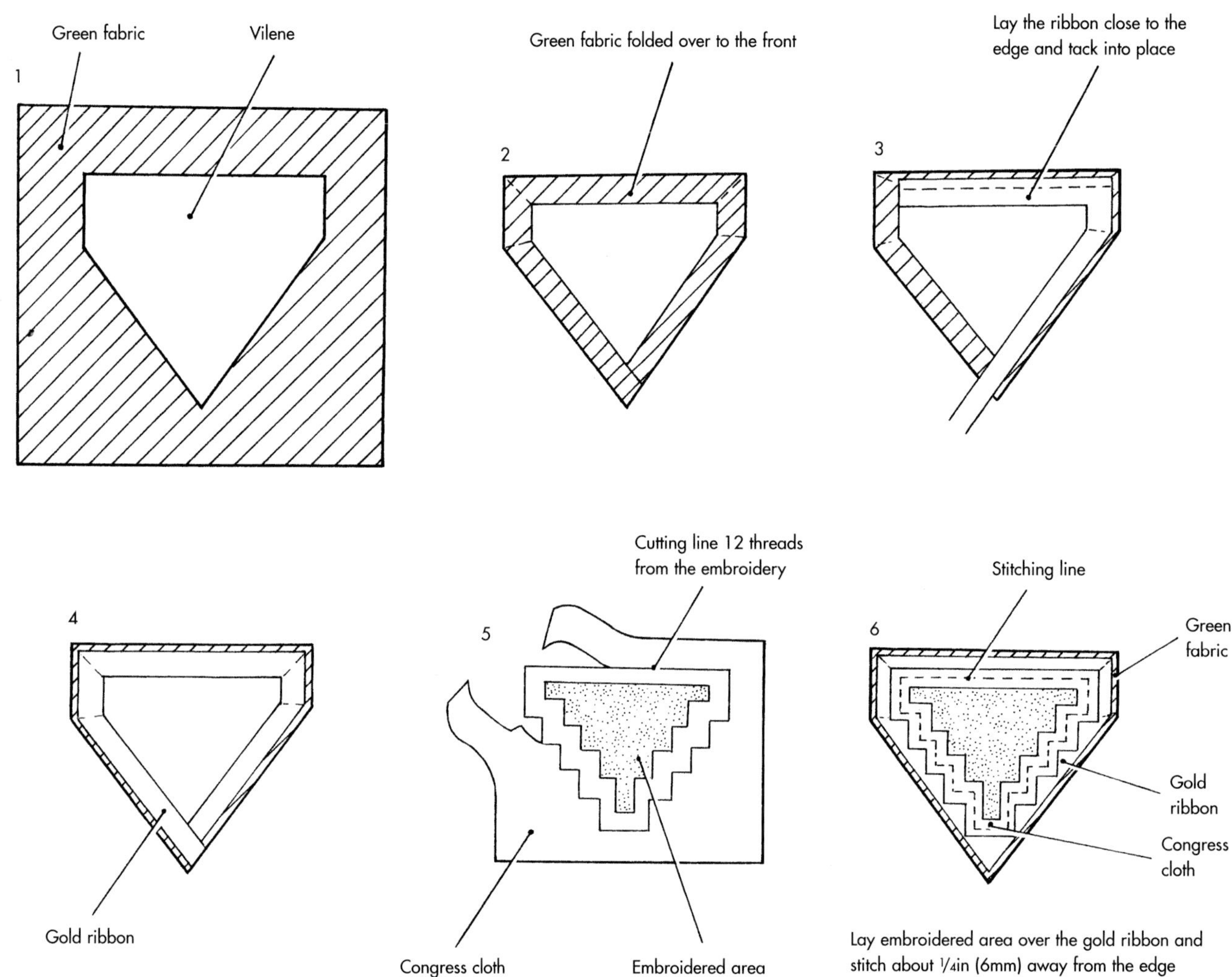

***Fig 14.12** Making up the triangles.*

Now take a 27in (686mm) length of the 35mm gold lamé ribbon and lay it close to the edge, on top of the overlapped green fabric. Tack the ribbon into place, again pleating the excess ribbon at the corners. Machine or hand stitch it in place. If you use a machine, thread the lower spool with green thread and use gold on the top.

Next, take one of the embroidered designs and, leaving a 12-thread margin all round, cut away the congress cloth to this dimension. Lay the embroidered piece over the top of the gold ribbon and stitch into place, 1/4in (6mm) away from the cut edge. (*See* Fig 14.12). Again, this can be done either by hand or machine. This time, if you use a machine, thread the lower spool with green and use black on the top.

Make loops from the 35mm ribbon to hang over the dowel. Cut lengths of 5¾in (146mm) for the loops at the pointed tops of the tree shapes, but only 4¾in (120mm) for the two lower edges of each shape and for the pot. Pin each loop into place and position over the dowels before stitching them, adjusting as necessary. Refer to the photograph of the finished piece and to Fig 14.13, for the arrangement of the pieces.

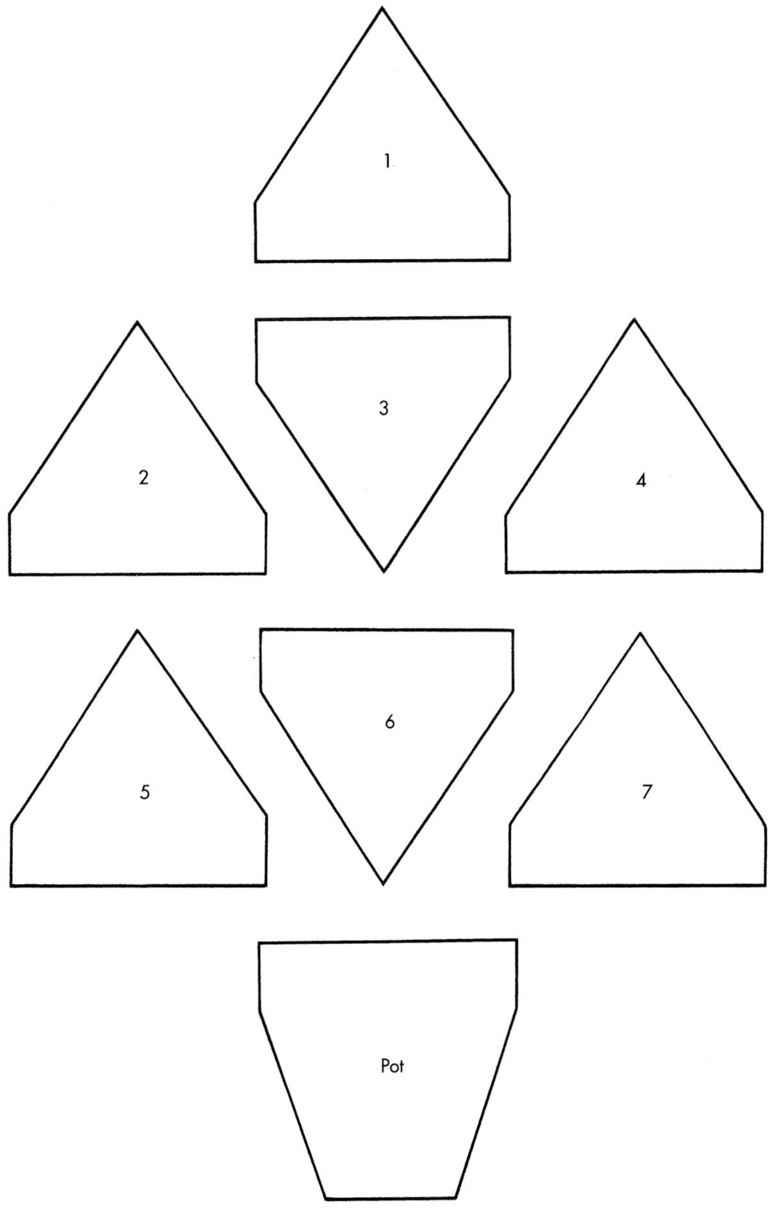

Fig 14.13 Wall hanging layout.

Using the same threads as for the embroidery, make tassels to go at each end of the dowels. (*See* page 155 for instructions on making tassels.)

Finally, use the narrow gold lamé ribbon to make a loop for suspending the completed wall hanging.

CHAPTER 15

EVENING BAG

Based on the classic Rhodes stitch, this eye-catching evening bag will attract many envious glances. The Celtic design is worked in black, grey and yellow threads, and is highlighted by metallic gold crosses. The 'fabric' for the bag is metallic gold ribbon and the final touches of elegance are the hand-made cord and the button covered with gold thread.

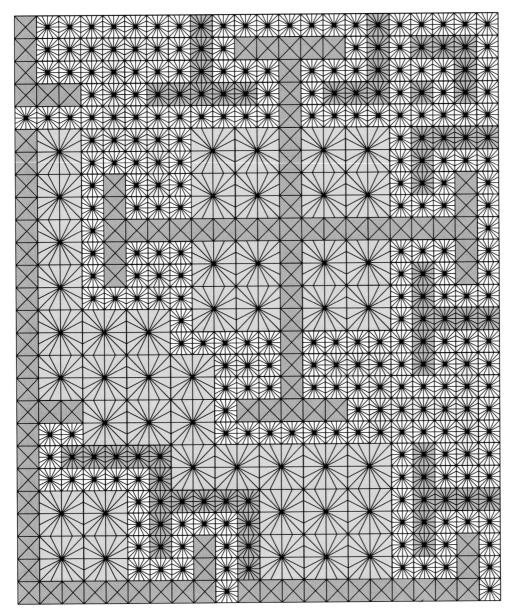

Fig 15.1 *Stitch chart for evening bag (quarter of design).*

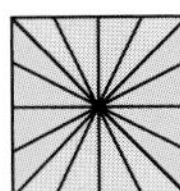

Variegated Rhodes stitch over eight threads in black; dark grey; pale grey; yellow; metallic gold

Diagonal stitches in metallic gold

Rhodes stitch over four threads

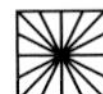

Black

Pale grey

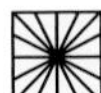

Yellow

THREAD KEY

1 cop each of Indian rayon in:
- Black
- Dark grey
- Light grey
- Yellow

2 reels of Madeira metallic gold no. 12, colour 33

MATERIALS AND EQUIPMENT

Threads as listed in key
Congress cloth, 12in (305mm) square
Gold button or glass bead (to be covered with gold thread)
Panda metallic gold ribbon, 35mm wide, 4½yd (4.1m)
Lining fabric, black, 24 x 10in (610 x 254mm)
Gütermann gold sewing thread, 1 reel
Vilene extra heavy interfacing, 19 x 8in (483 x 203mm)
Panda piping, gold, 3yd (2.7m)
Wooden embroidery frame, 12in (305mm) square
Tapestry needle, no. 24
Sewing needle
Embroidery scissors

PREPARATION

Stretch the congress cloth over the frame and secure with either staples or drawing pins. If pins are used, cover the heads with masking tape to avoid the threads catching.

EMBROIDERY

Use all the rayon threads in six thicknesses and the metallic thread double.

Work the panel from the chart given in Fig 15.1: note that only a quarter of the design is given. The small squares are worked in Rhodes stitch over four threads in the colours shown on the chart. The larger squares, over eight threads, are worked in variegated Rhodes stitch. For these, work the first three stitches of each square in black, the second three stitches in dark grey and the three remaining vertical stitches in pale grey. Follow this with four yellow stitches and complete the square with gold metallic threads.

The remaining gold work is done with diagonal stitches. Keep referring to the photograph of the finished bag to help with placing the colours.

Remove the congress cloth from the frame and trim away the edges, leaving an unworked area of ½in (13mm) all round.

MAKING UP

Cut four lengths of ribbon, two of 12in (305mm) and two of $10\frac{1}{2}$in (268mm). These will be used to bind the edges of the congress cloth.

Back stitch (or machine stitch) the ribbon to the right side of the work, allowing a $\frac{1}{4}$in (6mm) seam on the ribbon, using the last row of holes worked in the embroidered area to ensure that no canvas is showing. Do this on all four sides, using the appropriate lengths of ribbon, then fold back the ribbon and mitre the corners.

Next, cut two pieces of vilene interfacing, $9\frac{1}{2}$ x 8in (241 x 203mm). Place one piece centrally over the back of the work, fold the ribbon edges over it, and herringbone stitch into place.

To make the fabric for the back of the bag, cut eight lengths of ribbon, each 12in (305mm) long, and seven lengths of piping of the same length. Use the piping between the joins of the ribbon and stitch together, by machine or by hand, to create a fabric.

Lay the second piece of interfacing centrally over the back of the ribbon fabric you have created and again, turn over the edges of the ribbon, pin, tack and stitch into place.

Ladder stitch the lower edges of the front and back of the bag together, open out and lay the bag flat, inside uppermost. Use the piece of black lining fabric to cover the inside of the bag, pinning, tacking and stitching the lining into place about $\frac{1}{8}$in (3mm) away from the edges of the bag.

Fold the bag in half again, wrong sides facing, and ladder stitch the sides together. Attach a button to the centre of the top front edge of the bag. The 'button' shown here is a glass bead covered with gold thread but a purchased gold button could be used in its place. Stitch a button-hole loop at the centre of the back edge of the bag to fit over the button.

To make the cord handle, measure the length of the finished cord required and multiply this by four to arrive at the length of threads needed. Use the rayon threads and follow one of the methods for making cords described in Chapter 19 on page 154.

Double the cord and tie a knot at each end, leaving approximately 2in (51mm) after the knot – when the ends are cut, they will make a tassel. Attach the cord to the bag at each top corner. The bag in the photograph has a row of small beads over the stitching, added as extra decoration.

CHAPTER 16

GEOMETRIC PANEL

This panel would make a handsome wall feature in any room, varying the coloured rayon threads to suit the decor. The design uses several variations of cross-cornered cushion stitch and, with the addition of gold thread, makes a glittering panel, enhanced by a double mount and gilded frame.

This design was first published in *Needlework* magazine in March 1996.

THREAD KEY

1 cop each of Indian rayon in:
- Deep peach
- Pale peach
- Cream
- Deep turquoise

1 reel of Madeira metallic gold no. 12, colour 33

MATERIALS AND EQUIPMENT

Threads as listed in key
Congress cloth, 12 x 6in (305 x 152mm)
Rectangular embroidery frame, 12 x 6in (305 x 152mm)
Tapestry needle, no. 24
Embroidery scissors

PREPARATION

Stretch the congress cloth tightly over the frame and secure, either with staples or drawing pins. If pins are used, cover the heads with masking tape to avoid the threads catching on them.

EMBROIDERY

Throughout, use all the coloured threads in six thicknesses, and the metallic threads doubled. The design is worked over 48 threads across and 192 down.

All the overlaid threads lie in the opposite direction from the coloured threads. Keep referring to Fig 16.1 for the size of the square and direction of the stitching, and to the photograph for the colours used.

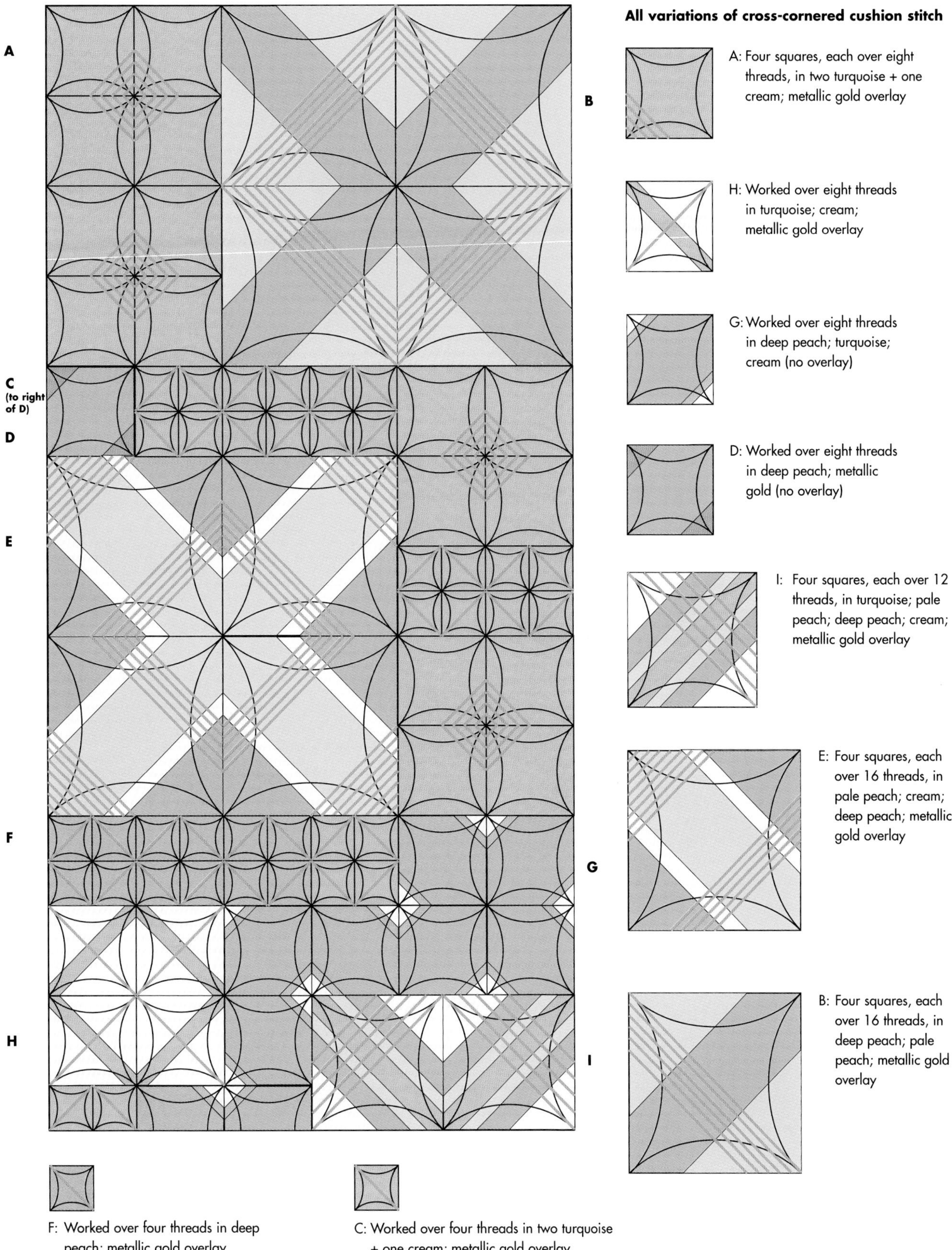
A
B
C
(to right of D)
D
E
F
G
H
I
All variations of cross-cornered cushion stitch
A: Four squares, each over eight threads, in two turquoise + one cream; metallic gold overlay
H: Worked over eight threads in turquoise; cream; metallic gold overlay
G: Worked over eight threads in deep peach; turquoise; cream (no overlay)
D: Worked over eight threads in deep peach; metallic gold (no overlay)
I: Four squares, each over 12 threads, in turquoise; pale peach; deep peach; cream; metallic gold overlay
E: Four squares, each over 16 threads, in pale peach; cream; deep peach; metallic gold overlay
B: Four squares, each over 16 threads, in deep peach; pale peach; metallic gold overlay
F: Worked over four threads in deep peach; metallic gold overlay
C: Worked over four threads in two turquoise + one cream; metallic gold overlay

Fig 16.1a Stitch chart for top half of geometric panel.

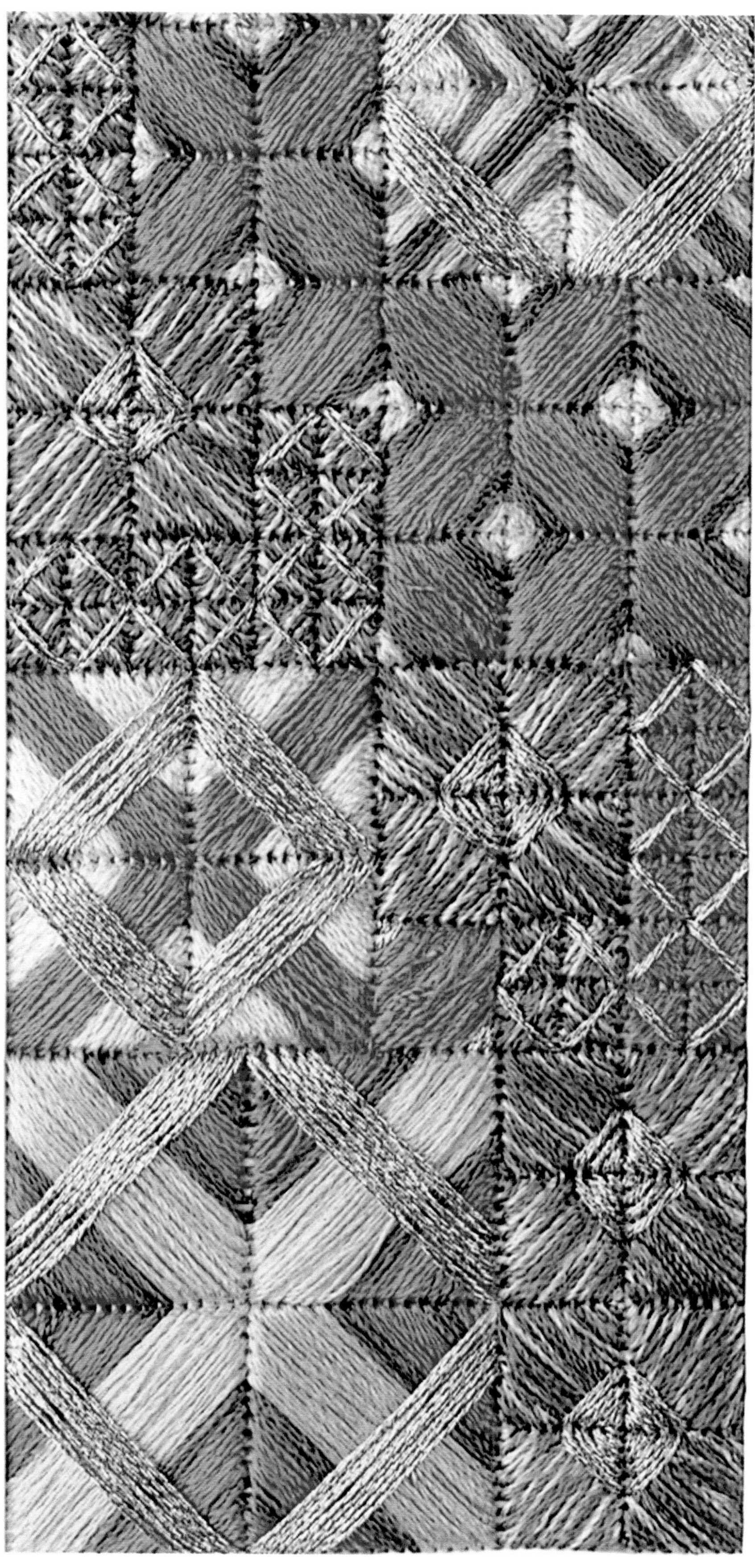

Fig 16.1b Stitch chart for bottom half of geometric panel.

All variations of cross-cornered cushion stitch

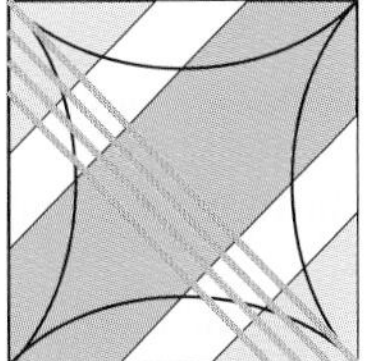

J: Four squares, each over 12 threads, in deep peach; cream; pale peach; metallic gold overlay

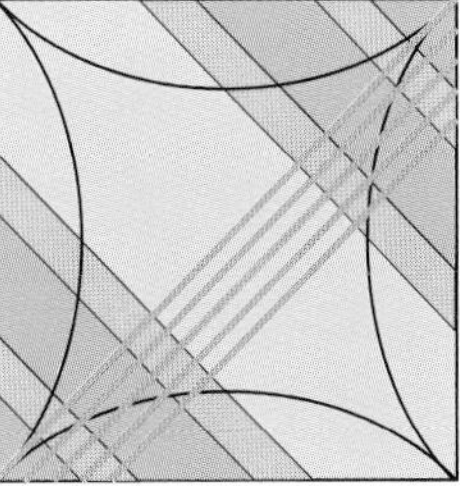

K: Four squares, each over 16 threads, in pale peach; turquoise; deep peach; metallic gold overlay

Start at the top left of the design. Follow the chart across and down, working any repeated stitches as they occur. This stitch (A) is worked with two threads of turquoise and one of cream, and each square is worked over eight threads. It is overlaid with gold threads across the four centre stitches.

Work the large stitch (B) at the top right corner next. The four squares making up this section are all worked in the same way, over 16 threads. Using deep peach, work the centre stitch and then add five diagonal stitches at each side. Work the remainder of the square in pale peach. Work across the square in the counter direction for the gold overlay, starting with the centre stitch and working five more stitches in towards the centre of the four squares.

The stitches (C) in the central row below these are worked over four threads with two turquoise and one cream thread in the needle. The gold is overlaid with only one central stitch across the square.

Work the square to the left of this (D) in deep peach with one central stitch plus five at each side. Finish the square with two stitches at each side in gold – there is no overlay.

The large stitch below these (E) is worked over a total of 32 threads. Start at the centre of each of the four squares with a central stitch, then add five on either side in pale peach. Outside this area, work two cream stitches on each side and complete the square with deep peach. The gold overlay is worked with eight stitches over the outside corners and five stitches in the centre, as shown on the chart in Fig 16.1.

Work the row of smaller stitches (F) below this one in deep peach over four threads and overlay one central gold stitch.

The stitches (G) to the right of this row have no overlaid threads. Work the central stitch and three on either side in deep peach, follow this with two turquoise stitches on each side, then finish the square in cream.

Work the stitches (H) below the row of smaller stitches with the coloured stitches in the opposite direction from that in which you have been working, and the overlaid gold stitches pointing to the centre of the four squares. The central stitch and the stitch each side are worked in turquoise and the remainder of the square is worked in cream.

The large stitch (I) to the right of these is striped. The central stitch and the stitch each side are turquoise, then two pale peach stitches are followed by two deep peach stitches on each side and the square is finished in cream. The gold overlay has five stitches, starting across the centre line and working outwards.

Moving back to the left-hand side of the chart, work the smaller of the two squares (J) using deep peach for the central stitch and the three on either side, then follow this with four cream and four pale peach stitches on each side. Start the gold overlay across the centre of the square and work inwards with three additional stitches.

The final square (K), at the base of the chart, is started with a pale peach central stitch then four more on either side. Progress outwards with two turquoise, four dark peach, two more turquoise and finally three dark peach on each side. The gold overlay consists of five stitches, starting at the centre and working out towards the corners.

MAKING UP

Once the embroidery is completed, the panel is ready for mounting and framing. For advice on mounting and framing to best effect, refer to Chapter 20.

CHAPTER 17

PANEL WITH BEADS AND RIBBON

This superb panel will enhance any room. In this particular version, rich hues of blue and bronze are surrounded by couched gold lamé ribbon. Glass beads in complementary colours add an extra dimension to this geometric pattern. The possible variations in design, using different combinations of Norwich and Rhodes stitch, are endless. Why not experiment for yourself and see what you can achieve.

Instructions are given for working both the smaller, quarter panel, and for working the full design.

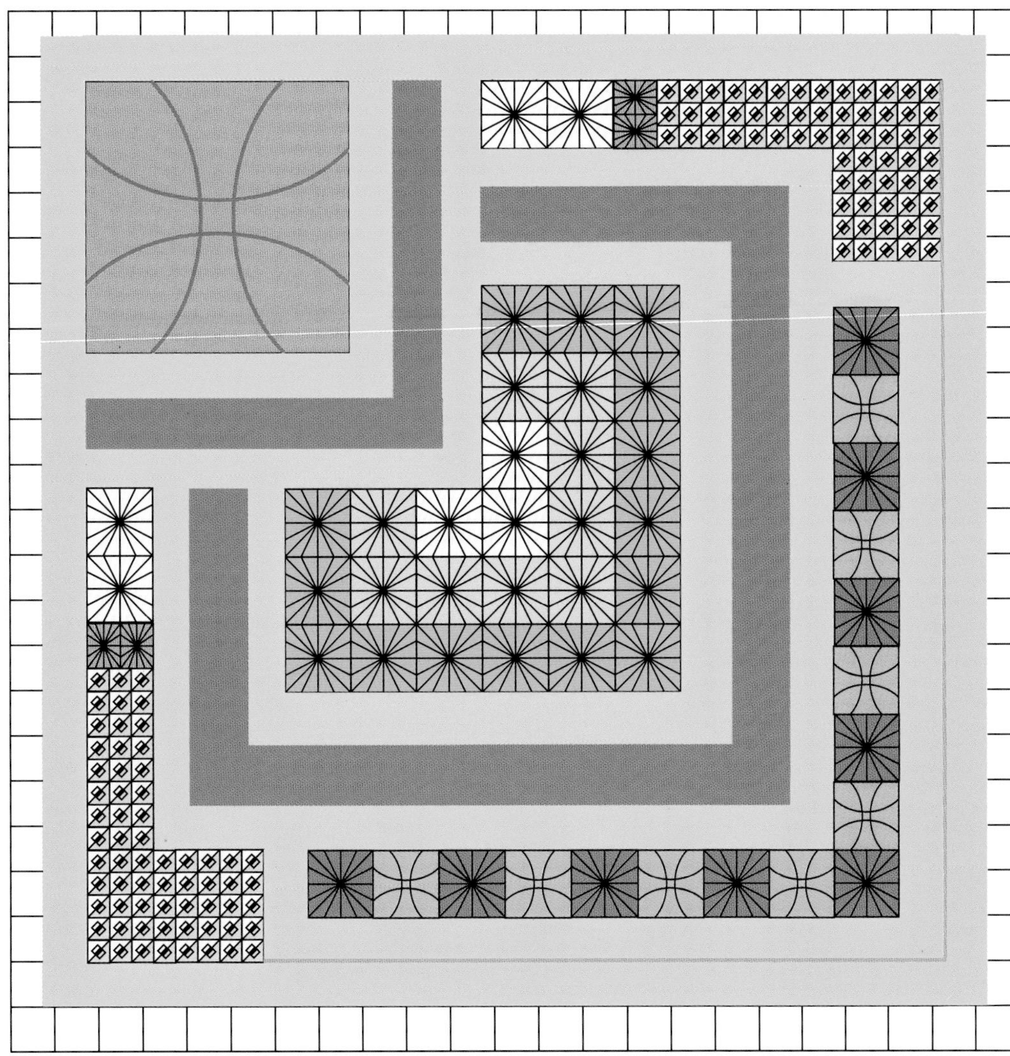

Fig 17.1 Stitch chart for quarter panel design.

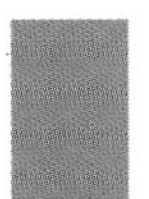

Bead border: repeat two straight stitches in peacock blue and one row of pearl and tan beads

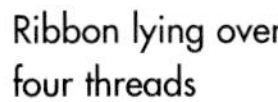

Ribbon lying over four threads

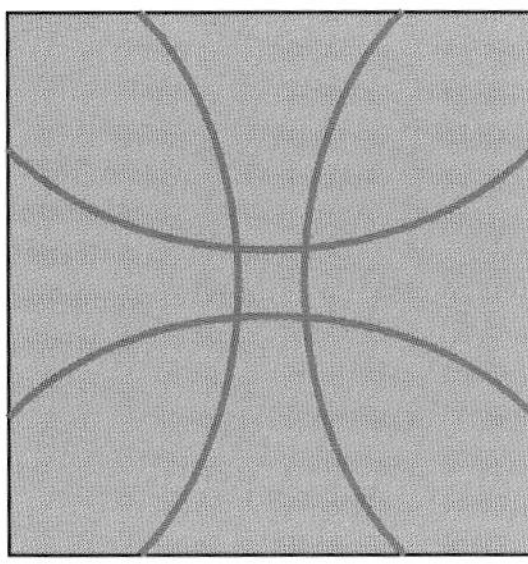

Rhodes stitch over three threads in metallic gold

Norwich stitch over 24 threads in turquoise; metallic gold; peacock blue

Rhodes stitch over six threads

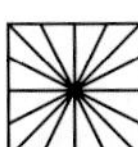

Cream

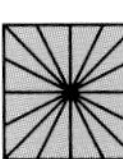

Turquoise

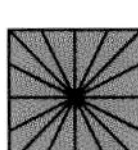

Peacock blue

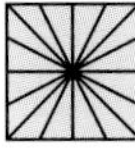

Two turquoise + one cream

Mosaic stitch (all over two threads except last stitch, over three) in two cream + one turquoise

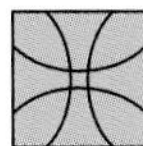

Norwich stitch over six threads in tan

THREAD KEY

1 reel each of Indian rayon in:
- Peacock blue
- Turquoise
- Tan
- Cream

1 reel of Madeira metallic gold no. 12, colour 33

MATERIALS AND EQUIPMENT

For all elements:

Threads as listed in key
Beadesign beads x 1 packet each of pearl no. 152 and bronze no. 181
Small gold sequins x 1 packet
Tapestry needle, no. 24
Fine beading needle
Embroidery scissors
Double card mount to fit
Card, slightly larger than mount
Double-sided tape

For quarter panel:

Congress cloth, 7in (178mm) square
Panda gold polyester lamé ribbon, 3mm wide, 2yd (1.8m)
Embroidery frame, 7in (178mm) square

For full design:

Congress cloth, 12in (305mm) square
Panda gold polyester lamé ribbon, 3mm wide, 6yd (5.5m)
Embroidery frame, 12in (305mm) square

Quarter Panel

PREPARATION

Attach the congress cloth to the frame, using either staples or drawing pins. If using pins, cover these with masking tape to avoid the threads catching on them.

The design is stitched over 86 threads across and down. Mark this area with tacking in the centre of the frame. Although the square in the photograph has been mounted as a diamond, work on the straight of the congress cloth.

EMBROIDERY

Throughout the design, use the rayon threads in six thicknesses and the metallic threads doubled.

Norwich stitch square

Keep referring to Fig 17.1 as you work. Start at the top left-hand corner, four threads in, and work a Norwich stitch square over 24 threads. Work the initial diagonal cross (points 1–4) and first round of four stitches (points 5–12) in turquoise. Stitch the next six rounds (points 13–60) in gold, and the final four rounds (points 61–92) in peacock blue. Figure 17.2 shows the order and pattern of stitches. On the last stitch, slip the needle under instead of over the top thread.

Fig 17.2 Working a Norwich stitch over 24 threads.

There will be one unused hole in the centre of each side because Norwich stitch should, to be correct, be worked over an odd number of threads.

Ribbon borders

Couch one length of ribbon, to cover a width of four holes, along the bottom and another along the right-hand side of the Norwich stitch square, making a stitch every third hole. These ribbons will cross at the corner (*see* Fig 17.3). Lay and couch a third length of ribbon outside this border, leaving a space of five threads for the addition of a bead border. This third ribbon will lie over the raw cut edges of the first ribbons. To get a neat corner, make a diagonal stitch into the corner, then fold the ribbon along the line of the stitch, away from the direction in which it will finally lie. Make a straight stitch in line with the outside edge, then fold the ribbon back to follow its final direction, and carry on stitching as before. (*See* Fig 17.4).

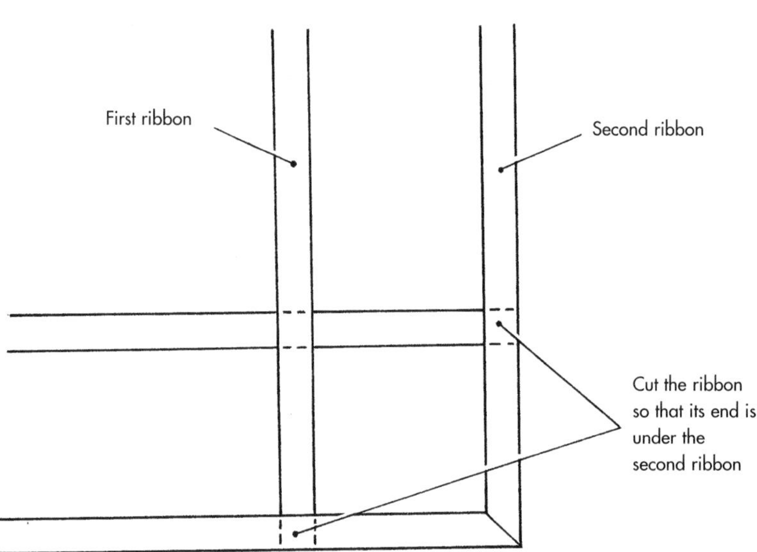

***Fig 17.3** Laying the ribbon borders.*

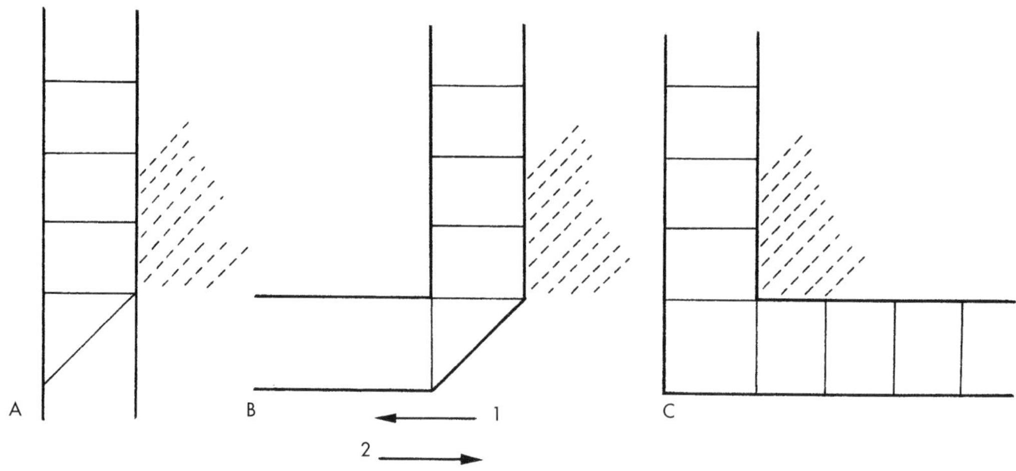

***Fig 17.4** Couching the ribbon.*

BEAD BORDERS

With peacock blue rayon, work straight stitches as shown in Fig 17.1. A detail of the placement of stitches and beads in this border is given in Fig 17.5. Leave a space, work two stitches, leave a space, work two stitches and continue repeating this until you reach the corner, then decrease each stitch by one hole to give a mitred corner. (Again, refer to Fig 17.1.) Using a beading needle and double rayon thread, attach the beads by bringing the needle up near the lower ribbon, threading one pearl, one tan and one pearl bead onto the needle, and taking it down by the upper ribbon.

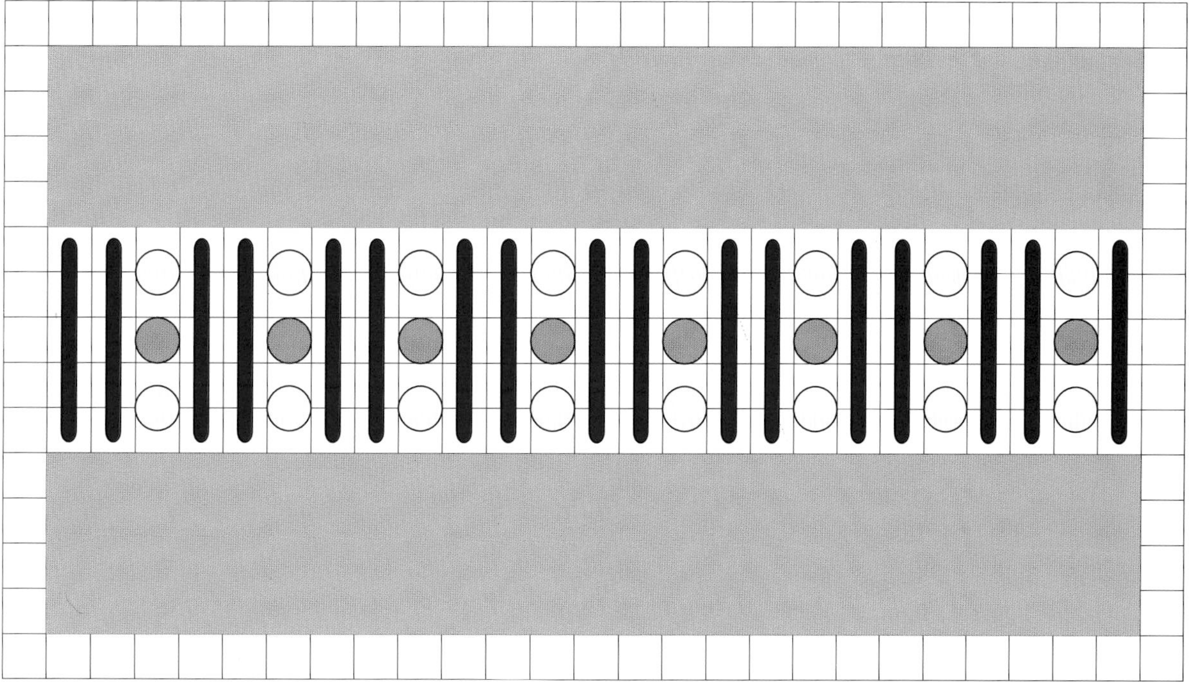

Fig 17.5 Bead border chart showing placement of beads, ribbon and stitches.

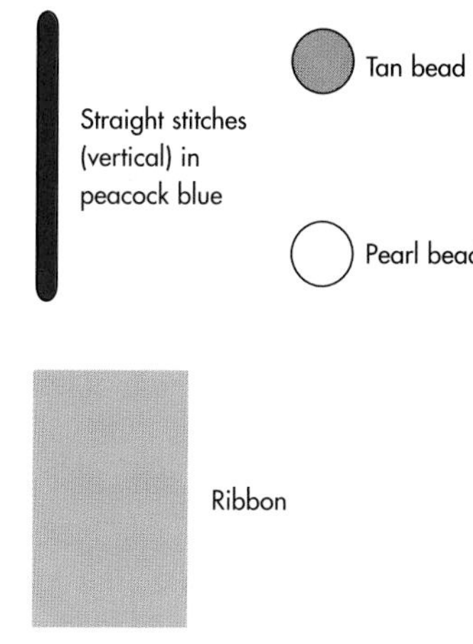

RHODES STITCH SQUARES

Now start to work the cream Rhodes stitch, over six threads, in the squares around the gold ribbon corner. Next, surround these with Rhodes stitch squares over six threads, worked in two turquoise and one cream thread, then add an outer row of squares worked completely in turquoise.

Surround this whole section of Rhodes stitches with two borders of ribbon, leaving five rows of threads between the ribbons as before, to add a second bead border. (*See* photograph of finished panel for placement of ribbons).

Work the four cream Rhodes stitches beside this ribbon border, again over six threads, then add smaller Rhodes stitches in gold, over three threads, beside these.

Now work the squares of alternating peacock blue Rhodes stitches and tan Norwich stitches, all over six threads. Surround this section with one couched gold ribbon, then surround the entire square with a final couched gold ribbon. (*See* Fig 17.4.)

Fill the two small remaining areas, in the top right and bottom left corners of the design, with mosaic stitch using two cream and one turquoise thread.

Finally, add a small gold sequin then a small bead to the corners of the ribbon borders as shown in the photograph. The stitching is now complete.

MAKING UP

Remove the work from the frame. Position and fix the work centrally on the card backing with double-sided tape: it is easier to start with a large piece of card and trim it to size when the mount is placed over it. Stick double-sided tape around the aperture of the mount and place this over the work, trimming the card to size (if necessary). Your design is now ready to be framed. (*See* page 160 for instructions on framing.)

Full, four-cornered embroidery

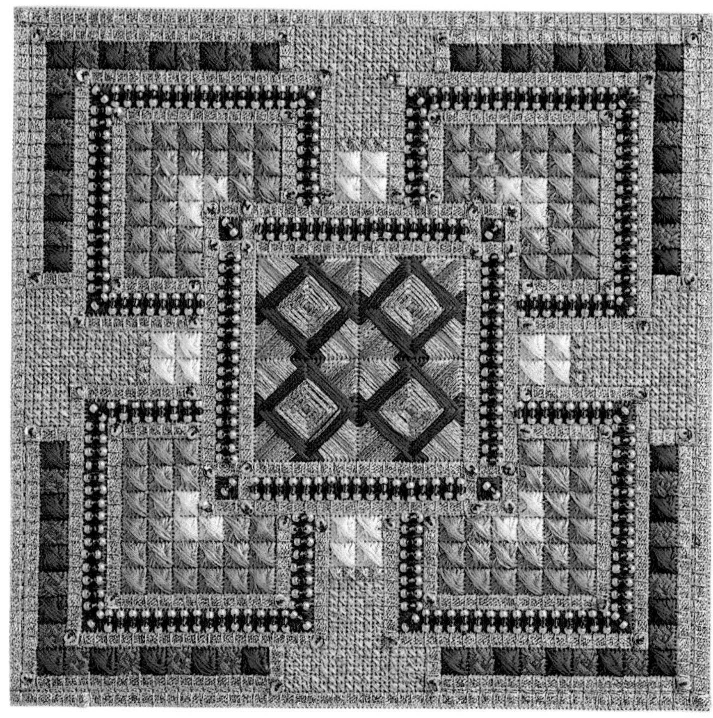

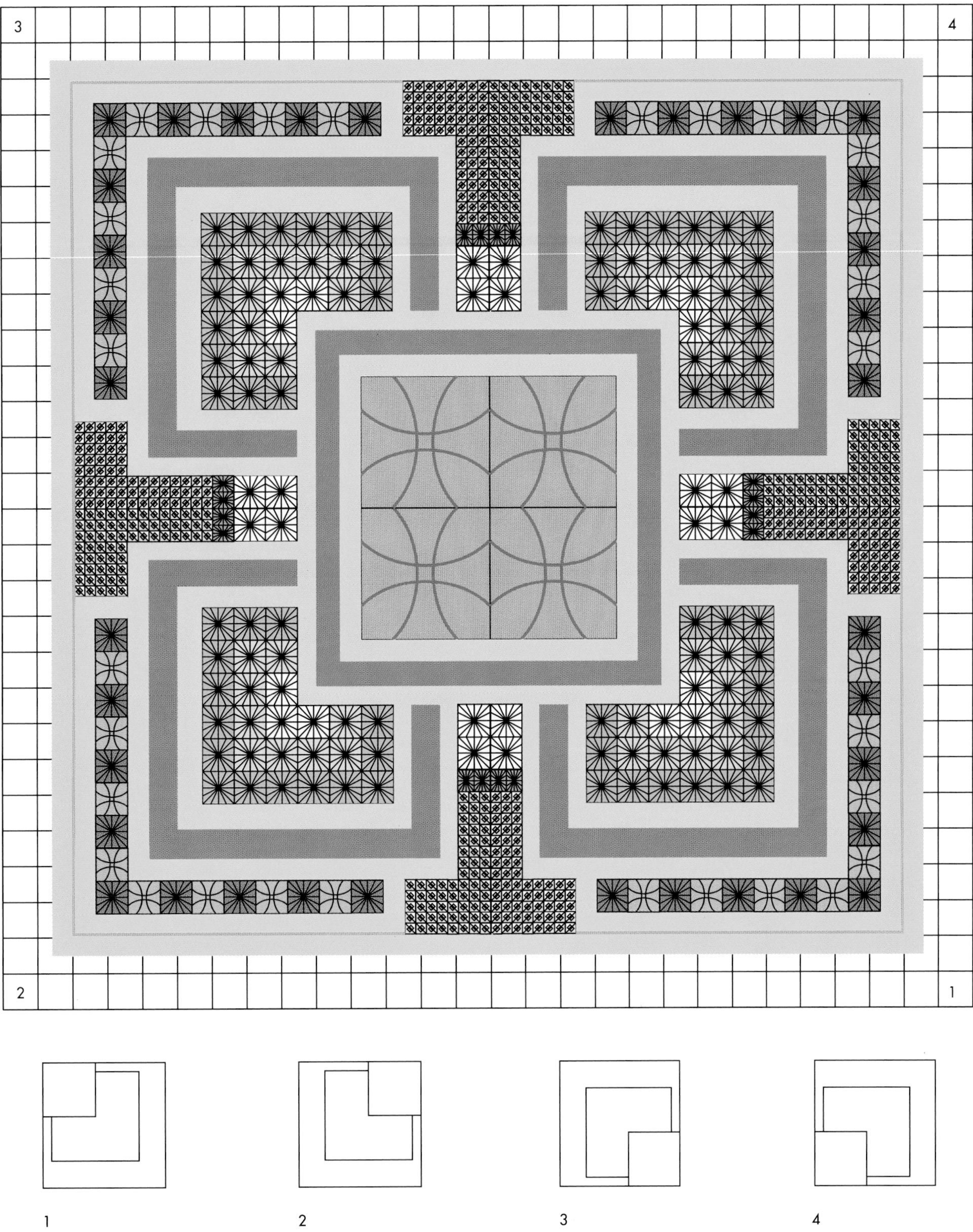

Fig 17.6 Layout of design for full, four-cornered panel.

PREPARATION

Attach the congress cloth to the frame in the same way as for the quarter panel. The full design is stitched over 172 threads across and down. Mark this area with tacking in the centre of the frame.

EMBROIDERY

To work the larger, four-cornered panel, omit the outside couched ribbon border and work the embroidery four times, turning the design through 90° each time. The first quarter worked will be the bottom right-hand corner of the finished design, the second quarter the bottom left-hand corner, the third the top left corner and the final section the top right-hand corner. If this placement is followed, the Norwich stitch section will always be worked in the centre of the completed design (*see* Fig 17.6). Notice what happens when you put four Norwich stitches together in the centre. Try putting other stitches together in this way – you will be surprised at the results you get!

MAKING UP

Follow the instructions given for mounting the quarter panel on page 146, and *see* page 160 for instructions on framing.

CHAPTER 18

Combining Techniques

Once you have experimented with the stitches and perhaps completed one or two of the items, you may like to use colour through gold in conjunction with other types of embroidery (for example, hand embroidery, machine embroidery and ribbon work) and with other crafts. The photographs on the following pages show how Daphne has used this idea.

HAND EMBROIDERY: NASTURTIUMS

To work a panel in the same way, you first need to complete the inner embroidery on a circular frame, but using it with the work at the bottom of the rings rather than over the top (*see* Fig 18.1). In order to avoid seeing expanses of white fabric around the flowers, Daphne stitches randomly, with matching thread, all over the background fabric, sometimes with a wavy line and occasionally in rows of stitches, but always following the contour of the embroidered flower. This technique is also a great help when working on fabrics, such as very fine silk, which require a cotton backing, as it ensures that there are no wrinkles when the work is stretched.

Fig 18.1 *Working the initial embroidery design.*

Adding the congress cloth

When the embroidery is complete, fix some congress cloth to a rectangular frame which is large enough to accommodate the finished border. Lay the round frame containing the embroidery on the congress cloth and, by holding them both up to the light, position the piece of work to achieve the border that you desire. It is usually better to leave a slightly larger border at the lower edge but, if a square border is preferred, this is not essential.

Now work a rice stitch area around the embroidery, using colours similar to those used in the embroidery for the base crosses and metallic gold thread for the crossed corners. This area needs to be at least two crosses deep and should be worked through both the embroidered fabric and the congress cloth (*see* Fig 18.2). You won't be able to see the holes of the congress cloth so, as you stitch, it is necessary to keep looking at the back of the frame to find the correct needle position. Once the first few base crosses are in position, the task will become easier and you will find you only have to refer to the back for a few of the holes. Having completed the base crosses, use metallic gold thread to work the four corner stitches, converting the crosses into rice stitch.

Now you can begin to cut away the excess fabric, but only a small piece at a time. Once this is done, work the next row of stitches to cover the raw edges of the fabric. By keeping to the 'multiples of four' count for all the colour through gold stitches, they will link together. Work in the same way until a border to the required width has been completed (*see* Fig 18.3).

Fig 18.2 *Fixing the embroidery to the congress cloth.*

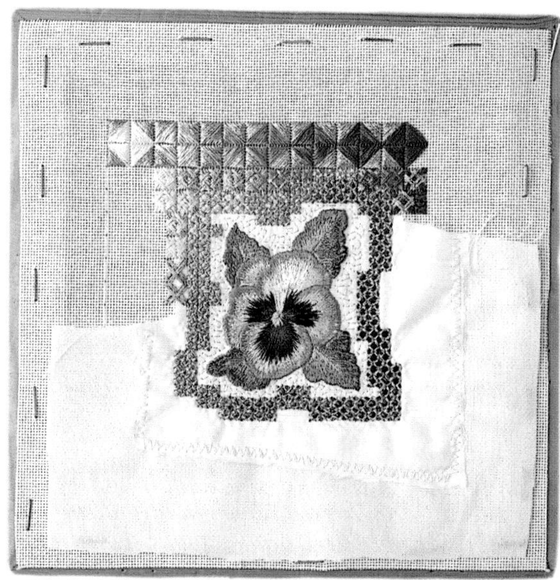

Fig 18.3 *Cutting away the excess fabric and covering the raw edges with rice stitch.*

***Fig 18.4** Colour through gold techniques combined with shaded embroidery.*

***Fig 18.5** Machine embroidery is combined with colour through gold to work this delightful pair of teddy bears.*

ADDITIONAL CRAFTS

Colour through gold can also be used successfully with crafts other than embroidery. The photographs below include samples of the technique incorporating mirror tiles, used as a decorative feature on fabric-covered boxes and combined with a three-dimensional model. Areas of different materials are worked into the overall design using the same method as for embroideries.

***Fig 18.6** Long and short stitch shading and dyed cloth are both incorporated in this piece.*

***Fig 18.7** Ribbonwork gives a three-dimensional aspect to this design.*

Fig 18.8 *A collection of embroidered box lids using colour through gold.*

Fig 18.9 *A wall hanging incorporating mirror tiles, ribbon and colour through gold techniques.*

Fig 18.10 *Colour through gold gives a dramatic background for this glorious, three-dimensional, embroidered bee.*

PART THREE

FINISHING

CHAPTER 19

Cords and Tassels

CORDS

Cords may be made, using rayon threads, either twisting by hand or with a hand drill, which will give a firmer cord.

Rayon threads are, of course, very fine, so select the colours you wish to use for the cord and experiment to see how many thicknesses you need to get the required cord size. To do this, wrap the cord around your outstretched hand several times, counting the number of times, then twist and double them over to see if that thickness is suitable. Keep doing this, adding or taking away threads, until you are happy with the result.

Fig 19.1 *Making a hand-twisted cord.*

Hand-twisted

When you are ready to make the cord and have assembled sufficient threads, each 2½ times longer than you require for the finished cord, knot them together at each end. Twist this band until it is taut and then double the threads over, allowing the two halves to twist together, before securing with a final knot.

Drill-twisted

Alternatively, to make a firmer cord, start as above, up to knotting the ends of the threads. Then, insert a cup hook into the drill in place of the drill bit, place one end of the threads over a support (a door handle or something equally secure) and the other over the cup hook. Turn the drill handle until the threads are tightly twisted and, keeping the twisted cord taut, take the loop from the cup hook and place it over the support. Find the halfway point and place this over the cup hook, then turn the drill handle in the opposite direction. This will give a locked twist to the cord. Remove the cord from the support.

TASSELS

For an attractive finish to a cord, make a tassel over each knotted end. Take fresh strands of the colours used in the cord and thread them into a large blunt needle. Hold one end of the knotted cord and keep passing the needle over the knot, making a series of loops to the length required for the tassel, until the knot is hidden by the threads. Draw the threads around the cord to cover the knot then wrap another length of thread around them a number of times, directly below the knot, and finish off securely. This forms the tassel head. Trim the lower edge of the tassel neatly to finish.

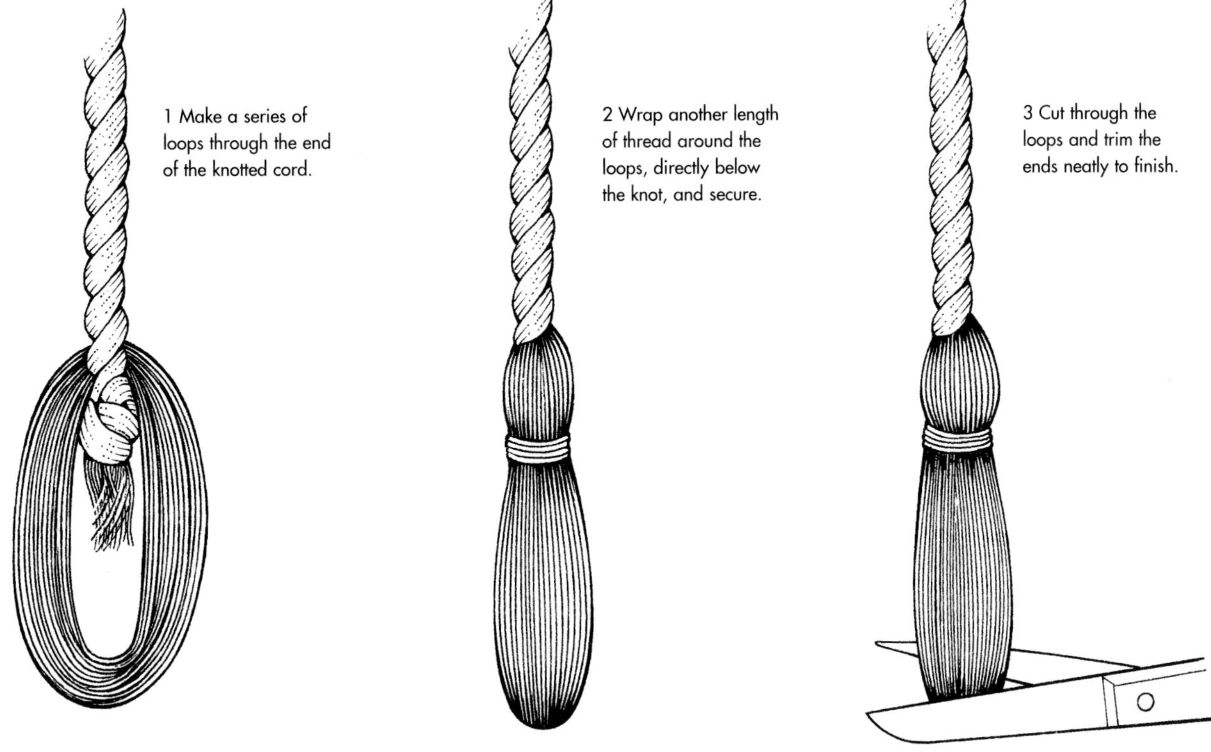

1 Make a series of loops through the end of the knotted cord.
2 Wrap another length of thread around the loops, directly below the knot, and secure.
3 Cut through the loops and trim the ends neatly to finish.

***Fig 19.2** Making a tassel.*

CHAPTER 20

Finishing and Presentation

STRETCHING THE WORK

It is not possible to stretch the work in the usual way when using congress cloth as it is too stiff and bulky to fold. If the item is not required as an 'heirloom', double-sided tape can be used to fix it in position. We give this qualification because tape may cause discolouration in the long term.

If you do use double-sided tape, cut the mounting card 3/4in (20mm) larger all round than the final mount required. Lay the piece of work in the centre of this card and mark, in pencil, where the edges of the congress cloth reach. Remove the work and position the double-sided tape inside the marked lines. Stretch the work over the tape and, using the mount, check that it is correctly stretched and that the edges are straight. Staple round the outside edges of the work when you are sure that it is in the correct position.

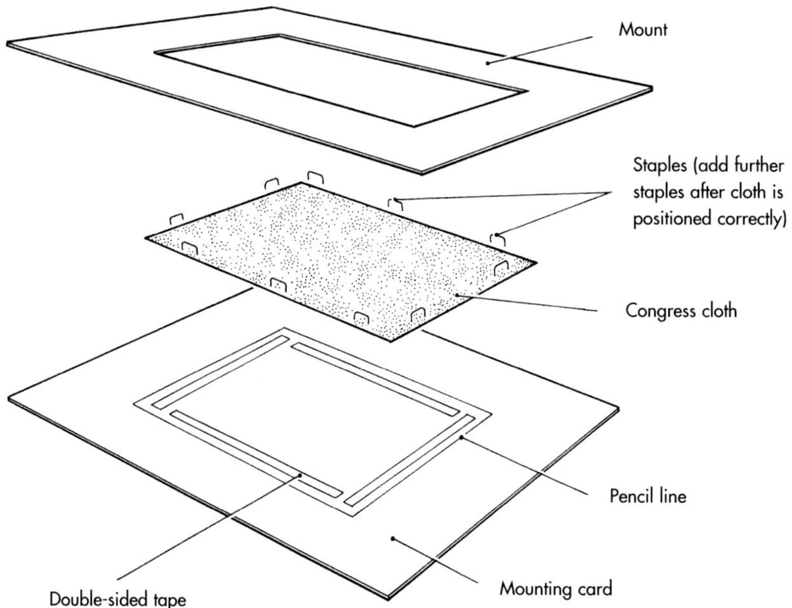

Fig 20.1 Stretching congress cloth using double-sided tape.

Alternatively, a longer-lasting method of stretching is to attach strips of cotton to each edge of the congress cloth. This cotton can be easily folded and the embroidery can be laced over the mounting card. The cotton and congress cloth together need to be 1/2–3/4in (13–19mm) larger all round than the mount card. Lace in accordance with the directions given in the next section.

LACING FABRIC OVER CARD

This is a method of covering card with fabric by sewing. Cut the fabric to be laced not less than 3/4in (19mm) larger all round than the card to be covered: the fabric should measure 1 1/2in (38mm) more than the card in each direction.

Lay the card on the wrong side of the fabric, on the straight grain, fold the fabric tightly over the card along two opposite edges, and pin securely. Always position the pins with their heads pointing inwards, as shown in Fig 20.2: this avoids the fabric riding up the pin when the thread is tightened to tension the fabric.

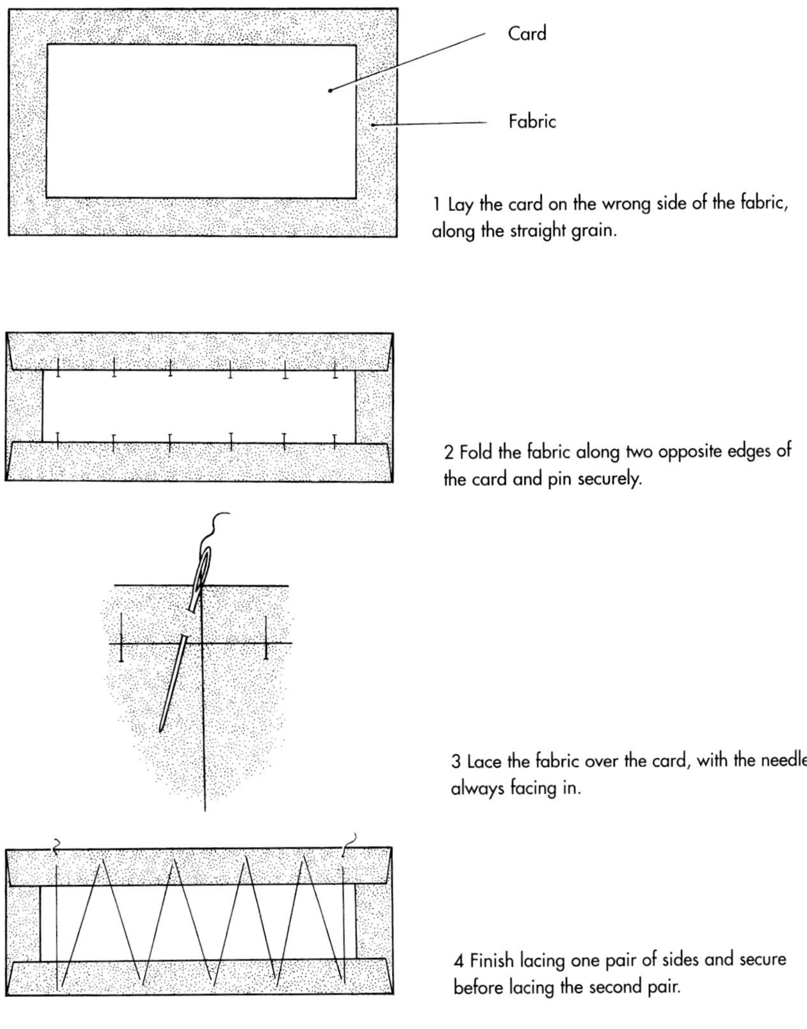

Card
Fabric
1 Lay the card on the wrong side of the fabric, along the straight grain.
2 Fold the fabric along two opposite edges of the card and pin securely.
3 Lace the fabric over the card, with the needle always facing in.
4 Finish lacing one pair of sides and secure before lacing the second pair.

Fig 20.2 Lacing fabric over card.

Use strong thread for lacing as this enables the fabric to be tensioned without wrinkling the surface. It is important to allow the needle to 'take a bite' from the fabric rather than just pass the needle through the fabric, as this could lead to a fine fabric fraying as the lacing thread is tensioned. Take a small stitch in the fabric with the large-eyed needle. Always have the needle pointing inwards as you stitch so that an even tension is maintained throughout. (*See* Fig 20.2.)

By threading the needle and leaving the thread attached to the reel, rather than cutting off a length, until the lacing has been carried the full length of the fabric, it is possible to tension the lacing by working backwards and also to avoid wasting or having to join the thread.

Lace one pair of opposite sides and fasten off the thread before repeating the process for the other pair of sides. For this second pair, mitre the corners carefully, following Fig 20.3, before lacing.

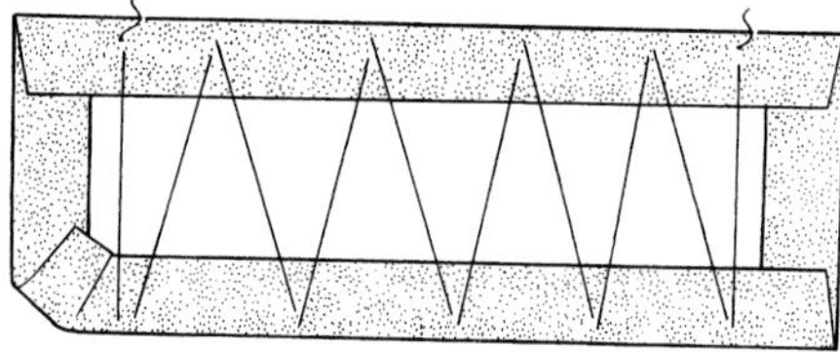

1 Pull the first corner down, tucking one edge under.

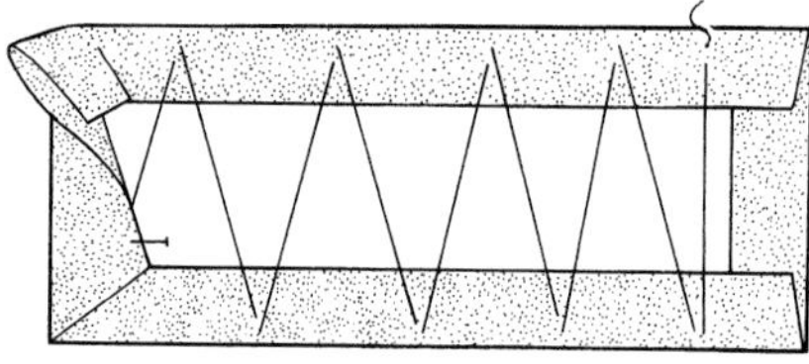

2 Pin this corner securely.

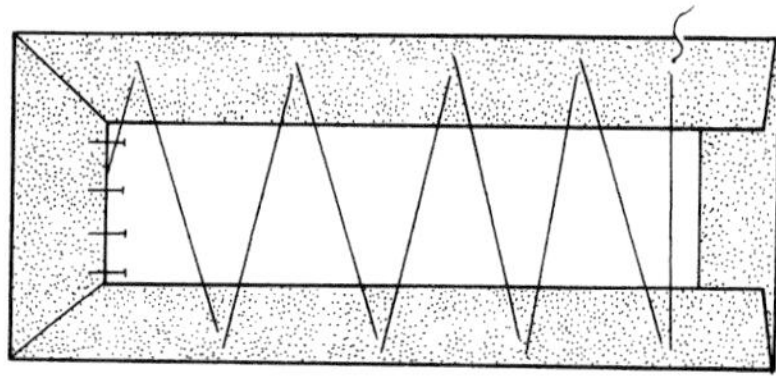

3 Repeat the process for the second corner, then pin along the length of that side.

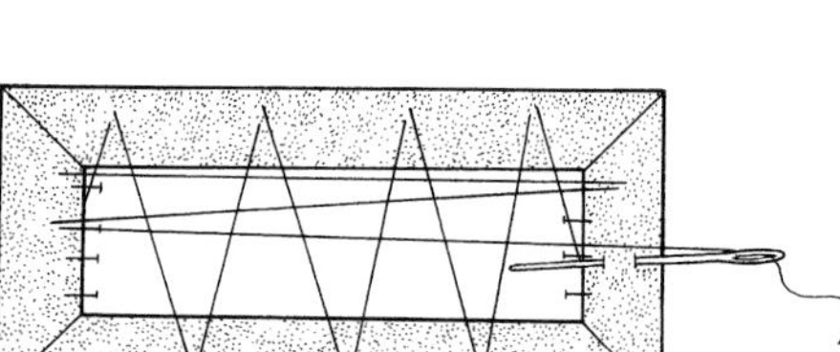

4 Follow the same procedure for the opposite side before lacing the two sides together.

Fig 20.3 Folding in mitred corners.

LADDER STITCH

This stitch is used to join invisibly, two fabrics or fabric-covered cards. Bring the needle up in one fabric then take it down in the second fabric, in line with the first stitch. Bring the needle up, still in the second fabric, a short distance away, then take it down in the first, in line with the previous stitch. Continue with this process along the fabric's length. The stitch between the two pieces should be at right angles to the seam, and when the seam is tightened, they should be almost invisible. (*See* Fig 20.4.)

Using a curved needle enables two flat, fabric-covered surfaces to be joined together invisibly with greater ease. Ladder stitch is employed still, but the curved needle makes the operation simple.

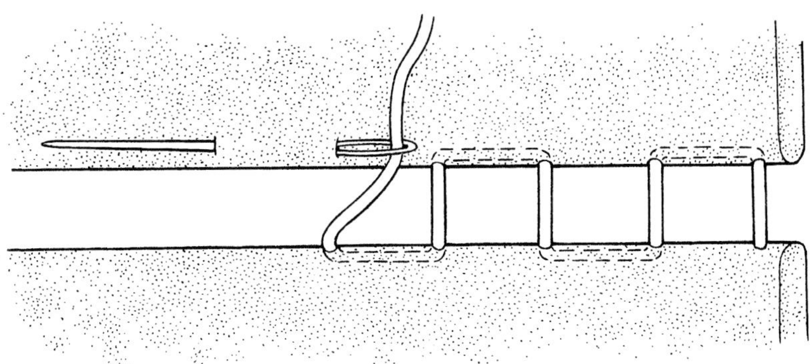

Fig 20.4 *Working ladder stitch.*

MOUNTING A PANEL IN A PADDED FRAME

Cut a piece of card to the outer dimensions of the required frame and from this cut out a panel to the exact dimensions of the embroidered panel. Cut a piece of extra heavy interfacing to cover this frame and position it carefully with double-sided tape. (*See* Fig 20.5.)

With this completed, cut a piece of firm, iron-on interfacing 3/4in (20mm) larger all round than the frame, and iron this on to the wrong side of a piece of outer fabric, cut to the same dimensions.

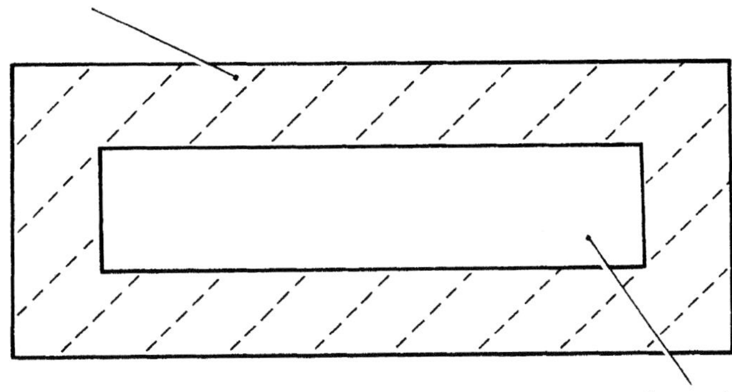

Fig 20.5 *Positioning wadding on the embroidery frame.*

Position the padded frame face down on the interfacing. Trace around the inner frame onto the interfacing, then carefully cut through the centre of the interfacing and outer fabric and into the corners as indicated in Fig 20.6.

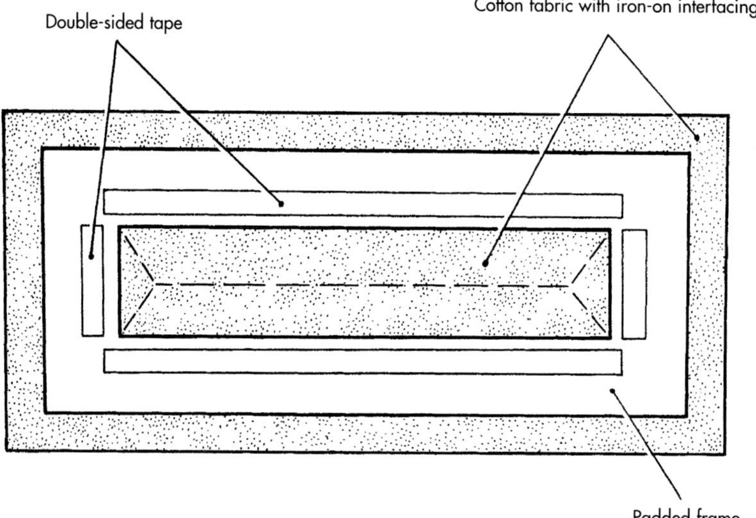

Fig 20.6 Fixing the outer fabric and interfacing in place over the frame.

Position double-sided tape on the card frame and, repositioning the fabric underneath, pull the cut fabric gently through the frame and fix in place on the tape.

Place the frame over the decorated panel and fix the panel firmly in place on the back with masking tape. Finally, lace the outer fabric over the back of the mounting card to complete the padded frame.

FRAMES AND CARDS

Unless you have had considerable experience in the mounting and framing of embroidered panels, it is a good idea to seek the help and advice of a professional. The choice of correct mount and frame can make or mar any project and it is worthwhile taking the time and spending the money to give an attractive finish to a piece into which you have put so much time and effort.

There are a host of cards on the market, offering cut apertures in a variety of shapes and sizes, such that it is possible to buy nearly anything that may be required. If the style you want is not available, then skilful cutting will enable you to create what you want from a blank card.

Place heavy interfacing, cut 1/4in (6mm) larger all round than the size of the aperture, behind the work prior to positioning it in the card, so that it will be slightly raised. This adds depth to the finished piece. For neatness and to prevent glue getting on the work, use double-sided tape to secure the embroidery and to fix the two faces of the folded card together.

Fig 20.7 *A greetings card with church window aperture.*

Fig 20.8 *A heart-shaped aperture for Valentine's Day.*

About the Authors

Daphne J. Ashby

After a career in teaching, mainly in Special Education, Daphne decided to take up embroidery seriously. She completed Part 1 of a City and Guilds Embroidery course and took a course on Goldwork at the Royal School of Needlework. She is now extremely busy lecturing and leading workshops all over Britain for Embroiderers' Guilds, Women's Institutes and private groups.

Daphne has also had many articles published in national magazines. In 1994 she was voted Designer of the Year and was presented with the Design of the Year Award by *Needlework* magazine.

Jackie Woolsey

Although arriving somewhat unexpectedly in the world of crafts – the result of moving to the country after retiring from a professional career – Jackie has taught fabric-covered box making and calligraphy for Adult Education for many years. She has also tutored courses for Embroiderers' Guilds, Women's Institutes and Townswomen's Guilds, as well as the National Federation of Women's Institutes' (NFWI) Denman College, and has contributed articles to a number of national magazines.

Jackie is a qualified Crafts' Judge, Demonstrator and Travelling Tutor for the NFWI, and is President of the South Cheshire Branch of the Embroiderers' Guild. She is the author of *Calligraphy for Beginners* (WI Books). A chance meeting with Daphne, through their mutual interest in embroidery, led to a friendship and to their collaboration in the publication of *Ribbon Embroidery* (David & Charles). This is their second title together.

METRIC CONVERSION TABLE

INCHES TO MILLIMETRES AND CENTIMETRES

MM = MILLIMETRES CM = CENTIMETRES

in	mm	cm	in	cm	in	cm
⅛	3	0.3	9	22.9	30	76.2
¼	6	0.6	10	25.4	31	78.7
⅜	10	1.0	11	27.9	32	81.3
½	13	1.3	12	30.5	33	83.8
⅝	16	1.6	13	33.0	34	86.4
¾	19	1.9	14	35.6	35	88.9
⅞	22	2.2	15	38.1	36	91.4
1	25	2.5	16	40.6	37	94.0
1¼	32	3.2	17	43.2	38	96.5
1½	38	3.8	18	45.7	39	99.1
1¾	44	4.4	19	48.3	40	101.6
2	51	5.1	20	50.8	41	104.1
2½	64	6.4	21	53.3	42	106.7
3	76	7.6	22	55.9	43	109.2
3½	89	8.9	23	58.4	44	111.8
4	102	10.2	24	61.0	45	114.3
4½	114	11.4	25	63.5	46	116.8
5	127	12.7	26	66.0	47	119.4
6	152	15.2	27	68.6	48	121.9
7	178	17.8	28	71.1	49	124.5
8	203	20.3	29	73.7	50	127.0

SUPPLIERS

Barnyarns Ltd.
PO Box 28
Thirsk,
North Yorkshire YO7 3YN
Tel: 01845 524344

Mail-order suppliers of threads, fabrics, ribbons, kits and needlework accessories.

Coats Crafts UK Ltd.
PO Box 22
The Lingfield Estate
McMullen Road
Darlington
Co Durham DL1 1YQ
Tel: 01325 365457

Suppliers of threads, fabrics, ribbons, kits and haberdashery products.

Fantasy Fabrics
Greenmantle
Plough Lane
Christleton
Chester CH3 7BA
Tel: 01244 335296

Mail-order suppliers of Indian rayon threads, congress cloth, metallic threads, ribbons and fabrics.

Framecraft Miniatures Ltd.
372–376 Summer Lane
Hockley
Birmingham B19 3QA
Tel: 0121 212 0551

Suppliers of frames, paperweights, boxes, cards, etc.

Impress Cards
Slough Farm
Westhall
Halesworth
Suffolk IP19 8RN
Tel: 01986 781422

Suppliers of cards, envelopes and other stationery items.

Kernow Crafts Woodturning
The Courtyard Shopping Mews
9 High Street
St Ives
Cornwall TR26 2HW
Tel: 01736 793628

Manufacturers of many items in wood.

Lowery Workstands
Bentley Lane
Grasby
Barnetby
Lincolnshire DN38 6AW
Tel: 01652 628240

Suppliers of workstands, stretching frames and magnifying lamps.

Madeira Threads UK Ltd.
PO Box 16
Thirsk
North Yorkshire YO7 3YX

Manufacturers of threads, kits and wooden frames and suppliers of fabrics and needles. Madeira Threads do not supply the general public but all Madeira materials can be obtained through Barnyarns Ltd. (details listed above).

Selectus Ltd.
Biddulph
Stoke-on-Trent
Staffordshire ST8 7RH
Tel: 01782 522316

Manufacturers of all types of ribbon.

The Voirrey Embroidery Centre
Brimstage Hall
Brimstage
Wirral L63 6JA
Tel: 0151 342 3514

All embroidery requirements.

INDEX

TITLES AVAILABLE FROM

GMC Publications

BOOKS

WOODCARVING

The Art of the Woodcarver *GMC Publications*
Carving Architectural Detail in Wood: The Classical Tradition *Frederick Wilbur*
Carving Birds & Beasts *GMC Publications*
Carving Nature: Wildlife Studies in Wood *Frank Fox-Wilson*
Carving on Turning *Chris Pye*
Carving Realistic Birds *David Tippey*
Decorative Woodcarving *Jeremy Williams*
Elements of Woodcarving *Chris Pye*
Essential Tips for Woodcarvers *GMC Publications*
Essential Woodcarving Techniques *Dick Onians*
Further Useful Tips for Woodcarvers *GMC Publications*
Lettercarving in Wood: A Practical Course *Chris Pye*
Making & Using Working Drawings for Realistic Model Animals *Basil Fordham*
Power Tools for Woodcarving *David Tippey*
Practical Tips for Turners & Carvers *GMC Publications*
Relief Carving in Wood: A Practical Introduction *Chris Pye*
Understanding Woodcarving *GMC Publications*
Understanding Woodcarving in the Round *GMC Publications*
Useful Techniques for Woodcarvers *GMC Publications*
Wildfowl Carving – Volume 1 *Jim Pearce*
Wildfowl Carving – Volume 2 *Jim Pearce*
The Woodcarvers *GMC Publications*
Woodcarving: A Complete Course *Ron Butterfield*
Woodcarving: A Foundation Course *Zoë Gertner*
Woodcarving for Beginners *GMC Publications*
Woodcarving Tools & Equipment Test Reports *GMC Publications*
Woodcarving Tools, Materials & Equipment *Chris Pye*

WOODTURNING

Adventures in Woodturning *David Springett*
Bert Marsh: Woodturner *Bert Marsh*
Bill Jones' Notes from the Turning Shop *Bill Jones*
Bill Jones' Further Notes from the Turning Shop *Bill Jones*
Bowl Turning Techniques Masterclass *Tony Boase*
Colouring Techniques for Woodturners *Jan Sanders*
The Craftsman Woodturner *Peter Child*
Decorative Techniques for Woodturners *Hilary Bowen*
Faceplate Turning *GMC Publications*
Fun at the Lathe *R.C. Bell*
Further Useful Tips for Woodturners *GMC Publications*
Illustrated Woodturning Techniques *John Hunnex*
Intermediate Woodturning Projects *GMC Publications*
Keith Rowley's Woodturning Projects *Keith Rowley*
Multi-Centre Woodturning *Ray Hopper*
Practical Tips for Turners & Carvers *GMC Publications*
Spindle Turning *GMC Publications*
Turning Green Wood *Michael O'Donnell*
Turning Miniatures in Wood *John Sainsbury*
Turning Pens and Pencils *Kip Christensen & Rex Burningham*
Turning Wooden Toys *Terry Lawrence*
Understanding Woodturning *Ann & Bob Phillips*
Useful Techniques for Woodturners *GMC Publications*
Useful Woodturning Projects *GMC Publications*
Woodturning: Bowls, Platters, Hollow Forms, Vases, Vessels, Bottles, Flasks, Tankards, Plates *GMC Publications*
Woodturning: A Foundation Course (New Edition) *Keith Rowley*
Woodturning: A Fresh Approach *Robert Chapman*
Woodturning: An Individual Approach *Dave Regester*
Woodturning: A Source Book of Shapes *John Hunnex*
Woodturning Jewellery *Hilary Bowen*
Woodturning Masterclass *Tony Boase*
Woodturning Techniques *GMC Publications*
Woodturning Tools & Equipment Test Reports *GMC Publications*
Woodturning Wizardry *David Springett*

WOODWORKING

Bird Boxes and Feeders for the Garden *Dave Mackenzie*
Complete Woodfinishing *Ian Hosker*
David Charlesworth's Furniture-Making Techniques *David Charlesworth*
Furniture & Cabinetmaking Projects *GMC Publications*
Furniture-Making Projects for the Wood Craftsman *GMC Publications*
Furniture-Making Techniques for the Wood Craftsman *GMC Publications*
Furniture Projects *Rod Wales*
Furniture Restoration (Practical Crafts) *Kevin Jan Bonner*
Furniture Restoration and Repair for Beginners *Kevin Jan Bonner*
Furniture Restoration Workshop *Kevin Jan Bonner*
Green Woodwork *Mike Abbott*
Making & Modifying Woodworking Tools *Jim Kingshott*
Making Chairs and Tables *GMC Publications*
Making Classic English Furniture *Paul Richardson*
Making Fine Furniture *Tom Darby*
Making Little Boxes from Wood *John Bennett*
Making Shaker Furniture *Barry Jackson*
Making Woodwork Aids and Devices *Robert Wearing*
Minidrill: Fifteen Projects *John Everett*
Pine Furniture Projects for the Home *Dave Mackenzie*
Router Magic: Jigs, Fixtures and Tricks to Unleash your Router's Full Potential *Bill Hylton*
Routing for Beginners *Anthony Bailey*
Scrollsaw Pattern Book *John Everett*
The Scrollsaw: Twenty Projects *John Everett*
Sharpening: The Complete Guide *Jim Kingshott*
Sharpening Pocket Reference Book *Jim Kingshott*
Space-Saving Furniture Projects *Dave Mackenzie*
Stickmaking: A Complete Course *Andrew Jones & Clive George*
Stickmaking Handbook *Andrew Jones & Clive George*
Test Reports: The Router and Furniture & Cabinetmaking *GMC Publications*
Veneering: A Complete Course *Ian Hosker*
Woodfinishing Handbook (Practical Crafts) *Ian Hosker*
Woodworking with the Router: Professional Router Techniques any Woodworker can Use *Bill Hylton & Fred Matlack*
The Workshop *Jim Kingshott*

UPHOLSTERY

Seat Weaving (Practical Crafts) *Ricky Holdstock*
The Upholsterer's Pocket Reference Book *David James*
Upholstery: A Complete Course (Revised Edition) *David James*
Upholstery Restoration *David James*
Upholstery Techniques & Projects *David James*
Upholstery Tips and Hints *David James*

TOYMAKING

Designing & Making Wooden Toys *Terry Kelly*
Fun to Make Wooden Toys & Games *Jeff & Jennie Loader*
Making Wooden Toys & Games *Jeff & Jennie Loader*
Restoring Rocking Horses *Clive Green & Anthony Dew*
Scrollsaw Toy Projects *Ivor Carlyle*
Scrollsaw Toys for All Ages *Ivor Carlyle*
Wooden Toy Projects *GMC Publications*

Dolls' Houses and Miniatures

Architecture for Dolls' Houses — *Joyce Percival*
A Beginners' Guide to the Dolls' House Hobby — *Jean Nisbett*
The Complete Dolls' House Book — *Jean Nisbett*
The Dolls' House 1/24 Scale: A Complete Introduction — *Jean Nisbett*
Dolls' House Accessories, Fixtures and Fittings — *Andrea Barham*
Dolls' House Bathrooms: Lots of Little Loos — *Patricia King*
Dolls' House Fireplaces and Stoves — *Patricia King*
Easy to Make Dolls' House Accessories — *Andrea Barham*
Heraldic Miniature Knights — *Peter Greenhill*
Make Your Own Dolls' House Furniture — *Maurice Harper*
Making Dolls' House Furniture — *Patricia King*
Making Georgian Dolls' Houses — *Derek Rowbottom*
Making Miniature Gardens — *Freida Gray*
Making Miniature Oriental Rugs & Carpets — *Meik & Ian McNaughton*
Making Period Dolls' House Accessories — *Andrea Barham*
Making 1/12 Scale Character Figures — *James Carrington*
Making Tudor Dolls' Houses — *Derek Rowbottom*
Making Victorian Dolls' House Furniture — *Patricia King*
Miniature Bobbin Lace — *Roz Snowden*
Miniature Embroidery for the Georgian Dolls' House — *Pamela Warner*
Miniature Embroidery for the Victorian Dolls' House — *Pamela Warner*
Miniature Needlepoint Carpets — *Janet Granger*
More Miniature Oriental Rugs & Carpets — *Meik & Ian McNaughton*
The Secrets of the Dolls' House Makers — *Jean Nisbett*

Crafts

American Patchwork Designs in Needlepoint — *Melanie Tacon*
A Beginners' Guide to Rubber Stamping — *Brenda Hunt*
Blackwork: A New Approach — *Brenda Day*
Celtic Cross Stitch Designs — *Carol Phillipson*
Celtic Knotwork Designs — *Sheila Sturrock*
Celtic Knotwork Handbook — *Sheila Sturrock*
Celtic Spirals and Other Designs — *Sheila Sturrock*
Collage from Seeds, Leaves and Flowers — *Joan Carver*
Complete Pyrography — *Stephen Poole*
Contemporary Smocking — *Dorothea Hall*
Creating Colour with Dylon — *Dylon International*
Creating Knitwear Designs — *Pat Ashforth & Steve Plummer*
Creative Doughcraft — *Patricia Hughes*
Creative Embroidery Techniques Using Colour Through Gold — *Daphne J. Ashby & Jackie Woolsey*
The Creative Quilter: Techniques and Projects — *Pauline Brown*
Cross Stitch Kitchen Projects — *Janet Granger*
Cross Stitch on Colour — *Sheena Rogers*
Decorative Beaded Purses — *Enid Taylor*
Designing and Making Cards — *Glennis Gilruth*
Embroidery Tips & Hints — *Harold Hayes*
Glass Painting — *Emma Sedman*
How to Arrange Flowers: A Japanese Approach to English Design — *Taeko Marvelly*
An Introduction to Crewel Embroidery — *Mave Glenny*
Making and Using Working Drawings for Realistic Model Animals — *Basil F. Fordham*
Making Character Bears — *Valerie Tyler*
Making Decorative Screens — *Amanda Howes*
Making Greetings Cards for Beginners — *Pat Sutherland*
Making Hand-Sewn Boxes: Techniques and Projects — *Jackie Woolsey*
Making Knitwear Fit — *Pat Ashforth & Steve Plummer*
Natural Ideas for Christmas: Fantastic Decorations to Make — *Josie Cameron-Ashcroft & Carol Cox*
Needlepoint: A Foundation Course — *Sandra Hardy*
Needlepoint 1/12 Scale: Design Collections for the Dolls' House — *Felicity Price*
Pyrography Designs — *Norma Gregory*
Pyrography Handbook (Practical Crafts) — *Stephen Poole*
Ribbons and Roses — *Lee Lockheed*
Rose Windows for Quilters — *Angela Besley*
Rubber Stamping with Other Crafts — *Lynne Garner*
Sponge Painting — *Ann Rooney*
Tassel Making for Beginners — *Enid Taylor*
Tatting Collage — *Lindsay Rogers*
Temari: A Traditional Japanese Embroidery Technique — *Margaret Ludlow*
Theatre Models in Paper and Card — *Robert Burgess*
Wool Embroidery and Design — *Lee Lockheed*

Gardening

Auriculas for Everyone: How to Grow and Show Perfect Plants — *Mary Robinson*
Bird Boxes and Feeders for the Garden — *Dave Mackenzie*
The Birdwatcher's Garden — *Hazel & Pamela Johnson*
Companions to Clematis: Growing Clematis with Other Plants — *Marigold Badcock*
Creating Contrast with Dark Plants — *Freya Martin*
Gardening with Wild Plants — *Julian Slatcher*
Hardy Perennials: A Beginner's Guide — *Eric Sawford*
The Living Tropical Greenhouse: Creating a Haven for Butterflies — *John & Maureen Tampion*
Orchids are Easy: A Beginner's Guide to their Care and Cultivation — *Tom Gilland*
Plants that Span the Seasons — *Roger Wilson*

VIDEOS

Drop-in and Pinstuffed Seats — *David James*
Stuffover Upholstery — *David James*
Elliptical Turning — *David Springett*
Woodturning Wizardry — *David Springett*
Turning Between Centres: The Basics — *Dennis White*
Turning Bowls — *Dennis White*
Boxes, Goblets and Screw Threads — *Dennis White*
Novelties and Projects — *Dennis White*
Classic Profiles — *Dennis White*
Twists and Advanced Turning — *Dennis White*

Sharpening the Professional Way — *Jim Kingshott*
Sharpening Turning & Carving Tools — *Jim Kingshott*
Bowl Turning — *John Jordan*
Hollow Turning — *John Jordan*
Woodturning: A Foundation Course — *Keith Rowley*
Carving a Figure: The Female Form — *Ray Gonzalez*
The Router: A Beginner's Guide — *Alan Goodsell*
The Scroll Saw: A Beginner's Guide — *John Burke*

MAGAZINES

Woodturning ◆ Woodcarving
Furniture & Cabinetmaking
The Router ◆ Woodworking
The Dolls' House Magazine
Water Gardening
Exotic Gardening
Outdoor Photography
BusinessMatters

The above represents a full list of all titles currently published or scheduled to be published.
All are available direct from the Publishers or through bookshops, newsagents and specialist retailers.
To place an order, or to obtain a complete catalogue, contact:

GMC Publications,
Castle Place, 166 High Street, Lewes, East Sussex BN7 1XU, United Kingdom
Tel: 01273 488005 Fax: 01273 478606
E-mail: pubs@thegmcgroup.com

Orders by credit card are accepted